THE RULE OF LAW IN
EUROPEAN INTEGRATION

The RULE OF LAW IN EUROPEAN INTEGRATION

The Path of the Schuman Plan

Stuart A. Scheingold

New Haven and London, Yale University Press, 1965

ONULP.

From an urban triangle
    to   420

     a

      swinging

  517 birch

   562   society

This book belongs to the establishment

   SHORTIE   MOSTLY

     RIP   the

    H *D* jr   junta

PREFACE

In the first ten years of its existence the Court of Justice of the European Communities handed down well over 100 binding decisions involving Community officials, member governments, and business enterprises—large and small. Never before have national governments undertaken and fulfilled such widespread "international" legal commitments. Ordinarily international politics is characterized by highly fluid relationships in which legal norms are out of place.

In this instance the legal commitments were, of course, undertaken as part of the general plan to integrate Europe—first within the framework of the European Coal and Steel Community and later in connection with the Common Market and Euratom. The common purpose of European union, and the solid economic foundations on which the Communities rest, give to European law a solidarity and a coherence which traditional international law lacks. Yet, as with all other facets of the European Communities, the legal systems are expediential—50 per cent compromise: the member states have given up only a portion of their sovereign prerogatives; and 50 per cent experiment: nobody knows what sort of system is best suited to community building.

After ten years, it is time to step back and assess the results of the experiment. Has the Court of Justice successfully adjusted to its environment? Conversely, has the Court made a real contribution to the success of the Communities? Previous studies of the legal and political aspects of European integration have tended to emphasize one to the exclusion of the other. The primary concern of this study is to document the reciprocal relationship between the two.

Accordingly, I have relied almost exclusively on primary sources. The Court reports and related documents, other official documentation, and interviews with attorneys and officials of the Coal and Steel Community and the national governments form the backbone of my research materials. Also vital was *Europe CECA*, the daily newsletter devoted to Community affairs; with its Common Market counterpart, *Europe CEE*, it is clearly the best source of information on the problems of European integration. A heavy reliance on primary sources often indicates a meager supply of secondary materials. This is certainly not the case here. My study draws upon only a tiny portion of the vast body of legal literature on the Coal and Steel Community. A sampling of these materials indicated that the points raised were often not *directly* relevant to the issues which concerned me. Moreover, as a non-lawyer I was reluctant to get involved in the many difficult and unresolved questions raised by the decisions of the Court of Justice. Finally, I wished to maintain the flow of my general arguments, and this was done by not pursuing interesting, but peripheral, matters.

In assessing the part played by judicial review in the growth of the Community, a detailed analysis of the case law of the Court has been combined with an institutional inquiry. The case law presents a virtually complete legal history of the first ten years of judicial review.* Thus, material not otherwise available has been brought together, but this legal history is not offered for its own sake. It was the means to an end— providing the necessary empirical springboard for a thorough treatment of the techniques and role of the Court of Justice.

Before turning to the study itself, let me acknowledge at least a few of my debts. Without the generosity and encouragement of the Social Science Research Council, which fi-

---

* But see infra, p. 53.

nanced a year's research in Europe and an additional year in Berkeley, the project would not have been possible. The first year's grant enabled me to gather my material at the source, and the second afforded me the intellectual luxury of unencumbered reflection and writing.

In Europe, the cooperation of Community officials was absolutely vital. While it would be impossible to acknowledge all those who assisted me, there are several whose help cannot go unmentioned. To Mr. H. Sperl and his staff at the library of the Court of Justice I owe a particular debt for their gracious assistance. I am also indebted to Mr. Charles Baré and Dr. Erich Zimmermann of the High Authority who opened the doors enabling me to speak with Community and national government officials. Special thanks are also due Me. Raymond Baeyens of the High Authority legal service for assistance and encouragement in Luxembourg, as well as in the United States after my return.

At the Court of Justice, initial introductions by Dr. Paolo Gori were invaluable, as was the social entrée provided for two damp and lonely Californians. Special mention must be made of Professor Sergio Neri, who combined friendship and intellectual companionship in generous proportions. To Madeleine Ledivelec, the Euratom librarian, untold thanks are due. Her seemingly unlimited generosity, hospitality, and warmth can never be adequately expressed—or repaid. Finally, I must offer a collective expression of gratitude to all national and Community officials and enterprise attorneys —particularly Me. Jean de Richemont, and Dr. Werner von Simson—who were so generous with their time and so patient in their responses to my questions.

My debts are not, of course, limited to Europe. From its inception, Professor Ernst Haas has guided the growth of this project. Moreover, the author owes to Professor Haas a major portion of his intellectual growth as a graduate student at the University of California. I must also mention

Professor Yosal Rogat, now of the University of Chicago, who sparked and nurtured an interest in public law and jurisprudence. At the same time, I am grateful to the other members of my dissertation committee—Professor Stefan Riesenfeld, who helped prepare me to tackle a venture in European law, and Professor John Schaar who prodded me to explore the jurisprudential possibilities of my study.

A Ph.D. dissertation is not necessarily a publishable manuscript, and in my case the transformation has been slow and demanding. It was again necessary to call for help and so I am, in many cases, doubly indebted to those mentioned above. In addition, there are four names to add to the list. Professor Eric Stein of the University of Michigan Law School provided me with a detailed and invaluable critique of the entire manuscript. Professor Richard M. Buxbaum of the Boalt Hall School of Law, University of California, and Professor Leon Lindberg of the University of Wisconsin have given friendship, counsel, and encouragement. And in long and detailed discussions, Richard E. Dudley has provided patient and discriminating criticism of all facets of this study. The editors of the *Journal of Public Law* have kindly permitted me to include here material which originally appeared in that journal.

Finally, for whatever stylistic grace and simplicity there may be in this work, I am indebted to Ruthie for her untold readings and countless battles with an author's stubborn pride. Moreover, without her unflagging faith through seemingly endless years of graduate work, neither this manuscript nor the dissertation from which it grew would have been successfully completed.

Rome
January 1965

CONTENTS

xi

ABBREVIATIONS

ALMA	Acciarieri Laminatoi Magliano Alpi
Assider	Associazione Industrie Siderurgiche Italiane
ATIC	l'Association Technique de l'Importation Charbonnière
Chasse	Compagnie des Hauts Fourneaux de Chasse
Cobechar	Comptoir Belge du Charbon
Comicoke	Italian Coke Industry
ECSC	European Coal and Steel Community
EEC	European Economic Community
Euratom	European Atomic Energy Community
Fedechar	Fédération Charbonnière Belge
GEORG	Gemeinschaftsorganisation Ruhrkohle
HA	High Authority
ISA	Industrie Siderurgiche Associate
JO	Journal Officiel des Communautés européennes
OCCF	Office Commun des Consommateurs de Ferraille
OKU	Oberrheinische Kohlenunion
SAFE	Société des Aciers Fins de l'Est
SNUPAT	Société Nouvelle des Usines de Pontlieue-Aciéries du Temple
SUTS	Société des Usines à Tubes de la Sarre
WES	Wirtschaftsvereinigung Eisen und Stahlindustrie

1 INTRODUCTION

1

SUPRANATIONALISM AND JUDICIAL REVIEW

This study is devoted to the Court of Justice of the European Communities. The Court is the single judicial organ of the three Communities comprising an incipient united Europe. The ultimate shape of an integrated Europe remains very much in doubt. Nevertheless, it seems fair to assume that the Court will remain an integral part of the final construction. If there is criticism of some of its work, nobody questions its legitimacy or threatens its existence.

It is my goal to define as precisely as possible the role which the Court has assumed, and to find standards by which to judge its success.

Although the Court serves as the judicial arm of three European Communities, it is with the Coal and Steel Community (the Schuman Plan) that we shall be concerned. This restriction is imposed by the extremely limited experience of the Court with the operation of the two newer communities, the European Economic Community—better known as the Common Market—and the European Atomic Energy Community (Euratom).

ADJUDICATION IN A FEDERAL SYSTEM

As David Easton has pointed out, it is the task of a political system to settle authoritatively the conflicting claims of individuals and groups which cannot be resolved through non-public procedures.[1] In his own terms, it is the task of the political system to provide an "authoritative allocation of values for a society." [2] There is no need to assume a "central governmental organization," and Professor Easton cites the authoritative allocation of values in international society by the major powers as a case in point.[3] However, given the existence of a central government, it can be assumed that conflicts are resolved according to established institutional patterns. The failure of interest groups and political parties to resolve conflicts privately focuses their efforts on the formal governmental institutions—legislative, administrative, executive, and judicial.

The choice is broadened somewhat under a federal form of government. Most simply defined, federal government divides political power between a central and local government. Consequently, groups and individuals may appeal to either level, although the particular division of powers may limit decisions on certain questions to either the central government or the local units. While the judicial power is an integral facet of both federal and unitary systems, its role in unitary systems is often sharply limited. Thus, it is the normal pattern in parliamentary systems to subordinate the judicial process to the legislative branch. Judicial review of legislation, to assure conformity with a constitution standing above both institutions, is an exception to the general rule of parliamentary supremacy.

On the other hand, "a constitutional judiciary is an integral part of any federal structure." [4] As Professor Paul Freund has pointed out: "Since the powers of government are by definition allocated, an arbiter is required to deter-

1. David Easton, *The Political System* (New York, Knopf, 1953), p. 137.
2. Ibid., p. 134.
3. Ibid., p. 139.
4. Carl I. Friedrich, *Constitutional Government and Democracy* (New York, Ginn, 1946), p. 222.

mine the limitations imposed by the Constitution, to check power which has not been conferred, and to authenticate power which has been granted." [5] Even where no explicit provision was made for judicial review—as in the United States and Canada—the prerogative has been asserted. Mr. Justice Holmes argued: "I do not think the United States would come to an end if we [the Court] lost the power to declare an Act of Congress void. I do think the Union would be imperiled if we could not make that declaration as to the laws of the several states." [6] However, in actual practice, judicial review once granted has not been so limited. Except in Switzerland, where review is restricted to cantonal law, judicial control extends to federal legislation. Moreover, no distinction is made between federal questions and other constitutional issues. [7] It is common for the court in a federal system to assert its authority against any constitutional infringement brought to it through proper channels.

The constitutional court—being a court of last resort—is the final mediator of conflicting claims among groups and individuals within the political society. In the same way that the entire political system resolves those disputes which cannot be settled through nonpublic procedures, the constitutional court resolves those disputes which the other organs of the political system cannot settle. Thus, the court must be studied as part of the political system in which it functions. In the first place, demands which are made on the political system, but which are unsatisfied, are likely to be clothed in legal wraps and taken to the court. This is a common experience for organs of judicial review. [8] But the problem is

5. "The Federal Judiciary" in Robert Bowie and Carl Friedrich, *Studies in Federalism* (New York, Little, Brown, 1954), pp 106–07.

6. As quoted in Edward S. Corwin, ed., *The Constitution of the United States* (Washington D.C., U. S. Government Printing Office, 1953), p. xxviii.

7. Bowie and Friedrich, pp. 132–72.

8. The current experience of the United States with the painful problems of integration is one example. The same thing can be seen in Germany where

deeper: not only is the court besieged by political questions, its decisions are judged by political yardsticks.[9] When the political institutions fail, or when the need for results overwhelms the respect for methods, courts are put under great pressure.

In other words, the court of judicial review is—in the current idiom—at the center of a system of inputs and outputs. However, at the same time that the court necessarily is part of its political system, its function is singular. Inputs are not restricted to demands but, in addition, include support for the political system.[10] Support, in turn, depends not only on the momentary gratification of demands but on long-run attachment to "a system or its ideals." [11]

Viewed from this perspective, judicial review takes on a different meaning. As the guardian of the system the constitutional court performs a dual function. On the one hand, it protects the system from disruption. On the other, the court legitimizes—provides the seal of approval for—action undertaken by the political institutions. In other words, the effective court decision not only puts an end to dispute but also resolves it.[12] As Louis Hartz has written of the United States: "Law has flourished on the corpse of philosophy in America, for the settlement of the ultimate moral question is the end of speculation upon it." [13]

---

the Social Democrats, failing to block rearmament politically, carried the case to the Constitutional Court.

9. Again, the experience of the U. S. Supreme Court is in point—not only in connection with desegregation but also, of course, during the early years of the Roosevelt administration.

10. David Easton, "An Approach to the Analysis of Political Systems," *World Politics, 9* (1957), 383–400 and 390–95.

11. Ibid., p. 391. Professor Easton also speaks of "building up a reserve of support." Ibid., p. 396.

12. In this distinction lies the kernel of the difference between adjudication and arbitration. Infra, pp. 8–13.

13. *The Liberal Tradition in America* (New York, Harcourt, Brace, 1955), p. 10.

Implicit in this analysis is the stabilizing role of courts. The adjudication of existing rights, not the reallocation of values, is the core of the judicial function.[14] The court sees to it that existing norms are enforced and that rule changes are made according to prescribed procedures and are kept within constitutional limits. By applying norms in a uniform and consistent manner, the court insures the equal administration of justice which is, of course, at the heart of any rule of law system. In addition, as a result of these norms, behavior of the participants becomes mutually predictable, thus forming the indispensable base of a stable social system.[15] While anchored in the status quo, this view of the judicial function does not commit the courts to a static system; it merely means that change will take place within a framework of predictability and continuity.

Obviously, in such a system it is politics and the political institutions which will be the engines of change. So long as these institutions work reasonably well, the court of judicial review can hew rather closely to the rules set forth above. However, inadequacies within the political system are likely to have immediate repercussions on the judicial process. Unsatisfied demands made upon the institutions of change are, as was mentioned above, likely to spill over into the judicial process. The specialization of the ideal pattern tends to break down and the institutions are tempted, or under pressure, to pull together in the service of the system.

This conflict between the normative and political roles of courts is certainly one of the permanent problems of law and to recognize it for what it is is not to debase the rule of law or the judicial process. Yet, two things must not be forgotten in coming to terms with the political role of courts. Courts are

14. See Charles DeVisscher, *Theory and Reality in Public International Law* (Princeton, Princeton University Press, 1957), p. 335.

15. See D. F. Aberle, A. K. Cohen, A. K. Davis, M. J. Levy, Jr., and F. X. Sutton, "The Functional Prerequisites of a Society," *Ethics, 60* (1950), 100–11.

not particularly effective organs of change—and most certainly they are not effective organs of democratic change. Secondly, whatever may be the political demands made upon it, if the court becomes indistinguishable in impact from the political branches, it undermines its most enduring source of support.

These problems, while not new, are of particular relevance to the study of the European Communities. The initial question is whether or not normative systems are possible in or even appropriate to regional integration. To the extent that the integrative base is economic, there is a strong presumption in favor of the normative system. Norms can provide the basic stability required for long-term business planning. Yet the whole program of regional integration is premised on changes of signal importance and broad but ill-defined dimensions. Needless to say, these changes are not solely or even principally economic.

The Court of Justice of the European Communities thus finds itself exercising the power of judicial review over a fluid and highly volatile process of political change. The parallel with international politics is clear. Accordingly, before examining the incipient European political system, let us turn to the judicial process in international affairs.

ADJUDICATION AND INTERNATIONAL POLITICS

Where power, not law, defines relations within a political system, negotiation is the paramount mechanism for resolving conflict. Moreover, when successful negotiation is formalized in a treaty, the parties are only partially restricted— "each state is the exclusive judge in its own suit." [16]

The implications for the judicial process in the interna-

16. Julius Stone, *Legal Controls of International Conflict* (New York, Rinehart, 1954), p. 75.

tional arena are obvious. Where it exists, international adjudication is a sort of halfway house between negotiation and adjudication as it is known in municipal law. The intimate association with negotiation is particularly marked in arbitration, this being true of labor arbitration as well as international arbitration. However, international adjudication, too, is deeply marked by its proximity to the negotiating process and the consent basis on which it rests.

In fact, the distinction between international arbitration and international adjudication is difficult to make. Historically, arbitration preceded adjudication, so that arbitration was until after the First World War the closest international approximation to the judicial process. With the creation of the Permanent Court of International Justice, however, international adjudication became distinct in form from international arbitration, which had been conducted by the Permanent Court of Arbitration, established under the 1899 Hague Convention for Pacific Settlement of International Disputes.[17] While there are distinctions between arbitration and adjudication on the international level, it remains possible to speak of the two collectively and thus to distinguish international adjudication from municipal adjudication.

The basis of the distinction is the element of consent. Consent is most prominently displayed in the freedom of parties to refuse to subject themselves to either process. Compulsory jurisdiction is about as foreign to international adjudication as to international arbitration. States have bound themselves under bilateral treaties to arbitration of future disputes. By the same token, the optional clause of the Statute of the International Court of Justice binds the parties to submit a wide range of disputes to adjudication. However, the sweeping reservations states have attached to their acceptance of

17. Ibid., p. 78.

the optional clause and the narrow range of compulsory arbitration arrangements serve to highlight the degree to which states remain free to refuse judicial and/or arbitral settlement of international conflict.

Consent is also reflected in the control of the parties over the "judge" and the norms he is to apply. In connection with these two elements, the distinction between international adjudication and arbitration is more marked. The parties to arbitration have complete freedom to choose the arbitrator. By the same token, they have complete freedom to specify the basis on which the award will be made. While international law is itself one possible basis, the parties can also prescribe justice, expediency, equity, etc.

International adjudication, on the other hand, is ordinarily based on international law. Thus, the first paragraph of Article 38 of the Statute of the International Court of Justice directs the Court to apply:

> a. international conventions, whether general or particular, establishing rules expressly recognized by the contesting states;
> b. international custom, as evidence of a general practice accepted as law;
> c. the general principles of law recognized by civilized nations;
> d. . . . judicial decisions and the teachings of the most highly qualified publicists of the various nations, as subsidiary means for the determination of rules of law.[18]

Moreover, the International Court is a permanent body, and the parties are accordingly not free to choose the "judge" who will resolve their dispute.

While the distinctions between international adjudication

18. *Charter of the United Nations—Statute of the International Court of Justice* (New York, 1946).

and arbitration thus seem clear and meaningful, they are in practice more blurred. As to the choice of arbitrator, some restrictions on free choice have grown directly from the institutionalization of the process. Thus, the Permanent Court of International Arbitration is made up of a panel of arbitrators, and it is from this preexisting panel that the choice of arbitrators is made. On the other hand, the International Court permits the addition to its ranks of ad hoc judges of the nationalities of the parties to each dispute brought before the Court.[19]

It is, therefore, clear that whatever the distinctions may be between international arbitration and international adjudication, the two stand together as a type, strongly rooted in consent and thus distinguishable from the judicial organs characteristic of federal states. The obvious corollary of the close control maintained by the parties to the dispute is that the tribunal is obligated to settle disputes with careful attention to the wishes of the parties. Development of international law or of a body of case law is, of course, secondary. While here, too, valid distinctions can be made between arbitration and adjudication, resolution of the case at hand remains the dominant goal. In discussing the arbitration process, Lon Fuller points out:

> Being unbacked by state power (or insufficiently backed by it in the case of an ineffective legal sanction) the arbitrator must concern himself directly with the acceptability of his award. He may be at greater pains than a judge to get his facts straight, to state accurately the arguments of the parties, and generally to display in his award a full understanding of the case. . . .
>
> As a special quality of contractually authorized arbitration . . . we may note that the contract to arbitrate may

19. Article 31.

contain explicit or implicit limits upon the adjudicative process itself. The arbitrator often comes to the hearing with a feeling that he must conduct himself in a way that conforms generally to the expectations of the parties, and that this restriction is implicit in the contract of submission. Thus, if both parties desire and expect a more "literal" interpretation than the arbitrator himself would prefer, he may feel obliged to adopt an attitude of interpretation that he finds intellectually uncongenial.[20]

Julius Stone—while not disregarding the obligation of the International Court to international law—cites with approval the following decision delivered by Judge Max Huber: "In contradiction to municipal tribunals, the Court has no jurisdiction independent of the will of the Parties and existing prior to such will." Professor Stone interprets the statement as follows: "In other words, the function of international law and of the Court was [in his view] to decide matters according to rules expressly or impliedly indicated in the Parties' submission. No more, no less." [21] In sum, then, the international process of adjudication is not obligatory, and its dominant element is resolution of conflict. It does not owe the same consideration to uniform application of the law or to the development of a consistent body of case law as does the municipal—or federal—court.

These limitations evidence and reflect the reluctance of states to be bound by a normative system. While states do accept some rules as binding, they have been unwilling to commit themselves to a complete and unified system in which virtually all disputes tend to become justiciable. International law thus resembles primitive law: although primary rules requiring performance of, or abstinence from, certain

20. *The Forms and Limits of Adjudication,* unpublished lecture (dittoed) delivered at The Center for the Study of Democratic Institutions, Santa Barbara, California (undated), pp. 60–61.

21. Stone, p. 159.

actions exist, secondary rules which confer powers to change and create rules as well as to adjudicate disputes are absent or rudimentary.[22]

SUPRANATIONAL EUROPE

The European Coal and Steel Community stands between the classic federal and international patterns. The Court of Justice is ostensibly an orthodox judicial institution. Its jurisdiction is obligatory and not restricted to states.[23] Moreover, the parties have no choice whatsoever as to judges. Still, the supporting institutional structure of the Community is incomplete. In order to appraise the operation of the judicial process it is necessary to understand the source of these structural peculiarities and their relationship to the goals and methods of regional integration.

The most common label applied to the Community is "supranational," meaning simply that the governments of the member states are—in matters specified by the treaty—bound by decisions of the Community institutions. However, by orthodox standards the institutions of the Community are deficient. Most prominently, there is no legislature. According to the treaty, it is the High Authority (HA)—the executive organ of the Community—which dominates the "legislative" process. Its decisions, which are binding and backed by sanctions, differ from ordinary legislation because the HA is in no way a representative body.[24] Consequently, there is no

22. See H. L. A. Hart, *The Concept of Law* (Oxford, Oxford University Press, 1961), pp. 77–79. "In form, international law resembles such a regime of primary rules, even though the content of its often elaborate rules is very unlike those of a primitive society, and many of its concepts, methods, and techniques are the same as those of modern municipal law." Ibid., p. 222.

23. In accordance with the structure of the international system, states alone are subjects of international law. Accordingly, only states have access to international tribunals.

24. Article 9 provides that, "The High Authority shall be composed of nine members designated for six years and chosen for their general compe-

assurance that its decisions will reflect the real balance of political power.

To the extent that any effective organ exists to reflect this balance of power, it is the Council of Ministers.[25] It is, in fact, the Council that has dominated the Community decision-making process.[26] However, the Council only mirrors the power alignment by nation. Unlike similar diplomatic bodies, Council unanimity is not as a rule necessary, so no government can veto measures with which it disagrees. In practice, however, the rule of unanimity has tended to prevail.[27] Thus, it is clear that the process of change in the Community operates under considerable handicaps.

The implications of this shortcoming are clearest when considered in light of the Community's essentially dynamic undertaking. The initial commitment of the member governments—formalized in the Treaty of Paris—is put under continual pressure by the process of building a common market. The Community was created to change habitual patterns, and yet the repercussions of these changes or their relation to the goals of the Community were not known at the

tence. . . . Each member State undertakes to respect this supranational character and not to seek to influence the members of the High Authority in the execution of their duties." Article 10 provides that, "The governments of the member States shall appoint members of the High Authority by agreement among themselves. These eight members shall elect a ninth member, who will be deemed elected if he receives at least five votes." All Treaty citations are taken from the English translation published by the High Authority. *Treaty Establishing the European Coal and Steel Community* (London, High Authority).

25. The Consultative Committee which is built along interest group lines is strictly an advisory body (Articles 18 and 19). The Assembly, made up of delegates from the parliaments of the member states (Article 21), has yet to assume a significant role.

26. See the article by Maurice Lagrange, former Advocate General of the Court of Justice, "The Role of the Court of Justice of the European Communities as Seen Through Its Case Law," *Law and Contemporary Problems*, *26* (1961), 405–06.

27. Ernst B. Haas, *The Uniting of Europe* (Stanford, California, Stanford University Press, 1958), p. 525.

outset and to some extent remain unknown. The initial commitment itself was left purposely vague. Consequently, the objectives and the methods of the Community—as spelled out in the treaty—are often ambiguous.

As concerns methods, the question marks left by the treaty cluster around the problem of partial integration. Obviously, it is artificial to cut off the coal and steel industries from the other sectors of the economy. Consequently, on the periphery of the Community are sectors like transport and general economic policy which are only partially regulated.[28]

Little would be gained by further detailing the ambiguities and uncertainties enveloping the implementation of the Coal and Steel Community Treaty. Certainly it is clear that the process is highly mobile, and a priori one could expect that immense pressures would be put on Community procedures for change and adaptation. However, as we have seen, it is at just this point that the Community's institutional structure is the most fragile. In addition to legislative weaknesses, the possibilities for amending the treaty are extremely limited. Amendments normally require ratification by *"all the member States according to their respective constitutional rules."* [29] The process is not only likely to be exceedingly time-consuming, but the unanimity requirement resembles more the inflexible procedures of international organization than the more adaptable methods employed on the national level.

The Court thus finds itself part of a unique governmental structure with weaknesses at critical points. To the extent that the institutions of the Community are unable to respond to the demands for change which are made upon them, the written law of the treaty and the "living law" of the Community are likely to become increasingly disparate. Questionable

28. By and large, national economic policy is left to the member states except insofar as it impinges on the Coal and Steel Community.

29. Article 96, paragraph 2 (italics supplied). For the exception to this rule see note 30, infra.

compromises with the requirements of the treaty can be expected. Alternatively, deadlock and paralysis may set in. For the Court—guardian of the treaty—the implications are clear: aggrieved parties are likely to call upon it to invalidate the compromises or to break the deadlocks by indicating the legally proper way to proceed.[30] The shortcomings of the system threaten to saddle the Court with a disproportionate and uncongenial role in the adaptation of the Community to changing circumstances.

THE TREATY OF THE COAL
AND STEEL COMMUNITY

The treaty itself compounds the difficulty of the Court. In addition to the institutional structure with which we have already dealt, the treaty specifies:

1. the broad goals of the Community: the Preamble and Article 1.
2. the specific measures to be taken: Articles 46–75.
3. the fundamental principles of the Community: Articles 2–6.

The preamble presents in their broadest form the goals of the Coal and Steel Community. A combination of rhetoric and purpose, the preamble points in appropriately ambiguous fashion to the ultimate goals of the Community. These are best summed up in the following provision:

Resolved to substitute for historic rivalries a fusion of their essential interests: to establish, by creating an

30. A restricted form of amendment is also possible with the support of the High Authority, two thirds of the Assembly, and five sixths of the Council. However, this change must "not modify the provisions of Articles 2, 3, and 4, or the relationship between the powers of the High Authority and those of the other institutions of the Community." (See Article 95, paragraphs 3 and 4.) Consequently, the Court is called upon to pass judgment on the proposal.

economic community, the foundation of a broad independent community among peoples long divided by bloody conflicts; and to lay the bases of institutions capable of giving direction to their future common destiny.

The preamble leaves no doubt that political goals exist, but the political consensus is particularly difficult to pin down. The common market is obviously to serve as an economic key for unlocking the door leading to political integration. Yet these political objectives are not clarified in the preamble or taken up in the body of the treaty.

While setting the tone and establishing an ideal, the broad generalizations of the preamble can hardly be expected to serve as operative rules for the Coal and Steel Community. On the other hand, the more specific measures inevitably contain certain ambiguities. Indeed, the unresolved problems of partial integration give the Coal and Steel Community more than its share of such ambiguity. Bridging the gap between the specific and the general are Articles 2 to 5 which spell out the fundamental principles of the Community.

Yet these principles, taken as a group, are too vague and contradictory to permit identification of a core consensus shared by the parties to the treaty. The goals are formidable —almost utopian—but they are to be realized with only limited Community action. A cataclysmic reordering of the economic structure of Europe's two most basic industries is to be accomplished "with limited intervention." [31] The tension between action and repose is the dominant theme of these opening articles.

Article 2 specifies the objectives of the Community in rather general terms, these goals being elaborated in Article 3. They fall roughly into three categories: (1) economic expansion; (2) improving living standards; (3) promoting international trade. It is the first of these goals which domi-

31. Article 5.

nates. There appears to be no more than a bow in the direction of expanded trade with the outside world. Moreover, it would seem that improved working conditions and living standards are to flow naturally in the wake of expanded production. However, the treaty does go on in later articles to specify protections and guarantees for the workers.

Expanded production is to be promoted by regular supply of the market, rational development of national resources, low prices, modernization of productive equipment, and the avoidance of fundamental and persistent disturbances in the economies of the member states. Specifically prohibited are discriminatory practices, subsidies or state assistance, import restrictions or export aids, and restrictive practices which divide or exploit markets.

The Community's task is to eliminate the proscribed practices and to insure conditions which "in themselves" promote the goals set out in Articles 2 and 3. In addition to information, consultation, and financial mechanisms, direct action is permissible, but "only when circumstances make it absolutely necessary." Moreover, the Community is to fulfill its obligations "with as little administrative machinery as possible." [32]

While the ambiguities and contradictions are apparent, they deserve some elaboration. The basic question is whether the far-reaching objectives can always be achieved with the laissez faire policies prescribed. Whether liberalism is to yield to planning when the conflict develops remains an open question. In addition, the goal of equal treatment is not necessarily compatible with competitive ideals to which the Community is attached. This contradiction has been amply demonstrated in connection with cases that have arisen over steel pricing practices. [33]

In sum, the fundamental principles of the treaty provide

32. Ibid.
33. Infra, Chapters 3 and 4.

something for everyone and the resolution of conflicting principles is left for the future. There is, of course, nothing wrong with this sort of solution. It is probably better to defer the answers to such explosive questions and get on to the practical problems of building a community. These articles do, after all, provide a sufficient framework to allow considerable constructive activity. Moreover, the operative sections of the treaty are in many respects clear enough to preclude recourse to the fundamental principles for directive guidance. Given the wide ideological gulfs separating the treaty fathers [34] there was every reason to choose the pragmatic approach to community building.

Yet this choice involves certain difficulties for the Court of Justice. It is, of course, in instances of textual ambiguity that the Court's opportunities to influence the development of the political system are most marked. However, the extent of judicial activism is likely to be a reflection of the judges' conception of the nature and function of courts and law. If law is viewed as a normative–ethical force, decisions will be strongly shaped by the judge's ethical evaluation of the situation. On the other hand, if law is seen as an agent of social control an attempt will be made to force the decision to conform as closely as possible to the judge's perception of social reality. By the same token, the judge's view of his own role is likely to influence his choice of alternatives. Where the tradition of judicial activism is strong, the judge is likely to be less hesitant to play a leading part in shaping legislation.

Certainly, the continental judge does not conceive of his role as expansive and directive. Nevertheless, the Court of Justice has engaged on occasion in its own variety of judicial activism. By undertaking a teleological process of interpretation, it has in fact adopted a rudimentary sort of functionalism. That is to say, it has looked primarily to "purpose" in order to ascertain the correct interpretation of the treaty.

34. See Haas, pp. 19–29.

FUNCTIONALISM

Functionalism visualizes law as a primarily normative institution, prescribing the rules of behavior necessary for achieving agreed upon objectives. It is predicated on—in the words of Gerhart Niemeyer—"transpersonal ends." [35] In other words, it rests upon accepted community goals, which are different from a simple sum of individual goals. In addition: "Since law is essentially a system of evaluative judgments of social behavior, it can be immanently evaluative only by reference to a common emotional structure, of a common pattern of culture." [36] In sum, it presumes agreement on ends and on common values which will determine the means for achieving those ends. In the functional pattern the court assumes a central position, because it is charged with measuring particular means against the transpersonal ends in the light of the community values.

How can these ideas be applied to the Coal and Steel Community? One could say that it is the Court's job to translate the "expansive logic of sector integration" [37] into standards for gauging particular decisions taken by the High Authority. In other words, the Court would then be charged with resolving the ambiguities in the treaty in terms of an imputed "purpose." Let us be more specific. It has been pointed out that the preamble, together with Article 1, spells out the goals of the Coal and Steel Community in their most general sense. Moreover, the body of the treaty contains in some detail the measures agreed upon for achieving those ends. Bridging the gap between the particular and the general are the fundamental principles of the treaty contained in Articles 2

35. *Law Without Force* (Princeton, Princeton University Press, 1944), p. 268.

36. Ibid., p. 285.

37. Haas, Chapter 8.

to 5. These articles are to guide the application of the treaty in the service of the broad goals of integration.

The Court is in a strong position to play a creative role when it is dealing with an unforeseen ambiguity in the detailed provisions which make up the body of the treaty. The so-called unprovided case can, indeed, be decided by reference to broad treaty goals in the light of the treaty's fundamental principles. This is the variety of judicial activism that no court can escape.[38] As Professor Hart has written: "When the unenvisaged case does arise, we confront the issues at stake and can settle the questions by choosing between the competing interests in the way which best satisfies us. In doing so we shall have rendered more determinate our initial aim." [39]

Of course, as we have seen, the fundamental principles of the treaty are sometimes in conflict. Accordingly, the Court is on less strong but not untenable ground when the unprovided case raises questions involving a choice between conflicting values, that is to say, where conflicts in the fundamental principles of the Community manifest themselves in a particular dispute. It is precisely at this point that functionalism becomes most useful. The Court can test the conflicting principles vis-à-vis their respective chances to effect treaty objectives. There is no need to permanently subordinate a given principle; the Court may well be called upon to reverse its priority in subsequent cases involving different factual problems. Yet the very process of measuring means against

---

38. The mechanical jobs of matching problems against rules are most often done by attorneys in consultation with clients and, consequently, seldom reach court. In a conventional judicial system those that are litigated are usually disposed of at the lowest levels. Since the Court of Justice is a court of first instance as well as a court of last resort, it might conceivably have more than its share of such cases. However, it is of no matter, because they are not likely to cause any trouble.

39. Hart, p. 126.

objectives entails at least an implicit value choice. It would be naïve to assume that there is no value commitment involved in the Court's choice of fundamental principles. While a given judgment may not yield conclusive results, the trend of decisions should disclose the ideological direction in which the Court is prodding the Community. Consistent emphasis on certain principles or regular disregard of others— where apparent—should enable us to understand how the treaty is being molded by judicial interpretation.

However, let us keep in mind the limits on such judicial activism. While "the human inability to anticipate the future" may be at the heart of the "indeterminacy" of the unprovided case,[40] it is not the whole problem. Where agreement on goals and methods has not crystallized, where the system is incomplete, the rendering more determinate of initial aims is a hazardous and perhaps an illusory undertaking:

> The truth may be that, when courts settle previously unenvisaged questions concerning the most fundamental constitutional rules, they *get* their authority to decide them accepted after the questions have arisen and the decision has been given. Here all that succeeds is success. It is conceivable that the constitutional question at issue may divide society too fundamentally to permit of its disposition by a judicial decision.[41]

While these fundamental difficulties can arise even in the municipal system, they tend to be endemic to international law. The Community system is, of course, characterized by only partial agreement on goals and methods. While some treaty provisions are indeterminate only because of the human frailties mentioned above, others reflect the incomplete and tentative character of the Community system.

40. Ibid., p. 127.
41. Ibid., p. 149.

Where the treaty offers no guidance, the Court—by functional standards—finds itself in Cardozo's "trackless ocean." Within the Coal and Steel Community, this difficulty is particularly marked in relation to the unresolved problem of partial integration. To what extent is transport subject to treaty rules? Are the member states free to pursue their own trading policies with respect to nonmember states? The Court cannot answer such questions authoritatively until the political powers have spoken. While the existence and character of the Community evidence a commitment to the common market, the ambiguities and lacunae of the treaty attest to the determination of the member states to keep a tight rein on the direction, pace, and intermediate goals of integration.

Moreover, in the European Communities the commitment to the integrative process seems to be based on a mélange of long-run hopes and short-run benefits, which fall into the category of reciprocal rather than joint goals.[42] In other words, the satisfaction of particular demands is likely to claim a disproportionate share of the energies of the member states and the Community enterprises. Commitment to the *ideals* of integration seems to be limited to a relatively small group which is identified, either in fact or in spirit, with the Monnet Committee. With others, interest in the Community is largely instrumental. As to the system itself, not even the farsighted few are committed: it is a hybrid, an expedient, which is expected to change and grow.

All this adds up to judicial review resting on rather shaky foundations.[43] Given the nature of things, the Court could

42. For a detailed analysis, see Haas, Chapters 4–7. Professor Haas concludes, "Our basic finding was that the acceptance of ECSC is best explained by the convergence of demands within and among the nations concerned, not by a pattern of identical demands and hopes." Ibid., p. 286.

43. Writing of international law, Stanley Hoffmann has said: "The law of community is strongest because it rests on a common positive purpose. The law of reciprocity is relatively strong because it is the law of a limited part-

devitalize the integrative process by curbing its flexibility and its freedom to act. While a normative pattern has much to contribute, its premature and indiscriminate introduction could inhibit rather than promote integration. Alternatively, restrictive judgments could be disregarded, in which case the Court would become a useless appendage to the Community's institutional structure.

---

nership, whose members' common end is a set of mutual interests. The law of the political framework is weakest, for it is the law of a collection of actors engaged in a struggle, and whose common end is both limited to a narrow sphere—the rules of the game—and subordinated to the fluctuations of the balance of power." "International Systems and International Law" in Klaus Knorr and Sidney Verba, eds., *The International System* (Princeton, Princeton University Press, 1961), p. 233.

2

THE JUDICIAL STRUCTURE OF SUPRANATIONALISM

Before beginning a detailed analysis of its work, a look at the Court itself seems in order. The Court of Justice is, of course, an institutional experiment. The rules set forth in the treaty to govern its operation reflect a combination of reasoned innovation and political bargaining. While the Court can safely be described as supranational, the designation raises more questions than it answers. Like the other organs of the Community, the Court is sui generis; it defies categorization.

In comparison with the standard international tribunal, the Court of Justice is impressively independent.[1] As we have already seen, judicial review in the Community rests on the solid foundation of compulsory jurisdiction and binding decisions.[2] On the other hand, the Court labors under handicaps growing directly from the member governments' determination to keep the reins of the Community in their own hands. Most strikingly characteristic of this ambivalence are the rules for choosing the members of the Court.

1. See Gerhard Bebr, *Judicial Control of the European Communities* (New York, Praeger, 1962), pp. 21–22: "It is a unique court which has very little in common with the International Court of Justice, if anything at all"; infra, p. 41.

2. See supra, pp. 13–16. Judgments are to be enforced "on the territory of member States by means of legal procedure in effect in each State." See Article 92 as referred to in Article 44. Enforcement has not really been a problem, but see Chapter 9, infra.

TABLE 1. OFFICERS OF THE COURT OF JUSTICE

DATE BORN	NAME	SERVICE	NATIONALITY	PROFESSIONAL BACKGROUND [a]
Judges				
1879 [b]	Massimo Pilotti, President 1952–58	1952–58	Italian	Judge
1888 [c]	P. J. S. Serrarens	1952–58	Dutch	International trade union leader
1894	Otto Riese	1952–63	German	Law professor
1896	Jacques Rueff	1952–59, 1960–62	French	Economist
1895	Louis Delvaux	1952 to date	Belgian	Attorney–Politician
1898	Charles Leon Hammes, President 1964 to date	1952 to date	Luxembourg	Judge
1899	Adrianus van Kleffens	1952–58	Dutch	Government official
1918	Andreas M. Donner, President 1958–64	1958 to date	Dutch	Law professor
1910	Nicola Catalano	1958–62	Italian	Italian Government and HA attorney

1889	Rino Rossi	1958–64	Italian	Judge
1907	Alberto Trabucchi	1962 to date	Italian	Law professor
1908	Robert Lecourt	1962 to date	French	Politician
1900	Walter Strauss	1963 to date	German	Government official
1909	Riccardo Monaco	1964 to date	Italian	Government official– Law professor

Advocates General

1900	Maurice Lagrange	1952–64	French	Conseil d'Etat
1899	Karl J. Roemer	1952 to date	German	Banking official
1913	Joseph Gand	1964 to date	French	Conseil d'Etat

Clerk

| 1914 | Albert Van Houtte | 1952 to date | Belgian | Government official |

a. Because a majority of the judges have pursued rather varied careers, I have sought merely to give an idea of the dominant strain in their professional backgrounds.

b. Deceased, 1962.

c. Deceased, 1963.

The Court is composed of seven judges and two Advocates General, all appointed for six-year, renewable terms.[3] The position of Advocate General is without an American equivalent. As an officer of the Court, one of the advocates must—prior to each judgment—make an independent assessment of the issues. His conclusions are read publicly and published alongside the Court's decision but have no legal weight; the Court is bound only to listen.[4] Finally, the Court is authorized a chief administrative officer, the Clerk.[5]

Quotas and Tenure

It is at once apparent that six-year renewable terms do not offer the members of the Court the secure tenure usually associated with high judicial office. There is no evidence that the governments have tried to take advantage of the leverage of limited tenure to influence the decisions of the Court. However, the system does enable the member states to retain ultimate and arbitrary power over the Court. Since no provision is made for dissenting opinions, the anonymity which attaches to judgments offers considerable protection to individual judges. However, the Court itself could be easily—and rather unobtrusively—decimated by dissatisfied national governments.

This possibility stems from a distortion of the treaty. According to Article 32, appointment of the judges and

3. Article 32, paragraph 1, of the Treaty and Article 12, *Protocol on the Code of the Court of Justice,* as published with High Authority's English translation of the Treaty. Hereafter cited as *Protocol.*

4. Professor Eric Stein has referred to the advocates as "institutionalized 'amici curiae.'" "The New Institutions," in Eric Stein and Thomas L. Nicholson, eds., *American Enterprise in the European Common Market: A Legal Profile* (2 vols. Ann Arbor, University of Michigan Law School, 1960), *1*, 69. For further discussion of the advocates general, see infra, p. 37.

5. Article 16, *Protocol.*

advocates is to be "by agreement among the governments of the member states." [6] In fact, it is common knowledge that each member government is free to choose its own appointees; the "agreement among the governments" has become a formality.[7] Until the fall of 1964 this possibility of an independent national choice seemed to be only the first of two distortions of the treaty. The second concerned the choice of a Court President. According to the treaty, the judges were to have made this choice themselves from amongst their own number.[8] However, in practice, the presidency became part of a complicated formula for dividing the seats on the Court. Moreover, leadership of the Court was linked to the division of the presidencies of the collegial executive organs of the three European Communities.

The ensuing problems can best be understood by tracing the changes which have taken place in the composition of the Court. At the outset, the judicial pie was cut up so that two pieces went to each member state except Luxembourg, which was limited to a single position. Both of Holland's places were filled by judges, but the four remaining states filled out their quotas in other ways. France and Germany each had a judge and an advocate general, while the Belgians had the Clerk of the Court in addition to one judicial position. Italy had only a single judge, but he was President of the Court. This strictly unofficial division of judicial places held constant despite numerous personnel changes during the Court's first twelve years. With one exception, each time an official has left the Court, he has been replaced by someone of his own nationality.

Paradoxically, it is the one exception that seemed to prove the rule. The Court continued intact while serving the Coal and Steel Community but in the fall of 1958—when the

---

6. Article 32, paragraph 1, of the Treaty and Article 12 of the *Protocol*.
7. Stein, pp. 68–69.
8. Article 32, paragraph 5.

Court of Justice became the judicial arm of the three European Communities—the two Dutch judges, Serrarens and van Kleffens, and the Italian President, the aged Judge Pilotti, were all replaced. However, the new Dutch judge, Professor Donner, was made President of the Court and, in compensation, the two places held by the Dutch were taken by the two new Italian judges, Rossi and Catalano.

In 1962 Judges Catalano and Rueff resigned and were replaced by Professor Alberto Trabucchi and Mr. Robert Lecourt, respectively. At the beginning of 1963, Professor Otto Riese's place was taken by Dr. Walter Strauss. Finally, in the fall of 1964, Advocate General Lagrange and Judge Rossi left the Court. The Advocate General, who returned to the *Conseil d'Etat,* was replaced by another member of that body, M. Joseph Gand. Judge Rossi's place was taken by Professor Riccardo Monaco.

What is most striking about the 1964 changes, however, is the fact that Judge Donner, who was reappointed to the Court, stepped down from the presidency. The job was assumed by Judge Hammes, one of the two judges who remain from the original court.[9] Obviously, this change of presidencies upsets the Court's traditional equilibrium, suggesting a degree of freedom from control of the national governments which had seemed quite out of reach. It was, for example, generally known that the Court, if it had been a free agent, in both 1958 and 1962 would have chosen as its President Judge Riese, the very highly respected German judge.[10]

There is other evidence of the rather tenuous state of ju-

9. The other is Judge Delvaux of Belgium. In addition, one of the original advocates, M. Roemer, remains, as does the Clerk of the Court, M. Albert Van Houtte. It was, however, rumored that M. Van Houtte would leave the Court to assume full time the presidency of the Community school system, which he has headed on a part-time basis since its inception.

10. Cf. Werner Feld, "The Judges of the Court of Justice of the European Communities," *Villanova Law Review, 9* (1963), 44.

dicial security. The Dutch–Italian trade of 1958 has already been mentioned. At the time it was rumored that the Dutch demanded this change because of dissatisfaction with the performance of the first Court. Whether or not this is true is beside the point. What matters is that the Netherlands—or any other national government—is in a position to refuse to reappoint a judge and is assured the choice of his successor.

Also symptomatic of the autonomy that member states enjoy with regard to their judicial appointments is the case of the well-known economist, Jacques Rueff, the original French member of the Court of Justice. Judge Rueff, while still a member of the Court, served as a vice-chairman of a study committee appointed by President de Gaulle to work out a program to overhaul the French economy. This impropriety was compounded by the failure of the French government to appoint a successor to Judge Rueff after he resigned under fire in November 1959.[11] As a final blow, Judge Rueff—having completed his work for the French government—was reappointed to fill his own vacancy.

Similarly unfortunate were the circumstances that surrounded the appointment of Dr. Walter Strauss. As the State Secretary in the German Ministry of Justice, Dr. Strauss certainly must be considered one of the Court's most prestigious appointees. However, his shift to the Court of Justice came hot on the heels of the sordid *Der Spiegel* affair in which he was apparently involved.[12] Whether Dr. Strauss was sent from the Ministry of Justice to the Court of Justice

11. The problem was rather delicately posed in the form of a parliamentary question by M. Vals, Chairman of the Budgetary and Administrative Committee of the European Parliamentary Assembly. The Council of Ministers responded evasively and based its reticence on the separation of powers. *Journal Officiel des Communautés Européennes, 3* (October 6, 1960), 1255–59. (Hereafter cited as *J.O.C.E.*)

12. Karl W. Deutsch, "The German Federal Republic," in Roy C. Macridis and Robert E. Ward, eds., *Modern Political Systems: Europe* (Englewood Cliffs, N.J., Prentice-Hall, 1963), p. 382. See also *The Observer* (London), 11 November 1962, p. 12, and 25 November 1962, p. 2.

as part of a political deal, or whether, as seems altogether possible, he had been for some time slated for a Court appointment, the fact remains that he came to the Court under something of a cloud.

Of course, there is no way to determine how a particular division of judicial positions affects the decisions of the Court. The Clerk, as the administrative director of the Court, is indisputably less influential than either the advocates or the judges. The role of the advocates is more difficult to appraise. Nominally, their rank is equivalent to that of the judges, and there is wide respect among attorneys and other students of the Court for their conclusions. However, it remains true that they have only an indirect influence on the judgments. The office of president is seemingly what one makes of it; the willingness of both sides to make the above-mentioned trade would indicate that assessments can differ. In practice, the personalities and abilities of individuals are of considerably more significance than estimates based on numbers. It is even possible that a particularly persuasive advocate general can be more influential than one of the less impressive judges.[13]

Judicial Independence

Against this background, what are we to make of the show of independence in electing Judge Hammes the third president of the Court of Justice? First it must be noted that, in the context of the politics of European integration in general, this change is considerably less troublesome than would have been a shift which put a German at the head of the Court. After all, the presidency remains in the Benelux group. More precisely, it does not give Germany a second presidency to add to its leadership of the Common Market Commission. Given the signal importance of President Hallstein's position, it is understandable that the German

13. See infra, p. 37.

government would not want to jeopardize this choice spot by taking on the presidency of the Court of Justice.

Still, a question remains. Why did the Dutch give up a position for which they had been willing to trade two places six years earlier? It seems inconceivable that the Dutch government was not forewarned that the Court was about to elect a new president. The judges' desire to have some control over the choice of the man who is to lead the Court dates back at least as far as the temptation to give the presidency to Judge Riese. If the other members of the Court preferred Judge Hammes, certainly Judge Donner would not have been ignorant of this preference. If, on the other hand, Judge Donner wished to step down from the presidency, it is most unlikely that he would have considered himself free to do so. Either way, it seems realistic to assume that Judge Donner felt some obligation to sound out his national government about the impending change. Accordingly, since Donner was reappointed for a new six-year term just prior to the selection of Judge Hammes as president, one must assume that the Dutch government accepted the new division of judicial posts.

As to the reason for the government's acquiescence, one can only speculate. The most plausible explanation is that the Dutch now look upon themselves as the possessors of a "credit balance" which they are free to draw upon in future negotiations. In other words, Holland's acceptance of the Court's decision represents at best only a small step forward in establishing the independence of the Court. Much depends on how the Dutch choose to use their credit. It may figure in the bargaining for seats on the new Commission, following the fusion of the executive organs of the three Communities. If so, the Court will be pulled closer to politics and its independence further threatened. On the other hand, if the Dutch simply claim the clerkship of the Court or a third advocate general's position, should one be authorized, then the change of presidents could mean some slight increase in the independence of the Court. The rigidity of the original distribution formula would be replaced by a more flexible procedure which would take account of the wishes of members of the Court, while at the same time keeping a reasonable division of judicial places.

With all this said, what are we to conclude about the independence of the judges and its effect on Court operations? To begin with, it is important to reiterate that there is no evidence of member governments having attempted to influence the deliberations of the Court. On the other hand, the governments show no signs of a willingness to change tenure arrangements and thus to establish more firmly the Court's autonomy. It can only be concluded that the member states are unwilling to relinquish whatever control—or potential control—the present system affords them. This, of course, is hardly surprising when viewed from the perspective of the strongly national orientation of the Community.[14] Accordingly and paradoxically, these personnel arrangements attest to the essential unity and coherence of the institutional framework of the Coal and Steel Community.[15]

Still, until recently it seemed possible to argue that the insecurity of tenure could stand in the way of prestigious

14. See supra, pp. 13–16.

15. Several members of the Court have told me that the generally advanced age of the judges mitigates the tenure problem. The argument is based on the assumption that men in the latter stages of their careers are not so concerned with stretching a six-year appointment into a term of twelve or more years. This is no doubt true, and there certainly has been a tendency for some governments to appoint older men to the Court. However, there has been a parallel tendency to appoint quite young men to the Court, men who might well view the Court as a stepping stone to bigger and better things—perhaps on the national level. Both developments have their dangers. The older men may well be beyond the age of professional commitment. Consequently, they may view the Court as a sinecure, a sort of retirement with both pay and work. The younger men, on the other hand, may be too sensitive to national interests. What the Court obviously needs is more judges who accept a seat on the Court of Justice as an end in itself.

judicial appointments. However, the last several appointees have been well-known and highly respected men. Significantly, one recent appointee had earlier refused a place on the Court. Also interesting is the fact that the last three judges chosen—Lecourt, Strauss, and Monaco—have all been men with considerable governmental and/or political experience.[16] While it is still too early to arrive at any definite conclusions, there seems at least some reason to believe that tenure difficulties are not interfering with the appointment of men of quality, prestige, and political sophistication.

JUDICIAL PROCEDURE

A case may be conducted in any of the Community's four official languages, French, German, Dutch, or Italian. In practice, the language is that of the enterprise or member government bringing suit.[17] As soon as the petition is filed, the suit is given a number which remains its official designation; the suits are numbered in sequence, by year. Thus, the first suit presented to the Court, in 1953, was numbered 1/53.[18] The defendant is notified of the suit and must then submit a memorandum in defense. The plaintiff follows with a rejoinder and the defendant closes out the written procedure with a surrejoinder. The correct French designations of the

16. Certainly the most puzzling of these appointments has been President de Gaulle's choice of Robert Lecourt, a leader of the MRP and a strong proponent of European integration.

17. In virtually all of the litigation under the Coal and Steel Community, the High Authority has appeared as the defendant. Cf. Eric Stein and Peter Hay, "New Legal Remedies of Enterprises: A Survey," in Stein and Nicholson, *1*, 502. All documents are translated into these four languages, and simultaneous translation is provided for the judges during all oral proceedings.

18. Unfortunately, the decisions of the HA are numbered in the same manner, and occasionally the numbers of the HA's decision and of the suit coincide. For example, suit 36/59 was against the HA decision of the same number. To avoid confusion, here the numbers of all HA decisions will be preceded by the initials HA (e.g. HA 36/59).

four parts are *requête, mémoire en défense, réplique,* and *duplique.*[19] The entire written procedure, as well as a transcript of the oral portion of the suit, is collected in a dossier which is on file in the Library of the Court of Justice.[20]

It is the president's job to choose a judge to act as rapporteur. The rapporteur keeps track of the documents and, when they are all submitted, works out a preliminary report including his suggestions on disposal of the case. This report and supporting documents which the rapporteur considers significant are then passed on to the other judges. It is also up to the rapporteur to suggest whether it is necessary to call in experts for technical advice or to hear witnesses. Usually, the Court decides against such preliminaries and moves on to the oral proceedings. Here, the parties again plead their cases and are questioned by the judges and the advocate.[21] The final stage of the suit begins when the advocate general reads his conclusions to the Court in public session.[22] The Court then retires to consider the case. After secret deliberations the judgment is delivered, also in public session. Both the decision and the conclusions of the advocate are later published in all four Community languages.[23]

It is difficult to generalize about the time required for the

19. Citations will often be made to these documents, using the French term and the number of the suit, for example, requête 1/54. The *mémoire en défense* will be referred to simply as mémoire.

20. An official dossier is retained by the clerk.

21. On the relative significance of the written and oral proceedings see Stein and Hay, pp. 500–01.

22. Only when the Court is considering minor revisions of the treaty, according to Article 95, paragraphs 3 and 4, are the advocates heard privately.

23. All references in this study will be to the French version. *Recueil de la Jurisprudence de la Cour,* published in annual volumes by *Services des Publications des Communautés Européenes.* The citations will include the number of the suit, the parties, the volume, the page, and the year decided, as, for example, 1/54, France v. H.A., 1 Rec. 7 (1954).

entire judicial cycle. The Court has considerable discretionary control over the rate at which the suit proceeds. Often the parties will decide on a delay, perhaps for negotiation; the Court will normally agree to a temporary suspension. At times, the Court itself will deem it expedient to slow down or speed up a suit. However, as a rule, the written procedure takes about five months.[24] The oral proceedings are of course quite short, usually lasting a single day, but the advocate and the Court must be given sufficient time to deliberate. On the average, a suit will be completed in about ten months, but extreme variations from the average can be expected; some suits finish in several months while others may take more than two years.

The Role of the Advocates General

The importance of the advocates is difficult to assess. The influence of their conclusions obviously varies from case to case, depending on the persuasiveness of their arguments and the difficulty of the problems facing the Court. However, my interviews lead me to believe that under President Donner the position of the advocates changed somewhat. Although never—I have been assured—had they been admitted to the deliberations of the Court, under President Donner they were not even kept au courant, as had been the practice during the tenure of President Pilotti.

But is there any reason to believe that this new pattern will continue? While President Hammes' course is still unknown, a strong argument can be made for maintaining the distance between the advocates and the judges. It is important to realize that the advocate general is patterned after the Commissaire du Gouvernement of the French Conseil d'Etat.[25]

24. See statement by President Donner as quoted in J. F. McMahon, "The Court of the European Communities," *Journal of Common Market Studies*, *1* (1962), 5.

25. See C. J. Hamson, *Executive Discretion and Judicial Control* (London, Stevens, 1954), pp. 79–81.

Significantly, the changing role of the advocates can be traced to an important distinction between the Court of Justice and the Conseil d'Etat. Because the decisions of the Conseil are inordinately brief, the conclusions of the Commissaire, which are considerably fuller and more nuanced, are heavily counted upon as a reliable reflection of the views of the Conseil. Naturally, this function puts a premium on close cooperation between the Commissaire and the Conseil.

The opinions of the advocates general are certainly more detailed and less evasive than the decisions of the Court of Justice. However, since the Court's decisions are not so spare as those of the Conseil, there is less need for the advocate to enlarge upon the words of the Court. Consequently, a somewhat different role—or perhaps, a different emphasis—seems called for. Because suits do not reach the Court of Justice on appeal, the advocates general can serve usefully as a kind of court of first instance. Their opinions can give the judges the benefit of a prior, public, and quasi-judicial resolution of the case.[26] If an improvised appeal procedure like this is to be followed, it would seem best for the work of the advocates to be set off rather strictly from the Court. Instead of the close cooperation which characterizes the relationship of the Commissaire and the Conseil d'Etat, independence and autonomy are called for.

DIMENSIONS OF JUDICIAL REVIEW

According to Article 31 of the Coal and Steel Community Treaty, the Court's function is "to ensure the rule of law in the interpretation and application of the present Treaty and of the regulations for its execution." This ambitious goal would seem to call for open access to the Court in order to assure that all legitimate claims are adjudicated. Of course, as might be expected, unlimited judicial review was not con-

26. Cf. Behr, pp. 24–25.

sidered feasible, and the treaty includes a number of restraints on the Court's power to extend the rule of law. The
ultimate importance of these restrictions will depend on how
they affect the work of the Court, and, accordingly, they must
be assessed in context. Nevertheless, a preliminary examination of each of the limitations in isolation will illuminate the
basic issues and, at the same time, afford a better view of the
milieu in which the Court must function.

If the prospective litigant is a member state, the road to
judicial review is relatively clear. The governments can use
court action to force the HA to observe the rule of law in
applying the treaty.[27] In addition, disputes among member
states over the application of the treaty can be brought directly to the Court of Justice for resolution.[28] For business
firms the path to the Court is, as we shall see, considerably
narrower. There is, however, one limitation on judicial review, applying equally to business firms and governments,
which should be considered at the outset.

Economic Issues

The Court is generally prohibited from reviewing the economic bases of HA decisions. The goal of this restriction was
obviously to keep the work of the Court of Justice within
proper boundaries—the judge of "legality" rather than "opportunity." [29] The parties have, in fact, often argued on this
basis that certain questions were not relevant to the Court's
determination.

However, the treaty provides several exceptions to this
rule. According to Article 33, the basic jurisdictional article,
the Court may examine economic facts when "the HA is
alleged to have abused its powers or to have clearly misin-
terpreted the provisions of the Treaty." In addition, court

27. Article 33, paragraph 1.
28. Article 89.
29. See Bebr, p. 89.

action initiated under certain other important articles of the treaty calls for more general judicial scrutiny. Article 95, paragraph 4, offers a method of making minor revisions to the treaty and provides that "the Court shall be fully competent to review any matters of law and fact." Article 37, which is designed to deal with "fundamental and persistent disturbances in the economies" of the member states, calls upon the Court to review "the cogency" of the HA's decision. Finally, Article 88, requiring the HA to take direct action against a member state which fails to fulfill one of its treaty obligations, authorizes "an appeal to the Court's general jurisdiction." [30]

The distinction between law and economic fact is, as a practical matter, very difficult to define. Given this fact and the significant exceptions to the rule that have been incorporated in the treaty, it is hardly surprising that the Court has been less than meticulous in accepting this restriction on its operations—as noted by Gerhard Bebr: "The Court has never felt restricted by this clause, particularly not when dealing with a very complex economic situation." [31] The limitation has, in fact, been left out of the Common Market Treaty.[32] At any rate, for all these reasons, the problem will be touched upon only very lightly in the course of this study.

30. Cf. Maurice Lagrange, "The Role of the Court of Justice of the European Communities as Seen through its Case Law," *Law and Contemporary Problems,* 26 (1961), 403.

31. P. 88, note 31.

32. Cf. Stein and Hay, p. 478. It can be argued that the failure to insert this limitation into the Common Market Treaty is tantamount to a tacit recognition that the distinction between law and economic fact is illusory. Accordingly, as I have suggested above, the judges should feel free to do whatever is necessary to apply the treaty. On the other hand, one can assume that in not specifying those situations in which the Court is free to consider the economic facts, the authors of the treaty intended to deny this prerogative to the judges.

Pathways to Adjudication

The rule of law requires not only that a court be able to deal with all the violations of legal rules but, in addition, that all injured parties be entitled to adjudication of their grievances. On the other hand, it is most unusual for private parties to have access to international tribunals. In the Coal and Steel Community, there is something of a compromise between traditional international legal procedures and the demands of the rule of law. Contrary to the practice in ordinary international tribunals, it is not only national governments that may bring suit; Community enterprises may also press their claims before the Court.[33] But this right is restricted, and these restrictions reflect the determination of the national governments to maintain their hold on the development of the Community.

In the first place, disputes among enterprises over the application of the treaty cannot be brought directly before the Court of Justice. In other words, an enterprise cannot use court action to pressure another firm to conform to the treaty. Similarly, enterprises are not permitted to bring suit against violations of the treaty by the member governments. Finally, while member governments may challenge both individual and general decisions of the HA, the right of firms to appeal general decisions is very narrowly confined. Of these three types of restrictions, the last is in practice far and away the most significant. Vitiating the effects of restrictions against *direct* appeal of disputes with other enterprises or

33. Article 80 specifies that all firms "engaged in production in the field of coal and steel" are subject to the treaty. Court access is also permitted to associations of Community enterprises, as defined in Article 48. For an explanation of the notion of enterprise embodied in the Coal and Steel Community Treaty as well as the disputes which have arisen with respect to implementation, see Bebr, pp. 59–65. Cf. 12/63, Mme. Marga Schlieker v. H.A., 1 Rec. 173, 185 (1963).

member governments is the indirect route that has been provided to judicial review of such disputes.

The HA may be sued not only for its actions but also for its failure to act.[34] Consequently, if the executive fails to inter-fere with unauthorized actions of the member governments or the enterprises, this lapse may be brought to the attention of the Court. The HA must first be asked to act in the desired manner, but the executive's failure to respond is considered an implicit negative decision.[35] By this indirect route mem-ber states and Community enterprises may bring grievances against one another to the Court of Justice. As an index of the convenience and effectiveness of such appeals, let us note that the member governments have preferred this method to direct appeal of disputes with other governments over the application of the treaty.[36] In these instances, the HA finds itself only the nominal defendant, or perhaps the code-fendant. Accordingly, the other defendant may, with the per-mission of the Court, submit its own brief. "Interventions" on the side of the plaintiff may also be permitted by the Court. According to Article 34 of the Protocol, parties wish-ing to intervene need only establish "an interest in the out-come of the dispute pending before the Court." [37] Perhaps it would clarify the explanation to present an example.

In a series of cases which will be treated in Chapter 7, some French enterprises objected to certain special rail rates which the state-owned German railroad, the Bundesbahn, gave to shipments of coal from the Ruhr to distant points *within* Germany. While not able to bring suit directly against the German government, the French firms were able

34. Article 35. See Thomas Buergenthal, "The Private Appeal Against Illegal State Activities in the European Coal and Steel Community," *American Journal of Comparative Law, 11* (1962), 327–41.

35. Stein and Hay, p. 476, note 81.

36. Article 89.

37. For a discussion of the problems with respect to interventions, see Bebr, pp. 169–77.

to call the Court's attention to the HA's failure to act against these special rates. Furthermore, they were able to persuade the French government to intervene in their behalf in the suit. In this case, the HA was in reality defending the interests of the German government, which could have intervened but did not.

Decisions: Individual and General

The most significant obstacle raised by the treaty against enterprises wishing to have their day in court is the distinction between individual and general decisions. As noted above, the businesses have only a very restricted right to appeal general decisions of the HA, but with respect to individual decisions, they and the member governments are on an equal footing. To get an idea of what is at stake, the following three questions will be successively explored:

1. What is the difference between an individual decision and a general decision?
2. What is the significance of this distinction?
3. What opportunity is there for enterprises to appeal general decisions?

The Court of Justice has characterized the distinction between the two types of decisions as follows: "General decisions are quasi-legislative acts, issued by a public authority and having a normative effect *erga omnes*." [38] On its face, the distinction seems clear enough. In practice, it is difficult to make, and the treaty is without guidance on the matter.[39] It might be said that the general decision has an abstract, nonspecific quality while individual decisions are determinate and particular. Instead of being generally applicable, the individual decision, "regulates . . . a specific, concrete situation, possibly even designating its addressee." [40]

38. 18/57, Firme I. Nold KG v. H.A., 5 Rec. 89, 113 (1959).
39. Bebr, p. 41.
40. Ibid., p. 44.

The difficulty of defining the border between individual and general acts should not obscure the importance of the distinction for Community enterprises. These firms have only a narrowly restricted right to test general decisions before the Court of Justice. Even if one of these quasi-legislative acts should impinge upon their interests, they are not assured of judicial relief. The essential criterion of justiciability is not injury per se, but the individual quality of the act from which the injury stems.

Accordingly, the line drawn by the Court circumscribes the area of legal protection afforded the enterprises. This line also defines the boundaries of the rule of law within the Community, in that parties are not always entitled to adjudication of legitimate grievances. It is not by accident that the enterprises' right of appeal is so restricted. In their determination to maintain a firm grip on the development of the Community, the member states have sought to exclude the enterprises from the big decisions, the general problems.[41]

According to Article 33, the HA can be held responsible before the Court of Justice for violations of the treaty, for substantial procedural violations, for abuse of power, and for acting without legal competence.[42] These four categories of infraction are drawn from French administrative law and were developed over the life of the French Conseil d'Etat.[43] The Conseil has sought to open its doors as widely as possible

41. These restrictions suggest the ambivalent position of the Court of Justice as a kind of supranational compromise between the national court and the international tribunal. This problem has already been discussed in the initial chapter, supra, pp. 1–16. Commenting on the enterprise's restricted access to the Court, Advocate General Lagrange has written: "The state is considered responsible for the normal safeguarding of its national interests. This is a principle of international law that has been maintained in the Treaty" (p. 406).

42. See D. G. Valentine, "The Jurisdiction of the Court of Justice of the European Communities to Annul Executive Action," *British Yearbook of International Law* (1960), pp. 185–200.

43. See Stein and Hay, p. 468. Note also the overlap with administrative law in the other member states. Ibid., pp. 468–70.

to individuals with grievances against the administration.[44] Therefore, in allowing appeal on all four grounds, the Coal and Steel Community indicated not just its heavy debt to the Conseil d'Etat, but also a determination to offer abundant protection to those subjected to the Community's administrative process.

Insofar as the enterprises are concerned this full range of protection is available against individual decisions of the HA; only when the executive abuses its authority may an enterprise appeal a general decision. Similar restrictions curtail the right of enterprises to bring suit against recommendations of the HA.[45] Only when the recommendation affects them—that is when it has an individual quality—or when it involves an abuse of power, may firms bring suit against recommendations.[46]

It is not clear why review against general acts is permitted only when an abuse of power is involved. It would be difficult to make a case for this infraction being any more serious in an objective sense than the others, although it is perhaps more insidious.[47] As evolved by the Conseil d'Etat, the no-

44. "The question thus arises as to what are the grounds upon which such annulment will be granted. What shortcomings of the act result in its elimination? There again the Conseil d'Etat has constantly extended the compass of judicial review in favor of the citizen and of the principle of legality of administrative action during the hundred and thirty-seven years of its functioning." Stefan Riesenfeld, "The French System of Administrative Justice: A Model for America? (Part II)," *Boston University Law Review*, 18 (1938), 424.

45. Recommendations differ from decisions in that they are binding only "with respect to the objectives" (Article 14, paragraph 3) while decisions are "binding in every respect" (Article 14, paragraph 1). What this means essentially is that parties are free to choose how they will accomplish the goals of the recommendation. Recommendations are concerned with ends rather than means.

46. Article 33, paragraph 2. It is not altogether accurate to identify the individual quality of the recommendation with its effect on the enterprise. See infra, p. 47.

47. Cf. Lagrange, p. 416: "Among the different tasks of the Court . . . the most important, according to the spirit of the Treaty, was most certainly

tion of abuse of power, *détournement de pouvoir*, has to do with the motivation of the administrator: "This principle was developed by the French Conseil d'Etat to control, to some extent, the discretionary powers of public authorities and prevent their arbitrary use. It is control of the administrator's motives which is largely alien to the practice of American courts." [48]

In practice, this ground has been something of a dead letter. It has often been alleged but never has the Court decided that the HA has abused its power.[49] Advocate General Lagrange accounts for the refusal of the Court to accept pleas of abuse of power as follows: "As a general rule, experience shows . . . that the only criticism that could possibly be leveled against the High Authority would not be that of having abused its power, but rather that of not having, in numerous cases, exercised its power with sufficient determination nor with sufficient promptness." [50]

Taken by itself, the failure of the judges to accept appeals claiming an abuse of power could have effectively sealed off the general decisions of the HA from court attack by the enterprises. This has not been the case. To fully understand why, some perspective is necessary. The development must be viewed as part of the rather flexible attitude that the Court of Justice has adopted with respect to the grounds of appeal and to procedural matters in general. The result has been that only two of the four grounds for appeal have proved effective bases for suits against the HA. The executive has been held

---

the task of safeguarding Member States and enterprises against possible *abuse of power* on the part of the High Authority."

48. Bebr, pp. 98–99. See also Riesenfeld, pp. 425–26. Any understanding of *détournement de pouvoir* within the Community must begin with Advocate General Lagrange's conclusions in one of the Court's initial cases. 3/54, Associazione Industrie Siderurgiche Italiane (ASSIDER) v. H.A., 1 Rec. 123, 143–75 (1954).

49. Buergenthal, pp. 338–39. See also Stein and Hay, p. 468. Cf. Bebr, p. 99.

50. Lagrange, p. 416.

responsible for substantial procedural violations in accordance with Article 33. However, all of the substantive grounds seemed to have been subsumed under the heading, violation of the treaty. Not only has abuse of power proved an unfruitful ground for appeal, but in no decisions has the HA been held to have acted without legal competence.

In reducing the avenues of approach, the judges have not sought to restrict the possibilities for judicial review. On the contrary, according to Advocate General Lagrange, the Court "has tried to open its forum as much as possible to private persons. It has been little inclined to attach undue importance to the rules of procedure, e.g., as regards the grounds of appeal." [51] There seems to be no reason to question this interpretation. To quote another commentator: "The Court has so far interpreted an individual act rather liberally to the detriment of a general act so as to ensure the widest possible protection of individuals." [52]

Specifically, the judges have leaned in the direction of the "interest" theory. Taken to its logical conclusion, the interest theory would give the enterprise access to judicial review whenever one of its interests is impinged upon by a general act.[53] However, the Court has not adopted the interest theory, it has merely indicated that it is receptive to claims based upon interest and, therefore, inclined to give the enterprises the benefit of the doubt.[54] In addition, firms have been permitted to raise objections to a general decision as part of a suit against an individual decision based upon that

51. Ibid., p. 407.
52. Bebr, p. 42.
53. See Stein and Hay, pp. 470–72, particularly note 67. Even taken this far, the interest theory would not put the enterprises on an even footing with member states, which may bring suit against all general acts without demonstrating a subjective concern.
54. For a compact review of Court practice, see Bebr, pp. 41–49. See also Lagrange, pp. 407–08. Cf. 12/63, Schlieker v. H.A., 9 Rec. 173, 186 (1963).

general decision.[55] If the individual decision is invalidated because of a defect in the general decision, for all practical purposes the general decision becomes inoperative.

While the judges have been sympathetic to the enterprises, there are obviously limits to how far they can go in opening the doors of the Court. It was clear from the beginning that particular interests were bound to be adversely affected by the convulsions attendant upon the opening of a common market. Since the member states—not the enterprises—are responsible for the process of building a community, it is understandable that precautions should be taken to avoid continued legal harassment by vested interests.

In this issue, the tension between community-building and the rule of the law is manifest.[56] To exclude the enterprises from judicial protection must be recognized as a significant blow against the rule of law in the Coal and Steel Community. Yet, sharply restricted access accords with both the letter and the spirit of the treaty: it is the logical extension of the distinction between individual and general decisions. As we shall learn,[57] there is evidence that the Court has tended to temper its initial commitment to the enterprises by an increasing awareness of Community values.

In closing, one must remember that despite the restrictions on the Court of Justice, its word is final. No appeal is possible, although the judges may be asked to clarify or reconsider a decision.[58] There is, thus, only a single judicial instance: the Court of Justice is the first judicial body to hear the suit, and there is no appeal from its judgments.

55. 15/57, Compagnie des Hauts Fourneaux de Chasse v. H.A., 4 Rec. 155, 184 (1958).

56. See supra, pp. 20–24.

57. See particularly Chapters 10 and 12, infra.

58. See Articles 37 and 38, respectively, of the *Protocol*. Reconsideration is possible only if decisive new facts emerge.

2 RULE FORMALISM AND JUDICIAL RESTRAINT

INTRODUCTION

The first two chapters of this study have highlighted the tension between the political and the legal roles of the Court of Justice. While under an effective obligation to accommodate its operations to the highly politicized setting of the Coal and Steel Community, the Court's primary duty is to the treaty. In Chapter 1 it was suggested that the functional technique might provide a satisfactory means of dealing with this judicial dilemma. By testing measures according to their purpose and in relation to treaty goals, functionalism enables the judges to bridge the gap between the practical demands of the political world and the textual rigidity of the legal world. It was argued that functionalism seemed to offer the most promising approach to stable rules and, accordingly, to effective judicial review.

The Court of Justice has, in fact, used functional methods for dealing with many of the problems presented to it. However, there is no evidence to suggest that this was a matter of conscious judicial choice. Indeed, insofar as I know, none of the judges has even recognized functionalism as a legitimate classification. Since the functional interpretation of the Court's work is solely the author's, it is hardly surprising that the course of judicial review has not been consistently within a functional framework. Moreover, the partial character of the Coal and Steel Community and the rather tentative nature of its institutional structure impose restrictions on the utility of the functional approach.[1]

1. Supra, pp. 20–24.

The basic goal of the chapters that follow will be to substantiate the argument that the Court has adopted functional techniques and to demonstrate the success of functional methods for imposing normative rules on the integrative process. But to understand fully the potential contribution of functionalism it will be necessary, on the one hand, to explore its limitations and, on the other, to establish the weaknesses of alternative methods adopted by the Court of Justice.

It is to this latter task that we shall turn in the next two chapters which comprise Part Two. Part Three will deal with the evolution of the functional technique and Parts Four and Five with its limitations—specifically, the problems of partial integration and political change. Each of these major sections will begin with an introduction which summarizes the findings of the preceding section and relates these findings to the problems about to be considered. Final conclusions will be reserved for Part Six.

To facilitate comparisons among chapters, a standard format will be used. The initial portion of each chapter will discuss the disputed provision of the treaty and indicate its bearing on the broader goals of the Community. It is, of course, upon this linkage of the specific with the general that the functional method ultimately rests. A second section of each chapter will explore the political background of the legal issues. Next, the arguments of the parties will be presented and the decision of the Court analyzed.[2] The concluding sections of each chapter will assess the practical impact of the judgment and explore its integrative consequences.[3]

2. It is important to note that in relating the positions of the parties there will be no attempt to develop—even in summary form—the complete arguments. Procedural questions will be consciously avoided, as will be matters which are deemed of limited importance to the broader purpose of this study.

3. It will not always be possible to stick strictly to this pattern. For example, when a series of cases is dealt with in a single chapter, some changes in sequence will be necessary. However, none of the steps will be left out: all of the problems will be taken up and clearly identified.

It is clear that this study is basically structured to highlight the uses and limitations of functionalism. There are, however, significant nonfunctional issues to be treated. Of particular importance are the ideological problems stemming from the Community's free market orientation.[4] Not unrelated to this matter—although certainly not identical—are the powers of intervention accorded to the Community's executive, the High Authority. At any rate, these questions will be accented as they arise in the course of litigation and summarized in Part Six. Finally, although virtually all of the Court's work will be treated, personnel problems which are confined to disputes over pay, retirement benefits, and job security will be excluded.[5]

Let me close this discussion with a few remarks about the two chapters of Part Two. These chapters are intended to illustrate and analyze two different kinds of problems. On the one hand, we shall see in Chapter 3 the pitfalls of strict adherence to the text of the treaty. While the temptations of textualism—the most obvious agent of certainty and stability—are understandable, its benefits are likely to be ephemeral. On the other hand, the importance of stable norms must not be underrated. Chapter 4 should clarify the importance of rules by indicating the difficulties that result when the Court fails to explore fully the important issues. Arbitral type settlements certainly have a place in the regional pattern, but it is important not to neglect their shortcomings. Taken together, the chapters of Part Two should demonstrate the need for an interpretive technique which combines appropriate shares of flexibility and certainty. It will be the task of Part Three to demonstrate that functionalism is that technique.

4. Supra, pp. 17–18.

5. In what was perhaps the only personnel dispute with political overtones, the Court held that the earnings of a Belgian national working for the HA were not subject to Belgian income tax. 6/60, Jean E. Humblet v. Belgium, 7 Rec. 1125 (1961).

3

FLEXIBLE PRICING: THE BIG PRODUCERS

I

It was more than two years after the Court began to function that it was given its first opportunity to render a decision. The litigation centered on Article 60 of the Coal and Steel Community Treaty, which defines the basic goals and methods of common market pricing policy. The first section of the article discusses procedures which are prohibited by the treaty:

> —unfair competitive practices, in particular purely temporary or purely local price reductions the purpose of which is to acquire a monopoly within the common market;
> —discriminatory practices involving within the common market the application by a seller of unequal conditions to comparable transactions, especially according to the nationality of the buyer.

At first glance, the provisions of the article seem clear and their relationship to the goals of the treaty apparent. If competition is going to be the integrative catalyst, predatory pricing practices directed at eliminating competitors must be suppressed. Moreover, pricing discrimination "according to the nationality of the buyer" is patently contrary to the idea of establishing a common market. To eliminate barriers and quantitative restrictions while permitting alternative measures capable of maintaining the isolation of national markets would, of course, be folly.

However, while Article 60 takes particular note of nationally oriented discrimination, its condemnation of discriminatory practices is general. The purposes to be served by this general prohibition are less clear, but it hardly seems likely to stimulate competition: "Monnet's specific proposals on market rules . . . were accepted in essence in the final version of the Treaty, including the rigorous interpretation of Article 60 which made 'non-discrimination' almost the equivalent of 'no price competition,' a deliberate device to limit the flow of German steel to the French market." [1] Moreover, at least insofar as the steel industry is concerned: "nondiscrimination and price publication involve an 'immense revolution' since the member countries themselves have no statutory limits on the freedom to contract in this field." [2] Accordingly, it is not surprising that litigation has arisen over the general prohibition of discriminatory pricing practices.

Initially, the HA chose simply to require prior publication of prices and rigid adherence to the published lists.[3] Publication was the simplest way to avoid discriminatory practices. So long as published prices were followed, equal treatment was assured. But publication is not a very sensitive test of discrimination. Price lists not only eliminate unequal treatment; they tend to stand in the way of proper distinctions

1. Haas, *The Uniting of Europe*, p. 245.
2. Louis Lister, *Europe's Coal and Steel Community* (New York, Twentieth Century Fund, 1960), p. 208.
3. HA 30 & 31/53, *Journal Officiel de la Communauté Européenne du Charbon et de l'Acier* (hereafter cited as *J.O.C.E.C.A.*), 2 (May 4, 1953), 109–11. Because most of the questions concerning coal prices were intimately connected with coal cartels, infra, Chapter 13, this discussion will deal exclusively with steel prices.

among buyers. If published price lists are the sole criterion of discrimination, sellers can be prohibited from deviating from price lists even to allow for valid cost differentials among buyers. In other words, strict enforcement of publication requirements inhibits rather than stimulates and protects competition.

Publication is particularly inhibitory of competition in periods of slumping business activity. If the published price reductions of one producer are followed by his competitors, no advantage is gained from the price cuts. All this is particularly true of industries like steel, where "the bulk of the output is provided by a few large sellers, the so-called 'administered price' industries. In these industries 'of the few' . . . each seller is acutely conscious both that he has some discretion over the price he charges and that his discretion is shared with rivals. No seller can gain a larger share of the market by cutting prices openly, for others would follow his lead." [4] The obvious alternative to uniform price reductions is secret rebating, which makes price reductions at least a somewhat effective means of attracting new customers. The result is likely to be lower prices, but at the cost of discrimination. Yet, so long as discrimination is not directed at eliminating competition or is not structured according to nationality, this would seem a small price to pay.

However, publication serves another purpose: it permits alignment of prices. Article 60 prescribes a multiple basing point system for the Community.[5] While in general held to published rates, each producer is allowed to align his prices

---

4. Eugene V. Rostow, *Planning for Freedom* (New Haven, Yale University Press, 1962), p. 222. As a matter of fact, uniform application of price reductions can be quickly ascertained by competitors even without publication and thus lose efficacy. See Derek C. Bok, *The First Three Years of the Schuman Plan*, Studies in International Finance, 5 (Princeton, 1955), 36–37.

5. For a discussion of the Community pricing system and of Article 60, see Lister, Chapter 7, particularly pp. 207–09.

on *lower* rates quoted at other basing points. Producers can thus maintain published prices and, at the same time, engage in a limited amount of price competition. This right of alignment serves a vital Community purpose, for it promotes inter-market penetration, thus advancing the cause of a common market: "Extensive alignment, if it occurred . . . would register a willingness of producers to 'invade' markets normally supplied by someone else." [6]

Even without penetration, alignment is likely to promote Community interests by driving Community prices down toward the level of the low cost producers. For example, when French prices dropped as a result of the 1957 devaluation, "demand remained high in France and there was no great push to export, but buyers in Belgium and elsewhere seem to have secured price concessions from their normal suppliers on the ground that the price of the *semi-fictitious* French deliveries had fallen." [7]

The connection between alignment and publication is clear.[8] However, if alignment is on a "semi-fictitious" offer, how does it differ from secret rebating? With 41 basing points to choose from,[9] alignment can offer the same obstacles to a transparent market as secret rebating. Moreover, as was noted above, rigid publication requirements go well beyond the needs of a viable policy against discrimination and stand in the way of fair competition. In other words, equal treatment itself is not an unmixed blessing. Neither secret rebating nor

6. William Diebold, Jr., *The Schuman Plan* (New York, Praeger, 1959), p. 278.

7. Ibid., p. 277, italics supplied. For an analysis of the beneficial effects of this price-reducing phenomenon in terms of European integration in general, see Tibor Scitovsky, *Economic Theory and Western European Integration* (Stanford, Stanford University Press, 1958), p. 39.

8. Article 60 #2(b) specifies that publication requirements must, inter alia, make "it possible to align the quotation with the price-list, based on another point."

9. Diebold, p. 275.

fictitious alignment is in accord with treaty rules against discrimination, but they do seem capable of producing a desirable measure of price flexibility.

II

Shortly after the opening of the Coal and Steel Community a steel slump led the HA to relax its own rigid publication requirements. It became common knowledge that published prices were being discounted by varying amounts in different Community markets. In Belgium and Luxembourg, for example, average discounts of 10 per cent were reported, while in France discounts ranged between 7 and 10 per cent and in Germany they were about 5 per cent.[10]

The HA's response was a decision which allowed a deviation of 2.5 per cent from published lists. By permitting discriminatory pricing within this limited range, it was hoped "to introduce greater flexibility in the rules governing the publication of price-schedules, and to induce enterprises to adjust their lists to the prices actually charged."[11] In other words, the HA was seeking publication requirements that would not inhibit price reductions. To enforce the more restrictive regulations at the cost of higher prices—even if it were possible—would have been a hollow victory, indeed.

The 2.5 per cent margin, named after Jean Monnet, the President of the HA, became known as the Monnet Margin. Other deviations were also permitted; the three decisions may be paraphrased as followers:

> 1. 1/54 permitted deviations from published prices where the transactions in question were not included in the categories specified in the price lists, or to the degree that the deviations were applied equally to all comparable transactions.

10. *Europe CECA* (Agence Internationale d'Information pour la Presse), 23 November 1953, pp. 1–2. See also Lister, pp. 220–21.

11. HA, *Second General Report* (1954), pp. 94–95.

2. 2/54 permitted an average deviation of 2.5 per cent above or below published prices.

3. 3/54 called for reports every 15 days on the deviations from published prices.[12]

When the HA first proposed the new regulations, there was opposition from many quarters, but following a series of meetings with industry and consumer representatives [13] and the obligatory consultation with the Council of Ministers,[14] only the Italian steel industry and the French and Italian governments remained opposed. Since the two governments were unable to block action in the Council of Ministers, they turned directly to the Court for relief.[15] Separate suits were brought by the French government (1/54), the Italian government (2/54), and two Italian steel associations (3 & 4/54).

The basis of Italian opposition by both the government and the steel associations is clear. According to Section 30 of the Convention, the Italian market was to be protected until February 1958. Consequently, no alignment was permitted on Italian prices. The new provisions, and particularly the 2.5 per cent margin, permitted a certain amount of price competition in the Italian market: non-Italian steel companies were provided with a margin for bargaining. Both the Italian government and the steel enterprises were interested in maintaining protection of the Italian market, and the result was three suits.

However, the situation is more obscure in France, where the government entered the contest alone. One can only speculate on the source of its opposition and the failure of the

---

12. HA 1–3/54, *J.O.C.E.C.A.*, *3* (13 January 1954), 217–20.

13. *Europe CECA*, 20 January 1954, p. 2, and 27 January 1954, p. 2.

14. Ibid., 21 December 1953, p. 1, and 22 December 1953, p. 1.

15. Article 60 required the HA to consult with the Council but did not necessitate the Council's approval. Moreover, a majority of the Council supported the HA. Ibid.

French steel industry to join the government's legal assault on the new decisions.[16] The postwar French battle against inflation resulted in tight government control of steel prices. These consistently low prices discouraged any marked penetration of the French market by other Community producers.[17] While the French steel industry was thus shielded from foreign competition, it was forced to pay the price of its own protection. Its low profit margins were a source of constant friction between steel and government.[18] More important than this cleavage, however, was the fact that the 2.5 per cent margin offered the steel industry some relief from government control, because it permitted deviations above as well as below published prices. This slightly inflationary potential of the margin incited government opposition but only benign silence from the steel industry.

In its first litigation the Court of Justice was, therefore, faced with a dispute of more than negligible political importance. Two member governments, dissatisfied with the response of the Community's political institutions, had turned to the Court for relief. Yet, it would be hard to argue that this price issue was of signal importance for either nation. In France the entire issue was obscure. In Italy the question was

16. My speculation is based primarily on an interview with an official in the steel division at the HA, 11 September 1961.

17. Lister, pp. 228–29.

18. At the time of the HA decisions, the French steel industry was engaged in a bitter dispute with the government. Over the years, some increases in basic steel prices had been permitted, but the 1952 Pinay Decree forbade producers of finished steel products to pass these increases along to the consumers. On the other hand, there was no such restriction on products produced from foreign steel. French producers of basic steel thus saw their markets threatened by foreign competition despite low prices. See *Europe CECA*, 16 January 1954, p. 2. They complained to the HA that the government action was contrary to Article 60, but the HA took no action. In order to emphasize their dissatisfaction, no French steel delegation was sent to the meeting explaining the changes in the HA's price policy. See *Europe CECA*, 20 January 1954, p. 1; 21 January 1954, p. 1; and 27 January 1954, p. 2.

less ambiguous, but hardly of great magnitude.[19] Moreover, the economic complexity of the question made the impact of the HA's actions—particularly at this early date—difficult to assess. It was, in fact, this economic complexity which made the case particularly difficult for the Court.

III

The key to the appeals against the HA was the inextricable connection which the plaintiffs claimed existed between discrimination and publication. The French argued that the paramount goal of Article 60 was to eliminate discriminatory practices. Accordingly, the HA's pursuit of lower prices, a more flexible steel market, and an end to price cartels was rejected.[20]

In support of its basic argument, the French government denied that the HA could attain its objectives by the methods chosen, thus making the sacrifice of the antidiscrimination goals of Article 60 even more unpardonable. The HA had hoped to release the natural flexibility of the steel market. According to the French, markets like steel, where highly concentrated firms predominate, are just not naturally flexible. On the contrary, the argument continued, price leadership is endemic to the steel market. Consequently, the HA should have been concerned with breaking down at least some of the barriers between the six national markets by eliminating national discrimination.[21]

Since the French went so far as to contend that *any deviation* from published prices was *automatically* discrimina-

19. There were rumors that Belgium would also appeal to the Court. *Europe CECA,* 18 February 1954, p. 1.

20. *Droit Social,* January 1955, p. 10. This article contains the full text of the oral argument made by Professor Paul Reuter for the French government. See also 1/54, France v. H.A., 1 Rec. 7, 16 (1954).

21. *Droit Social,* January 1955, pp. 10–11 and 1/54, France v. H.A., 1 Rec. 7, 16 (1954).

tory,[22] their attack against the HA's decisions was uncompromising. It was claimed that publication served not only the purposes of equal treatment, but also made possible the alignment of prices guaranteed by Article 60. Without publication, alignment ceased to be a right and became instead proportional to the effectiveness of a firm's commercial espionage system.[23]

Finally, all the parties attacked the HA's motivation, charging that the new decisions were actually ex post facto efforts to validate prior violations.[24] There was, of course, no doubt that it was the violations of the original regulations— engendered by the steel slump—which precipitated the HA's new decisions. As Advocate General Lagrange put it: "The High Authority could, of course, have pronounced sanctions; but these would have had to be invoked against practically all enterprises of the common market." [25] Yet the defensive posture of the HA did not automatically discredit the new rules.

The HA's response was pragmatic, an ad hoc defense of an obviously expediential program. It was, for example, pointed out that alignment was to be made on prices practiced, not on prices published, and that nobody could doubt that steel firms had discovered methods to align under the new rules.[26] By the same token, the HA held that the Italian market was sufficiently protected by geographical factors and by the right, under Section 30, to maintain protective tariffs.[27]

22. 1/54, France v. H.A., 1 Rec. 7, 15 (1954).

23. *Droit Social*, January 1955, p. 8. The Italians, of course, were protected against alignment by Section 30 of the Convention. However, they argued that, because price competition was possible within the limits of the rebate, their protective wall was in fact breached by the new rules. See 2/54, Italy v. H.A., 1 Rec. 73, 80, 81 (1954) and 4/54, Industrie Siderurgiche Associate (I.S.A.) v. H.A., 1 Rec. 177, 190 (1954).

24. See 3/54, Associazione Industrie Siderurgiche Italiane (ASSIDER) v H.A., 1 Rec. 123, 126 (1954) and 2/54, Italy v. H.A., 1 Rec. 73, 82 (1954).

25. "The Role of the Court of Justice," *Law and Contemporary Problems*, 26 (1961), 409.

26. 1/54, France v. H.A., 1 Rec. 7, 17 (1954).

27. 4/54, I.S.A. v. H.A., 1 Rec. 177, 190 (1954).

However, the cornerstone of the HA's defense was the separability of discrimination and publication. Rejecting the French contention, the HA argued that publication was merely a means, and that the elimination of discrimination was the end. Publication was useful only insofar as it was effective in avoiding discrimination. In a slumping market, buyers who were benefiting from secret rebates could hardly be expected to complain about this discriminatory treatment. Article 60 had specifically provided for such contingencies in specifying that prices "shall be published to the extent and in the form prescribed by the HA." [28] Since stringent publication requirements had, in fact, proven an ineffective means of controlling discrimination, other methods had been sought.

Moreover, the HA pointed out that the first line of Article 60 reads, "Pricing practices contrary to the provisions of Articles 2, 3, and 4 are prohibited." Since the fundamental principles set forth in these articles sought both lower prices and elimination of restrictive market practices, the HA was not only entitled but obligated to pursue these goals along with the control of discriminatory pricing practices. Finally, the HA defended its rules as economically realistic, i.e. capable of permitting flexibility while at the same time avoiding producers' price cartels.[29] Obviously, the HA was anchoring its position in the text of Article 60, while at the same time attempting to persuade the Court to look beyond—or beneath—that text to the purposes to be served by the article.

The Court's resolution of the problem was rather curious.[30] The Court seemed to approve of much of the HA's

---

28. 1/54, France v. H.A., 1 Rec. 7, 17 (1954). The HA thus rejected the contention of the plaintiffs that, although Article 60 allowed the HA some leeway as to form, economic necessity dictated the substantive limits of publication. See, for example, 2/54, Italy v. H.A., 1 Rec. 73, 81.

29. Ibid., p. 84.

30. Four decisions were delivered by the Court (1–4/54), but they were virtually identical and so will be treated together.

argument, but proceeded to annul two of the three decisions in question.[31] It accepted HA 1/54 which permitted deviations for categories of transactions not included in the price lists, so long as they were applied equally to comparable transactions. The Court excused the HA from defining the meaning of comparability, a concept which, it was held, did not lend itself to definition in the abstract. The idea of comparability was, according to the Court, inextricably linked with the market. If the market remained stable, transactions weeks apart could be comparable. Moreover, far from leaving producers free to establish their own criteria,[32] the HA's decision placed the burden of proof for establishing comparability on the producers.[33]

The limited concessions made by the Court to the HA's search for price flexibility and increased competition were based on a crucial distinction: "It is indisputable that deviation of any size from the price or conditions of sale prescribed in the price list is not discriminatory when it is a question of a unique transaction or when the deviation is applied to all comparable transactions." [34] In other words, the Court recognized the propriety of distinguishing between discrimination and publication. Moreover, the HA's contention that publication was instrumental was also accepted in the judgment.[35] Still, the Court proceeded to reject the Monnet Margin as a derogation of Article 60.

Publication, while only a means to an end, was an essential means.[36] The Court derived its argument from the following statement, taken from Article 60 #2(a): "The price-lists and conditions of sale applied by the enterprises within the com-

31. See supra, pp. 58–59.
32. This was a charge made by the plaintiffs; see 1/54, France v. H.A., 1 Rec. 7, 15 (1954).
33. Ibid., p. 21.
34. Ibid., p. 20.
35. Ibid., p. 25.
36. Ibid.

mon market *shall be published* to the extent and in the form prescribed by the High Authority." [37] By stressing the italicized words, the Court drained much of the significance out of its acceptance of the idea that publication was instrumental. Whatever significance may have remained was obliterated by the Court's claim that even if publication does not serve to control discrimination during a period of falling prices, it still serves the goal of alignment. The Court's solicitude for securing the right of alignment stands out. Of course, neither the plaintiffs nor the Court argued that the new rule *prevented* alignment. The HA's claim that the enterprises had found ways to align, even with the 2.5 per cent margin, went unchallenged. Alignment, the Court held, was not presented as a possibility but guaranteed as a right, and publication was the means provided by Article 60 for securing this right.[38]

IV

The economic impact of the Court's invalidation of the Monnet Margin has been nil. The HA's scheme was, of course, designed to deal with price rigidity in a falling market. By the time the Court's decision had been rendered, the steel market had picked up to the point that German steel was selling at published rates, and the Belgians were already demanding the permissible premium on sales.[39] Moreover, the HA now seems satisfied that, even in a slumping market, prices are sufficiently flexible.[40] The key to this flexibility is the right of alignment, which entitles producers to align their prices with lower quotations made at other basing points.

37. Italics supplied.
38. Ibid., p. 27.
39. *Europe CECA,* 29 December 1954, p. 1.
40. This assessment stemmed from a study of the 1958 slump. The HA compared rates in Great Britain and the United States with those of ECSC and concluded that the Community market had demonstrated substantially more flexibility. HA, *Seventh General Report* (1959), p. 113.

Because French prices have been the lowest in the Community since the 1957 and 1958 devaluations,[41] it has been consistently possible to align on French rates. In the slack period which began in 1963, conditions changed slightly. In the first place, French firms began to lose their price advantage to Belgian steel makers.[42] Secondly, the Community producers in general found themselves under pressure from lower priced third-country imports. Accordingly, alignment practices changed, refocusing particularly on third-country rates.[43] But regardless of the point of alignment, producers were enabled to reduce prices in individual transactions without revisions of published price lists.

There is, of course, no way of determining how flexible prices might have been, had the HA been able to employ the 2.5 per cent margin. However, the opportunities provided by alignment seem at least to have done away with secret rebating per se. On the other hand, in the early part of 1963 the HA was forced to take steps against fraudulent alignment.[44] This practice seems to involve deviations from published prices in order to "compete" with nonexistent quotes from third countries.

The problem of fraudulent alignment raises a significant issue. Needless to say, such tactics do not represent a noticeable improvement over secret rebating and could, in fact, be considered tantamount to the proscribed practice. No evidence of fraudulent alignment was turned up during the 1958 slump. However, there are some grounds for suspecting that this was a reflection of lax enforcement. One authoritative observer argues that in 1958 the steel market

41. Lister, p. 241 and HA, *Seventh General Report* (1959), p. 113.

42. *Europe CECA,* 6 March 1963, pp. 1–2.

43. See ibid., 18 January 1963, p. 3; 8 March 1963, p. 1; and 9 March 1963, p. 1. Article 60 also permits alignment on "quotations . . . of enterprises outside the Community."

44. See, for example, ibid., 18 January 1963, p. 3, and 26 March 1963, pp. 2–3.

was still divided along national lines.[45] If this is true, then alignment was not serving the cause of market interpenetration. Nor was it a defensive reaction to a French invasion or a threatened invasion, because during this period France was increasing its imports from other Community countries.[46] It is possible, therefore, to argue that alignment on French prices was fraudulent, an expediential substitute for the prohibited secret rebating. Moreover, it was an open-ended dodge without the built-in limitations of M. Monnet's 2.5 per cent rebate.

V

While the economic consequences of the Court's first judgments appear negligible, their legal and organizational aspects are, of course, extremely interesting. In the first place, the Court put sharp restrictions on the discretionary power of the HA. Thus, the provisions of Article 60 #2(a) [47] were interpreted as giving the HA the power only to choose the means of publication—for example, the amount of notification required to change prices, or the breakdown of items included in the price computation. On the other hand, the Court held that the HA could not relax the requirement for publication of exact prices.[48]

The Court also refused to deal with the HA's claim that the enterprises had found ways to align, even with the 2.5 per cent margin. In this way, the Court denied to the HA the discretionary power, implied in Article 60 #2(b), to allow a margin of deviation from the price lists: "The methods of

45. Diebold, pp. 278–86.
46. HA, *Seventh General Report* (1959), p. 110.
47. "The price-lists and conditions of sale applied by enterprises within the common market shall be published to the extent and in the form prescribed by the High Authority."
48. 1/54, France v. H.A., 1 Rec. 7, 28 (1954). See also Lazare Kopelmanas, "Note doctrinale," *Revue du droit public et de la science politique en France et à l'étranger, 71* (1955), 91.

quotation applied must not have the effect of introducing into the prices practiced . . . reductions below . . . [the price list] . . . whose amount exceeds . . . the margin making it possible to align quotations." [49]

Perhaps more interesting than the Court's systematic exclusion of discretionary power for the HA was the formalized, textual exegesis which characterized its judicial technique. Thus, in defending its declaration that publication of price lists necessarily entails publication of exact prices, the Court held that it had to be assumed that the treaty use of the term price list was in accordance with standard commercial usage, i.e. that it was an offer to sell.[50] It thereby followed that publication must be preliminary to sale and must be exact. Even more revealing is the following:

> It is necessary first to repeat that the system of preliminary publication of exact prices constitutes the imperative principle prescribed by paragraph 2 of Article 60. It follows that this principle cannot be evaded, even on behalf of rules more appropriate to the ends pursued. It is not up to the Court to express itself on the advisability of the system imposed by the Treaty, nor to suggest amendment of the Treaty.[51]

By limiting itself to textual analysis and disclaiming responsibility for the economic consequences of its acts, the Court opens itself to charges of formalism.[52] Yet this approach

---

49. The truncated nature of the above citation is required by the rather involved form of the article.

50. It was, in fact, the French word *barèmes* which is referred to and defined by the Court.

51. 1/54, France v. H.A., 1 Rec. 7, 30 (1954).

52. As summarized by one commentator, critics felt that the decisions exhibited "the prudence and neutrality of a civil judge interpreting a contract" when the Court's posture should have been that of an administrative tribunal seeking "a constructive solution." Fernand-Charles Jeantet, "Note doctrinale," *Revue du droit public et de la science politique en France et à l'étranger,* 71 (1955), 619–20. See also Bok, *The First Three Years,* p. 40.

fits well with a rather modest exercise of power of judicial review. Having accepted the propriety of the HA's goals,[53] and the deviation for noncomparable transactions,[54] the Court was hard pressed to justify cutting away one segment of the HA's program, the Monnet Margin. Either the judges had to demonstrate that the Margin could not achieve its purpose and thus engage in economic analysis, or they had to distinguish the provision textually. The Court chose the latter alternative.

But why did the members of the Court feel compelled to rule against the Margin? It has been suggested that the judges, particularly in the questions raised by the rapporteur, Judge Riese, indicated both a concern for, and a grasp of, the economic problems. Accordingly, the real reason for rejecting the margin was that the Court was simply not convinced that the HA plan would work.[55] If this analysis is accurate, there were good reasons—both legal and practical—for hiding judicial activism beneath a textual covering. Legally the Court was denied the right to review the HA's evaluation of the economic situation, except under conditions which were not here fulfilled.[56] Practically, it is understandable that the Court—with but a single economist—would not at this early date wish to involve itself overtly in complicated economic questions. Indeed, one must not forget that this was the beginning of supranational judicial review. To criticize without taking into account the novel and delicate position of the judges would be grossly unfair.[57]

53. 1/54, France v. H.A., 1 Rec. 7, 23 (1954).
54. HA 1/54, see supra, p 58.
55. See Jeantet, p. 623 and Kopelmanas, pp. 94–95.
56. See supra, Chapter 2, pp. 39–40.
57. Professor Jeantet describes the predicament of the Court as follows: "If the Treaty is a constitution, it is indeed a special kind of constitution. . . . One can imagine that a court feels less freedom in the presence of these precise and technical rules and in the presence of States which defend their rights and prerogatives, than it would have in the presence of a constitution defining in broad principles the rights and obligations of citizens and of the principal organs of the State" (p. 624).

While it is important to understand the plight of the judges, it is equally important not to overlook the difficulties raised by these initial decisions. We have no certain way of knowing whether or not the Court's recourse to textualism was merely a smokescreen. Nevertheless the judgments were certainly anchored in the text of the treaty, and the Court was willing to argue that words must be taken at face value, whatever the economic consequences.[58] The rigidity inherent in this approach is hardly capable of providing a solid foundation for stable rules.

In this instance, the judges heavily emphasized the right of alignment and apparently subordinated equal treatment. Alignment may well be a crucial aspect of pricing rules,[59] more significant than equal treatment—at least where the discrimination is not nationally oriented or directed at eliminating competition. However, the judges made no attempt to sort out and weigh these goals. Instead, they turned their backs on the dilemma, rejecting the HA's attempt to seek a balance and implying that such compromises were gratuitous.

Accordingly, a complex and contradictory article of the treaty remained obscure and its links to the fundamental principles of the treaty indefinite. In addition, it seems likely that the judgment has not really eliminated discriminatory pricing; only its form has been changed. The steel industry has, in other words, responded to an unrealistic and unworkable decision by finding an alternative route to its goal. Fraudulent alignment would seem to be at least as undesirable as secret rebating and not nearly so satisfactory as the Monnet Margin which the Court invalidated.

58. See Kopelmanas, pp. 88–97, for a sympathetic analysis of the Court's position, based upon both legal and economic grounds.

59. See supra, pp. 56–58.

4

THE MUTE COURT

FLEXIBLE PRICING: THE MARGINAL FIRMS

I

The Court has had two opportunities to apply and amplify the rules set forth in the Monnet Margin judgments. Again, steel pricing practices were at issue but, rather than big firms and member governments, marginal Italian enterprises were involved. The first of these cases was little more than a police action conducted by the HA against Acciarieri Laminatoi Magliano Alpi (ALMA), which had failed to forward its prices to the HA. In a letter taking note of ALMA's infraction, the HA indicated an intention, according to the provisions of Article 64, to assess a fine and invited ALMA to respond to the HA's charge. When no response was received from ALMA, the HA imposed a penalty of 800,000 lires.[1] ALMA then brought suit against the fine, arguing that Article 64 authorized penalties only for substantive violations like discrimination, not for failure to forward prices.[2]

1. 8/56, ALMA v. H.A., 3 Rec. 179, 186–87 (1957).
2. Ibid., p. 188. Subsidiarily, ALMA argued that the HA's letter of notification had never reached the company's plant. The Court admitted ALMA's claim but held it irrelevant. Although incorrectly addressed, the registered letter had been received at the firm's office in Turin where it had been signed for and marked by ALMA's stamp. Whether or not the letter had been forwarded to the plant, in a little town about 100 kilometers away, was legally of little import. Ibid., p. 190.

The Court ruled that Article 64 authorizes fines for the failure to publish prices, a requirement of Article 60 #2(a).[3] The judgment seems fairly routine and without significant consequences—except for ALMA, of course, which found itself facing a bill of 800,000 lires. Yet, the willingness to sanction fines for failure to publish is an index of the primary position assigned by the Court to the rules requiring publication of prices: "The rules on the disclosure of prices are not minor, on the contrary they constitute a fundamental principle of the common market." [4] Almost exactly two years later, the Court was given an opportunity to elaborate on and re-emphasize its concern for publication in a more interesting case.

II

The Italian enterprise, Macchiorlatti Dalmas e Figli, was fined 2,500,000 lires by the HA for selling at prices above those published by the firm. Macchiorlatti based its defense on the HA decision which permitted deviations from the price lists for noncomparable transactions.[5] It argued that the price increases covered extra services performed, and that the charges had been computed at standard, nondiscriminatory rates.[6] Macchiorlatti alleged that the HA had never established criteria of comparability and offered to provide whatever proof the Court wished that its billings were, in fact, proper.

The HA claimed that there were enormous differences in charges according to the client and according to the service performed. If the charges were standardized they should have been published. On the other hand, if they were not applied

3. Ibid. Article 64 is somewhat ambiguous in that it permits fines for all violations of the provisions of Chapter V of the treaty (Articles 60–64).
4. Ibid., p. 191.
5. Supra, p. 58.
6. Requête, 1/59.

uniformly, to justify them on the basis of their singularity was to make the price lists useless.[7] The Court accepted the HA's contention, and the judgment covered much the same legal ground as the earlier cases.

The Court again distinguished between publication and discrimination and concluded that each deviation from published prices violates the treaty rule requiring publication, even if there is no discrimination in evidence.[8] While admitting that discrimination is a more serious offense than the failure to publish, the Court made clear its conviction that "this latter infraction should not be considered secondary." From its own examination of the invoices—those claimed irregular by the HA—the Court concluded that in a majority of cases the rules of publication had been violated and, significantly, that several of the invoices evidenced discrimination.[9]

III

The Court's argument demonstrated a continued emphasis on the importance of publication. Here the new Court, dealing with a marginal steel enterprise, again saw publication as an imperative means. While the Court did not actually repeat this term, the emphasis was made abundantly clear when contrasted with the conclusions of Advocate General Lagrange. Highlighting this contrast was the advocate's determination that Macchiorlatti should be penalized only 100,-000 lires, instead of the 2,500,000 lires assessed by the HA and approved by the Court. The differences between the Court and its advocate general are best illustrated by the following excerpt from the conclusions of the advocate:

> To violate the rule of non-discrimination, one of the basic principles of the common market, appears much more grave to us, *a priori* at least, than to disregard the

7. Mémoire, 1/59.
8. 1/59, Macchiorlatti Dalmas e Figli v. H.A., 5 Rec. 413, 425 (1959).
9. Ibid.. pp. 426–27.

rules relative to publication which have no other goal than to facilitate the observation of the former; and it is especially so, when, as in this instance, one is dealing with small or average sized enterprises, which are not affiliated with powerful associations, and which are thus much more subject to the real fluctuations of the market and naturally much more obliged to assent to effective competition and whose more or less limited radius of commercial action renders less necessary official publication within the whole of the common market.[10]

As in the earlier cases, what stands out is not the Court's position, but its failure to defend its stand in really meaningful terms. In the first place, the Court failed to come to grips with the very interesting problem of discrimination presented in the case. Perhaps the most damaging piece of evidence against Macchiorlatti was a letter sent by the plaintiff to the HA in connection with a dispute over the assessment of the general levy.[11] As Advocate General Lagrange pointed out, the letter presented with "some vigor and much candour" the firm's pricing policies.[12] The picture that emerged from this letter was of a small firm competing as best it could in a hostile environment dominated by much larger business units and dependent for its electric power on a quasi-monopoly. Macchiorlatti's marginal position forced it to follow market conditions very closely, sometimes even pricing below cost in order to retain a workable share of the market. By the same token, it was necessary to reward customer loyalty.[13]

In other words, these small enterprises were forced into competitive pricing practices. Let us recall Lagrange's char-

10. Ibid., p. 435.
11. The enterprises are assessed a tax which finances the operation of the Community. Infra, pp. 75–77.
12. 1/59, Macchiorlatti v. H.A., 1 Rec. 413, 434 (1959).
13. Mémoire, 1/59.

acterization of the smaller independent enterprises as "more subject to the real fluctuations of the market and naturally much more obliged to assent to effective competition." [14] To force rigid rules of nondiscrimination and publication on these firms is perhaps to drive them out of business. But what Community goals would be served by such results? Certainly there can be no thought that these price variations were in the service of acquiring a "monopoly within the common market," nor were charges made that the discrimination was "according to the nationality of the buyer." [15] It is true that these two goals are merely emphasized in Article 60; they are not exclusive. Discriminatory practices are, in general, ruled out. However, in this instance, the only apparent result of ruling out discrimination would be to make the steel market less competitive.

It can, of course, be argued that marginal firms which cannot survive "honestly" in the competitive environment of a common market should not be allowed to linger on. If this was the Court's position, it was never made clear or even explicitly suggested. In other words, the Court failed to elaborate or even propose a working analysis of the treaty regulations against discrimination. No attempt was made to clear up the considerable ambiguity occasioned by the wording of Article 60 #1, or to relate the rules of equal treatment to the fundamental principles of the treaty or to the goals of integration.

THE POWER TO TAX

I

Articles 49 and 50 of the Coal and Steel Community authorize the HA to raise funds by means of a general levy assessed directly against the Community enterprises on their

14. Supra, p. 74.
15. Article 60 #1.

production of coal and steel. The tax is assessed annually, and while the Council of Ministers must be consulted Council approval is not necessary. The taxing power of the HA thus offers double testimony to the supranational character of the Community. The HA has direct financial access to the enterprises, and this access is free of control by the Council of Ministers.

Given its novel character, it is hardly surprising that five suits have been filed with the Court against various phases of the HA's taxing power. For the most part, they were appeals against the Authority's refusal to exempt specific products from the levy.[16] It is, of course, understandable that at the outset small enterprises, to whom the Coal and Steel Community was more phantom than reality, would have sought ways to escape their financial obligations. However, the issues raised by such disputes are significant only to the firms in question and need not detain us.

Yet, almost from the beginning, some of the larger enterprises—particularly the Germans who shoulder a major share of the tax burden—have raised more fundamental objections to the HA's exercise of its taxing power.[17] The regulatory possibilities of the general levy are extremely limited. Given the ceiling of one per cent of the value of Community production,[18] there is no chance that the power to tax could become the power to destroy. However, the general levy does add measurably to the HA's supranational base. If the HA can establish a strong financial position through an accumulation

16. One of the suits (22/59) brought by Macchiorlatti, Dalmas e Figli questioned the HA's power to tax on the basis of its own estimates and computations, in the event that the enterprises failed to forward their production data. The Court, while not ruling on the issue in this case, has made clear its position in another decision, 36–38/58 & 40–41/58, Società Industriale Metallurgica di Napoli et al. v. H.A., 5 Rec. 331, 354–56 (1959). Consequently, there seems little reason to deal with Macchiorlatti's suit here.

17. See Diebold, *Schuman Plan,* pp. 317–19.

18. Article 50 #2.

of funds, these funds can be used to extend the executive's influence in matters where the treaty authorizes only limited action. For example, a broader financial base would enable the HA to undertake a more vigorous social policy, a direction urged by the Parliamentary Assembly and particularly by labor interests in the Community.[19]

II

The objections of the producers culminated in a suit, filed late in 1959, by two German coal mining firms, Hamborner Bergbau AG and Friedrich Thyssen Bergbau AG (41 & 50/59). The enterprises were interested in reducing their tax burden but, more significantly, were anxious to restrict the HA's power to accumulate funds. As Louis Lister has written:

> The coal and steel producers favored the progressive reduction of tax rates. They were afraid that the High Authority might otherwise try to influence their decisions by means of a large loan program coupled with strict scrutiny of individual investment projects under Article 54. They expressed their distaste for such an eventuality by attacking "dirigisme and bureaucracy." [20]

Specifically, the German firms wanted the general levy funds limited—as a general rule—to current expenses, with excesses from one year being used to reduce the levy for the following year. At issue was a $100 million *guarantee fund* which the HA had built up to establish its credit rating, and a *special reserve fund* which the HA was using to help finance workers' housing projects.[21]

Despite some ambiguity in the wording of Article 50, the plaintiffs did not directly challenge the HA's right to use the

19. Diebold, pp. 317–18 and Chapter 16.
20. Lister, *Europe's Coal and Steel Community*, p. 71.
21. Unless otherwise noted, the following arguments are taken from the Requête, 41/59.

proceeds of the general levy for loan guarantee purposes.[22] What was in question was the size of the fund, which the mining firms claimed was far in excess of what was demanded by the international money market. A more modest fund was possible, it was held, because the HA's taxing power could in itself serve as a loan guarantee. In other words, if for any reason the HA found itself unable to meet its financial obligations, the necessary funds could be raised through the general levy. Moreover, in accordance with Article 51 #3, this smaller fund could and should be financed in part from the proceeds of loan operations, thus reducing the need to draw on the general levy.[23] Accordingly, the German firms objected to the HA's use of interest proceeds for its special reserve fund.[24] Indeed, the whole special reserve fund was held to be contrary to the treaty. Textual arguments were advanced in support of the contention that the special reserve should be dissolved, but it was clear that plaintiffs rested their argument on a more fundamental position.[25]

The Court was asked to play a particularly active role in HA financial operations. The German firms advanced a sweeping theory of Community political organization, claim-

22. The relevant portion of Article 50 #1 reads as follows: "The levies are intended to cover . . . *payments required* in fulfilment of the High Authority's guarantee on loans obtained *directly by enterprises*" (italics supplied). However, in support of the guarantee fund, see e.g. Paul Reuter, *La Communauté Européenne du Charbon et de l'Acier* (Paris, Librairie Générale de Droit et de Jurisprudence, 1953), pp. 70 and 73, and Lister, p. 70.

23. Article 51 #3 reads: "The High Authority may adjust its terms for loans or guarantees in order to build up a reserve fund, for the sole purpose of reducing the size of the levy provided for in the third subparagraph of section 1 of Article 50."

24. The HA responded that the interest earned on loans, which had been added to the special reserve, included only loans made on the special reserve itself.

25. Specifically, it was claimed that just as the proceeds of the general levy could not be used for loan operations, so, too, the interest earned on deposits which were raised entirely from the general levy were subject to this restriction. The same argument was made in connection with the remaining component of the special reserve, penalty money.

ing that the HA's position differed from that of a national executive in that the Community system included virtually no parliamentary control of the purse strings. Consequently, the Court was obliged to protect the interests of the enterprises by a strict construction of the limits imposed by the treaty. While the argument was advanced in terms of checks and balances, it was clear that the goal of the attack was to limit the supranational independence of the Community's executive organ. The HA, it was held, had no general fiscal power comparable to that of national governments, but was instead bound by the doctrine of *affectation stricte:* it could raise money only for specific purposes.

The HA answered this assault on its position by both functional and textual arguments. Both the guarantee fund and the special reserve were defended as appropriate undertakings. While in normal times the general levy combined with its interest earnings would enable the HA to meet its obligations, the guarantee fund was set up for emergencies. When poor business conditions prevailed, it was more likely that the HA would have to make good on its guarantees. Yet, it was just at this time that it would be most difficult to increase the levy. The HA had, therefore, prepared for bad times during good times. Additionally, it was the guarantee fund that had given the HA the prime credit rating that made possible loans to Community enterprises at low interest rates.[26] The same sort of practical argument justified the HA's special reserve fund: money to finance workers' housing was not available on the money market. Moreover, the HA pointed out that the question of the special reserve fund was not relevant, because the money to create the reserve did not come from the general levy.

26. Lister writes (p. 72): "Thanks to the $100 million guarantee fund, the High Authority was able to borrow at interest rates of from 3.5 to 5 per cent and to lend money to the firms at the same rate plus a small charge for service. These interest rates were lower than those then prevailing in most European countries."

While thus defending on practical grounds its financial programming, the HA argued that these questions were not open to judicial scrutiny. Rejecting the argument of *affectation stricte,* the HA directed the Court's attention to the first line of Article 49: "The High Authority is empowered to procure the funds necessary to the *accomplishment of its mission.*" [27] Accordingly, within the one per cent ceiling imposed by Article 50, the HA was free from judicial review; its economic and social assessment of the Community's financial needs was final.[28] Article 33, paragraph 1, prohibited the Court from dealing with these questions, and the HA, of course, rejected the enterprises' claims to special rights on tax questions. The industries were entitled to complain to the Court if the HA violated any limitations imposed by the treaty on its power to tax. However, if it was felt that controls on the HA were inadequate, it would be necessary to amend the treaty.

The issues raised by the parties were, thus, broad and provocative; they struck at the heart of the HA's supranational position and, more particularly, at its possibilities for growth. It was, in fact, the future much more than the present strength and possibilities of the HA that concerned the German firms.[29] Unfortunately, none of these interesting questions were dealt with by the Court, which rejected both appeals on procedural grounds.

27. Italics supplied.

28. The plaintiffs had argued that if there was any validity in a category of "political questions" not subject to judical review, it was not applicable to the Coal and Steel Community. Such immunity was granted to national governments charged with high policy decisions involving the future of their nations. The enterprises denied that an analogy could be drawn with the HA which had limited economic responsibilities and was without such general competence. Réplique, 41 & 50/59.

29. This assertion is based on an interview with a reliable party intimately involved in the suit.

III

Whereas in most of its judgments—even those based on formal grounds—some clue is given to the Court's position on the substantive issues, here the slate was left completely blank.[30] The HA remained free to continue its financial operations according to customary patterns. On the other hand, it would be relatively simple for the enterprises to eliminate the procedural defects and file another suit. While it is perhaps significant that the HA reduced the rate of taxation shortly after the Court's decision, it is more likely that the reduction resulted from general pressure within the Community for lower rates.

Advocate General Roemer—while also rejecting the suits on procedural grounds—went on to deal with the substantive issues. Although Mr. Roemer approved of the guarantee fund, he accepted the principle of *affectation stricte,* explicitly distinguishing the limited financial powers of the HA from the general budgetary competence of national governments. The advocate concluded that neither the general levy nor interest earned by the HA from loan operations or from deposits could be used to finance workers' housing projects; he suggested amendment of the treaty.

While the conclusions of the advocate are of no legal significance, they might well encourage further suits by the enterprises or a more conciliatory attitude on the part of the HA. Although the firms had most vigorously assailed the guarantee fund, the special reserve question must be considered the more important. The guarantee fund has been

30. The procedural defects in the suits brought by the German firms need not detain us. Suffice it to say that in the first suit (41/59) the enterprises had questioned the legality of the wrong decision: the Court decided that the real basis of HA action was a 1953 decision establishing procedures for assessing the levy, not the June 1959 decision which the plaintiffs had attacked. 41 & 50/59, Hamborner Bergbau AG et al. v. H.A., 6 Rec. 989, 1014 (1960).

stable since the spring of 1956 and there seems little likelihood of an increase. Now that the Community's financial reputation is established and loans are increasingly easy to secure, a reduction in the guarantee fund seems more likely than an increase. Of course, the enterprises were interested in its dissolution because a large sum of money would thereby have been made available for reduction of the levy.

The special reserve fund was of less immediate interest because of its smaller size; however, it involves a principle which is of far greater significance than can be measured by size alone. The advocate rejected the special reserve fund because he decided that the HA was bound by *affectation stricte*. In the measure that the HA is, thus, limited to raising money only for specific purposes, it will be prevented from accumulating and employing large funds. Of course, Advocate General Roemer accepted the guarantee fund, so his interpretation was not as restrictive as that of the German enterprises. Nevertheless, the advocate explicitly denied to the HA the general fiscal competence that it sought. At present, this question remains unresolved. The enterprises seem satisfied with an ambiguous situation, which would seem to bear out the theory that they are primarily concerned with the future and, more specifically, with keeping the HA's financial power within limits. They have put the HA on notice that they will not hesitate to turn to the Court if the Authority abuses its taxing power.

The Court, in its turn, remains uncommitted. The immediate dispute has been resolved, but the basic question remains unanswered; the matter has been postponed. Since the settlement of disputes is certainly one of the functions of the Court, it is not necessarily open to criticism for failure to treat the vital issues. Moreover, issues raised in this suit were more prospective than present. The suit was, in fact, largely by way of warning—an expression of potential rather than current grievance. Accordingly, the Court's delaying action was perhaps appropriate. Yet, it must be borne in mind that this is more a negotiated settlement—a temporary truce—than a legal action. In other words, it is an arbitral operation, not a judicial settlement. The normative element is nonexistent; no rules have been articulated nor have any begun to take shape; there is not even any assurance that the Court will deal with the crucial issues in a suit from which procedural defects have been purged.

3 THE FUNCTIONAL APPROACH

INTRODUCTION

The judgments discussed in the preceding chapters range over a variety of issues, and extend from the opening of the Community through 1961. What they have in common is a marked reluctance to develop and articulate Community norms. The Court's unwillingness vigorously to assert rule-making power was most apparent in Chapter 4. Substantive issues were either left completely untouched, as in the general levy decision, or treated only in a limited fashion, leaving major questions unresolved.

Such judgments tend to allow the political authorities broad, if not unlimited, leeway to respond to problems that subsequently arise. When successful, this arbitral technique does manage to settle disputes without coming to grips with the underlying issues. However, parties finding themselves in analogous disputes on subsequent occasions are without guidance as to the legally proper way to proceed. Obviously —and ironically—this judicial deference to the political authorities is likely to lead directly to additional litigation.

At first glance, it might seem that the Court's veto of executive action in the Monnet Margin cases was hardly an example of judicial restraint. After all, the judges had thwarted the HA's effort to realize the significant Community goal of fair but flexible steel pricing. However, let us recall that the ruling was based on a strict construction of the text of Article 60. By showering an inordinate amount of respect on the words of the treaty, the Court sought to generate an air of reverence for the original compact entered into by the member states. In other words, judicial caution was characterized by heavy-handed textualism which suggested a minimum of activism and just happened in this instance to entail rigorous restrictions on the discretionary power of the HA. Of course, as soon became clear, the certainty and stability conveyed by these judgments was illusory—as it had to be in the dynamic setting of regional integration.

The series of cases presented in Part Two thus serves to demonstrate the problem confronting the Court: it must find a path between self-defeating reliance on the text of the treaty, and self-effacing reluctance to come to grips with vital issues. The rule of law calls for norms, and the Court must accept its share of responsibility for establishing them. It has already been suggested that functional tools provide the most promising technique for rule building. The remainder of this study will be devoted to exploring the province of functionalism in supranational judicial review.

5

SHORING UP THE BELGIAN COAL INDUSTRY

I

At the opening of the common market, the Belgian coal industry was weak and noncompetitive. Belgium's entry into the Coal and Steel Community was, in fact, hinged upon the grant of special assistance to its collieries: [1] the Convention on Transitional Procedures provided for various subsidies to the Belgian coal industry.[2] These subsidies were to be financed by a compensation levy assessed against the "coal production of those countries whose average costs are less than the weighted average of the Community." [3]

The proceeds of the levy—together with matching grants from the Belgian government—were made available to the Belgian mine owners. The money was to be used to lower Belgian coal prices to a competitive level. Additionally, it was *generally understood* that this assistance would help finance a rationalization of the Belgian mines.[4] By the end of the transitional period, Belgian costs were to be in line with competitive prices, thus eliminating the need for a subsidy. As stated in the Convention, the objectives of the compensa-

1. Haas, *The Uniting of Europe*, p. 87.
2. Section 26. Similar provisions were made for Italy (Section 27), and protection was also offered to French coal (Section 28).
3. *Convention on Transitional Procedures*, Section 25.
4. William Diebold, Jr., *The Schuman Plan*, p. 206.

tion plan were "to make it possible to bring the price of Belgian coal to all consumers in the common market as close as possible to prices in the common market, generally, so as to reduce Belgian prices to a level near that of estimated costs of production at the end of the transition period." [5]

The HA was given considerable responsibility for carrying out the plan, but the executive's authority for the anticipated reduction in Belgian costs was never spelled out. As Louis Lister has written: "The Convention for the Transitional Provisions contained no explicit policy regarding the use to which the subsidy was to be put, although it was understood that the operators would do whatever was necessary to put the mines on their feet by February 1958." [6]

Specifically, the HA was to:

1. "address to the Belgian Government recommendations on the shifts in production which it considers possible" according to its own production and trade forecasts.[7]

2. in consultation with the Belgian Government, "jointly determine the appropriate means and procedures [for] integration of the Belgian coal market into the common market." [8]

3. based on the above needs and with specified limits, "periodically fix the amount of the levy actually imposed." [9]

In sum, a program of market intervention was called for, its goals spelled out, and some of the methods specified. But at least two big questions were left unanswered. What could the mine owners be *required* to do in the service of rationaliza-

5. Section 26 #2 (a).
6. That is, by the end of the transitional period. *Europe's Coal and Steel Community*, p. 118.
7. Section 26 #1.
8. Section 26 #4.
9. Section 25.

tion? Was the HA free to use the compensation program as an instrument of rationalization? In other words, the scope of supranational authority was uncertain.

Initially, the HA confined its action to price ceilings for Belgian coal. These prices were set at a level below the formerly uncompetitive rates. The subsidy was then computed to give the mining companies the same return on their investments as they had earned under the old prices. While no controls were established over the use of the subsidy, it should be noted that the Belgian government and coal industry were already engaged in something of a rationalization program.[10] In the spring of 1955, on the basis of the report of a joint HA–Belgian government commission, the HA made some changes in an effort to increase the effectiveness of the program. Price ceilings were reduced; compensation payments were either decreased or withdrawn from those producers able to face competition without assistance; and the Belgian government was given permission to end the subsidy for enterprises not undertaking rationalization measures.[11]

The revised program was, of course, directly related to the ultimate treaty goal of integration. The Belgian coal industry had to be prepared to face common market competition. While the HA changes had come at a time when a coal shortage offered assurance that even the weakest Belgian firms would be able to market their coal, many enterprises could not hope to compete in a buyers' market. Accordingly, without rationalization, any lowering of trade barriers was bound to be tentative.

Still, the method prescribed by the Convention was to some extent contrary to the generally free market approach

---

10. Diebold, p. 206.
11. HA 22/55 and HA letter to the Belgian government, 28 May 1955, both in *J.O.C.E.C.A., 4* (31 May 1955), 753. For this information, as well as a summary of the programs undertaken during the transitional period, see HA, *Sixth General Report, 2* (1958), 27–46.

of the Treaty.[12] The Belgian coal industry was to be subsidized to health. Moreover, the HA was—in attempting to influence the utilization of the subsidy—moving outside the *text* of the Convention which nowhere explicitly authorized such action. Not only had the Court already indicated the significance of textual considerations [13] but the whole spirit of the treaty was one of limited intervention.

II

At any rate, the changes in the program resulted in suits by the Belgian Coal Federation (8/55) and by the three mining companies from whom the compensation had been withdrawn (9/55). It is, of course, clear why the three strong companies which had lost the subsidy were inclined to complain to the Court. Yet the whole industry had a stake in fighting changes. In the first place, the reduced ceilings came at just the time when the coal shortage made it possible to command higher prices. On more general grounds, the revision meant unwelcome interference by the Community, which was certain to upset a long standing modus vivendi with the Belgian government. The plans of the HA heralded a more stringent policy of rationalization, likely to take the form of closing the least profitable mines.[14]

While the complaints of the Belgian coal industry were thus understandable, they were not received with great sympathy by the Community. Since the revised program had been designed to insure more purposeful and effective use of

12. Supra, pp. 17–18.

13. Supra, Chapter 3.

14. Since prices prior to the Coal and Steel Community had always been the same throughout the country, the stronger companies had something of a common cause with their less fortunate colleagues: "Although Belgian coal prices seem to reflect less than average cost in the southern field, they are nevertheless high enough to give the mines in the Campine, which have usually sold at the same prices as the southern mines, a comparatively large economic rent." Lister, p. 116.

the subsidies granted to the Belgian mines, the other Community enterprises—particularly the German and Dutch coal producers who were financing the plan—were not inclined to support the Belgian enterprises.[15] The mining companies were also in opposition to their own government, which was committed to the changes largely because they called for price reductions which would result in lower costs for the Belgian steel industry.

III

The arguments raised by the plaintiffs questioned both the wisdom and legitimacy of the HA's revision.[16] Since the treaty pledged the HA to limited intervention, it was contended that the producers should be allowed to take full advantage of the favorable market conditions. If the HA's ceilings were eliminated, the extra income gained from higher prices would provide the necessary funds for rationalization. The HA had gone well beyond its powers, it was contended, in continuing ceilings for enterprises no longer benefiting from the compensation program: the compensation system had been established to enable coal firms to bear the burden of price ceilings.[17] Indeed, the whole process of withdrawing benefits from certain firms was challenged as discriminatory.

The HA, it was pointed out, had initially set prices according to Section 26 of the Convention, that is, according "to a level near that of estimated costs at the end of the transition period." The plaintiffs held that these estimates, based on

15. Because the new program resulted in lower prices, there were rumors that the competitive French industry might join the Belgian enterprises in opposition. See *Europe CECA*, 1 April 1955, p. 1. However, this support never materialized, probably because the coal shortage assured the French of sales outlets.

16. The following arguments are taken from the Requête, 8/55 and the Réplique, 8 & 9/55.

17. Although the HA can also fix prices under Article 61, this power is hedged with procedural restrictions not imposed by the Convention.

objective calculations, were not subject to change. Moreover, the new prices were certainly below the costs which would prevail at the close of the transitional period. It was argued that the HA had disregarded cost questions and structured its price ceilings on Ruhr levels, the lowest in the Community. Instead, the HA should have allowed prices to rise naturally in the favorable market; the correct mix of price and cost factors would then have resulted, allowing Belgian prices to reach the level of estimated costs.

The HA defended its program according to the goals it was called upon to pursue during the transitional period. The HA began by accepting the responsibility and assuming the authority for adapting the Belgian coal industry to the common market. While there was no intimation that this authority was without textual limits, the HA denied a controlling obligation to maintain the receipts of the Belgian coal mining enterprises and set forth functional tests of executive power.[18] The compensation payment was to enable enterprises to make the necessary price reductions. Since Section 25 of the Convention called for a progressive reduction of the levy which finances the compensation payments, there could be no excuse for allotting those decreasing resources to enterprises which were in a position to lower their prices without assistance.[19]

Similarly, because the HA was charged with the structural changes necessary to integrate the Belgian coal industry, the temporary opportunity to sell coal at high prices was irrelevant. The HA pointed out that it had chosen Ruhr prices as a base—rather than prices of the higher cost French basin suggested by the Belgians—because the Ruhr was not only the

18. Except where otherwise noted, the HA's arguments are drawn from its Mémoire, 8/55.

19. Section 25 reads as follows: "The upper limit of the compensation levy shall be 1.5% of such receipts during the first year of the operation of the common market, and shall be lowered each year by 20% of that figure."

Community price leader, but Belgian coal's main competitor.[20] As to the cost estimates, the HA argued that the Belgian figures had failed to take into account the rationalization called for during the transitional period. The reduced ceilings were defended as a lever. It was expected that the pressure of increasingly lower returns would convince the mining companies to abandon or, where possible, to modernize their high cost operations.[21]

The decision rendered by the Court represented a sharp departure from the stand taken in the Monnet Margin cases. The Court resolved the textual ambiguities in the provisions of the treaty by reference to the purposes of the Belgian coal program. Moreover, particular measures were judged according to the needs of successful operation. Both in substance and in principle, the decision was a complete victory for the HA.

In assessing the program, the Court held that it would be improper to think of the compensation payment either as a subsidy to finance modernization, or as an effort to maintain a particular level of receipts. Rather, the payment was to "neutralize to some extent" the disadvantages of the Belgian coal industry in order to permit lower prices during the rationalization process.[22] By thus emphasizing the goal of lower prices, the Court laid the groundwork for much of the remainder of its decision. There could be no justification for doling out money to enterprises which could maintain lower prices without assistance. The Court held that the payment would be transformed into an illegal subsidy "to the extent that it would be accorded to enterprises whose productive

20. Duplique, 8 & 9/55.

21. The HA's case rested, in part, on the conclusions of the joint committee which had reported that necessary rationalization was not taking place and recommended a concentration of compensation payments on enterprises which really needed them.

22. 8/55, Fédération Charbonnière de Belgique v. HA., 2 Rec. 199, 314–15 (1956).

conditions would not be exposed to the disadvantages which are the very premises of the compensation." [23]

Moreover, because a lower price level was the goal of the program, prices could not be left to the free market forces of supply and demand which might at times be inflationary.[24] By the same token, the Court—in the absence of express provisions to the contrary—accepted the HA's right to establish price ceilings. While not denying the plaintiffs' contention that the treaty favored indirect action rather than direct intervention, in this instance the Court decided in favor of the HA because *direct measures were necessary for success:*

> An indirect intervention by the High Authority, as, for example, a reduction in the compensation payment, is insufficient to assure the realization of the objective prescribed by Section 26, #2(a) of the Convention.
>
> In these circumstances, it is necessary to hold that only direct intervention by the High Authority is likely to guarantee the immediate realization of the lower prices which must necessarily go with the compensation.[25]

On the other hand, the Court acknowledged the dual limitations imposed by Section 26 #2(a) on the HA's power to fix price ceilings: estimated costs and the competitive level. The Court conceded that realistic cost estimates, rather than airy hopes for integration, had to serve as the basis of the HA's computations. However, after examining figures supplied by the parties, the Court concluded that the HA had made an effort to ascertain the costs at the close of the transitional period, and that it was on this basis that ceiling prices had been established.[26] As to the HA's choice of the Ruhr

23. Ibid., p. 314.
24. Ibid., p. 303.
25. Ibid., p. 304.
26. Ibid., p. 310. The figures were submitted to the Court just prior to the final decision. Some months earlier the Court had rendered a partial opinion (ibid., p. 199) pending receipt of cost forecast data. In this earlier

prices as a guide to the competitive level, the Court's response was again practical. Whether or not these prices were artificially low, Ruhr price leadership remained an objective factor that the HA could not ignore. Moreover, the Belgian and Ruhr prices were not identical; the HA had properly used Ruhr prices only as a guide to the common market level.[27]

Finally, the judges turned to the HA's attempt to control the use of compensation payment by allowing the Belgian government to withdraw the subsidy from those firms not undertaking the necessary steps toward rationalization. The Court noted that financial assistance was premised on the possibility of integrating the Belgian firms but denied that the payments were in themselves to finance rationalization measures. Accordingly, if the enterprises were not devoting sufficient effort to rationalization, the assistance would become without purpose and the HA was entitled to withdraw its benefits.[28]

IV

The result of the Court's ruling was to permit the HA to continue its attempt to make the Belgian compensation project into an effective instrument of rationalization. The agreement worked out by the HA and the Belgian government was thus left intact, and the immediate interests of the Belgian coal enterprises were sacrificed to the longer run needs of the Community and the enterprises themselves.

In retrospect, it can be argued that the Court paved the way for continuation of a program destined to failure and, at least indirectly, contributed to the squandering of a great deal of money collected from German and Dutch mining firms. The failure of the program and the squandering of the

---

decision, it was held (p. 228) that the HA was not only entitled, but obligated, to revise prices in accordance with changes in cost forecasts.

27. Ibid., p. 308.
28. Ibid., p. 316.

money seem beyond dispute. In its *Sixth General Report,* the
HA summed up the disappointing results of the Belgian coal
scheme as follows:

> At the end of the transition period, the Belgian coal-
> mining industry is still in difficulties. . . .
>
> It is extremely sensitive to market fluctuations and
> tends in particular to accumulate stocks on a consider-
> able scale when business is slack.
>
> The problem of the integration of Belgian coal there-
> fore remains unsolved.[29]

The HA then added, somewhat wistfully, "The results of the
action taken to further integration are certainly not com-
mensurate with the efforts made." [30]

Still, it is difficult to see how the Court can be held to
account for this failure. Indeed, it was the inadequacy of the
initial program that gave rise to the changes which the Court
approved. The shortcomings of the revised program were
never raised before the Court, and the Court was, of course,
in no position to raise the question on its own. Since those
enterprises which were contributing to the compensation
plan failed to complain, the blame must be placed on them
rather than on the Court.

The failure to integrate the Belgian coal industry was
demonstrated when, two years after the close of the transitional period, the Belgian market had to be insulated from
the competitive pressure of the coal crisis by import quotas.
At about the same time, the assistance provided by the treaty
to workers injured by dislocations incident to the introduction of the common market was extended to cover the structural dislocation resulting from the 1958 coal surplus crisis.
Both of these measures resulted in litigation and once again

29. HA, *Sixth General Report,* 2 (1958), p. 45.
30. Ibid., p. 46.

threw the Court into the center of efforts to integrate Belgian coal into the common market.[31]

V

There is much more of interest in this judgment than its impact on the Belgian coal industry. The Court indicated a willingness to allow the HA considerable leeway in managing the market, recognizing that when the HA properly intervenes it must be permitted to do so effectively. In discussing the HA's right to fix prices, a right not expressly authorized by the treaty, the Court noted:

> It is permitted . . . to apply a rule of interpretation generally admitted, as much in international as in national law, according to which the norms established by an international treaty or by a law imply the norms without which the former would be without sense or could not be reasonably and usefully applied.[32]

The extent of the Court's departure from its initial tack can hardly be more graphically illustrated than to recall the words of the Court in the Monnet Margin cases:

> It is necessary, first of all, to repeat that the system of preliminary publication of exact prices constitutes the imperative principle of paragraph 2 of Article 60. It follows that this principle can not be evaded, even in the service of a regulation more appropriate to the ends pursued.[33]

Of course, the Belgian coal program was a particularly effective vehicle for this change of direction. There could be no doubt about the validity of the program itself or the goals

31. Infra, Chapters 11 and 12.
32. 8/55, Fédération Charbonnière v. H.A., 2 Rec. 199, 305 (1956).
33. 1/54, Gouvernement de la République Française v. H.A., 1 Rec. 7, 30 (1954).

it was pursuing. Moreover, the textual ambiguity of the relevant provisions of the Convention, while real, was without
highly charged political implications. Finally, there was
no doubt that the HA was, in fact, attempting to make the
program more effective and that the Belgian mine owners
were fighting the rationalizing tide of the common market.

Ironically, the fact that the compensation program was
based on subsidies—under normal circumstances forbidden by
the treaty—reinforced the HA's need for "a certain autonomy."
The program could not be allowed to go beyond the limits
"strictly necessary" to its basic purpose—to provide a "certain
measure of protection." [34] The Court's acceptance of a considerable margin of freedom for the HA thus came in particularly propitious circumstances: intervention was in the
interest of the free market. But these circumstances did not
prove unique; judicial support of executive intervention received explicit reaffirmation and was, in fact, extended two
years later in a series of suits dealing with another compensation mechanism, the Community scrap program.

34. 8/55, Fédération Charbonnière v. H.A., 2 Rec. 199, 305 and 315 (1956).

6

THE SCRAP SHORTAGE

I

At the end of World War II, Europe was well supplied with scrap, a necessary component in the making of steel.[1] But European steel production was at a low ebb and the demand for scrap was high in both Great Britain and the United States. Consequently, large quantities of scrap crossed the English Channel and the Atlantic Ocean. When steel production began to pick up the Continent found itself faced with a serious scrap shortage.

At the time the Coal and Steel Community Treaty was drafted, the balance had not yet shifted. Therefore, despite a whole series of special measures for dealing with other problems, no provision was made for the impending scrap crisis. Yet almost from the moment that it began to function the HA was faced with a shortage. The HA's initial response was based on the conclusion that the scrap shortage would be neither long-run, nor of serious dimensions. Ceiling prices were established and a consumer board was set up. The board—composed of the Community's steel firms—was authorized to collect information, negotiate joint import contracts, and, most significantly, create a compensation system. This equalization program called for payments by users of

1. For a summary of this problem, see Diebold, *Schuman Plan*, pp. 287–90.

low-priced Community scrap into a fund used to compensate producers employing high-priced imported scrap.[2]

It soon became apparent that the HA's hopes for a quick and easy resolution to the scrap problem were illusory. The executive responded with a series of progressively more rigorous measures designed to curb the shortage. Each new step raised significant constitutional issues. Before looking into these developments, let us examine the legal implications of the compensation system which remained the central feature of the program throughout.

Article 57 specifies that "in the field of production, the High Authority shall give preference to the indirect means of action at its disposal." A compensation system falls under the heading of indirect action. Instead of stepping into the market and allocating the available supplies of scrap among the steel firms, the HA used a financial mechanism in an attempt to influence consumption patterns.[3] The HA's choice of indirect intervention was dictated not only by Article 57 but by the general orientation of the treaty.[4]

The particular provision under which the compensation system was set up was Article 53(b):

> The High Authority, with the unanimous agreement of the Council may itself set up any financial arrangements . . . which are considered necessary for the accomplishment of the objectives defined in Article 3.[5]

Most of the legal problems of the scrap program centered on the difficulty the HA had in attempting a simultaneous pur-

2. See HA, *The Activities of the European Community* (1953), pp. 86–89.

3. During a very brief period of transition in 1953, the HA did allocate scrap directly. Ibid., p. 87.

4. See particularly Article 5. "The Community shall accomplish its mission . . . with limited intervention."

5. The second segment of the citation is from Article 53(a), to which reference is made in Article 53(b), which reads as follows: "The High Authority, with the unanimous agreement of the Council, may itself set up any financial arrangements answering the same purposes."

suit of the long list of goals specified in Article 3. In other words, conflicts developed among the fundamental principles set forth in the article as the HA sought to realize its primary objective—development of a workable scrap program. Let us briefly trace these difficulties as they unfolded.

Among the various objectives of Article 3, those of most immediate relevance to the scrap program were regular supply of the market and "the lowest possible prices." [6] The compensation system stabilized the price of scrap, thus repressing the natural tendency of Community prices to rise to the import level. However, by making scrap available at more favorable prices, the program stimulated demand and intensified the shortage. In order to shore up this weakness in the program it was decided in 1955 to offer a bonus to those who substituted pig iron for scrap in the production of steel.[7] This move tended to curb consumption but the bonus did not fall evenly on all producers: Germany was favored, while Italy and France were disadvantaged. Consequently, this action jeopardized another of the goals of Article 3, "equal access to the sources of production." [8] Moreover, experience demonstrated that the bonus was incapable of stemming the increasing demand for scrap. Accordingly, more stringent measures were adopted.

The compensation plan had tended to make third-country scrap cheaper in Italy than Community scrap. In order to discourage these imports, an adjustment was made in 1956 which raised the price of non-Community scrap in Italy. While dictated by the circumstances, this double-pricing mechanism intensified the problem of equal access by sad-

6. Articles 3(a) and (c).
7. HA 26/55, *4 (J.O.C.E.C.A.)*, 26 July 1955, 869–72. While exact comparisons are difficult, pig iron was more expensive than the compensated price of scrap, and the bonus was to enable steelmakers to use pig iron without a penalty. Diebold, pp. 293–94.
8. Article 3(b).

dling Italian imports with special burdens. A second revision of the program in 1957 raised more general questions. The salient aspect of the revised program was a penalty charge added to the compensation payment. This surcharge was to be paid on scrap purchases in excess of those bought during a base period. Given the shortage of pig iron and the rising demand for steel, producers generally expected that base period consumption would be surpassed and that penalty charges would be incurred. In addition, no concessions were made for new productive equipment put into service after 31 January 1958: a surcharge would have to be paid on *all* scrap used. It could, of course, be persuasively argued that these extra charges would discourage the "expansion and the modernization of production." [9]

The methods of the scrap program thus raised significant legal questions. More generally, it could be asked whether the goal of the program was in itself consistent with the fundamental principles of the Community. This goal was to encourage the use of pig iron and to discourage a high scrap ratio, thus promoting the regular supply of the market. Yet, a high scrap ratio can lead to a more flexible steel market. "In a buyers' steel market, the scrap price falls more rapidly than the price of other raw materials. The steel producer who uses a large amount of scrap is at such times also less burdened with idle capital-intensive facilities for pig iron production." [10] Moreover, the tendency of the compensation fund to equalize scrap prices was open to question; it could have inhibited the rationalizing forces of the free market, which the common market was intended to release. "The question remains whether or not the use of a subsidy to spread the cost of imported scrap during periods of peak demand retards the long-run locational adjustments that a free scrap market

9. Article 3(g).
10. Lister, *Europe's Coal and Steel Community*, p. 66.

might have induced and prolongs the operation of high-cost plants, especially in Italy." [11]

Generalizations about the changing pattern of the scrap program are not easy, but some observations should be made before beginning a detailed analysis of the litigation. The various programs introduced complex technical and legal questions, and it is this complexity which dominates the issues brought to the Court. There was not, as will be apparent in the cartel issue,[12] an underlying layer of patent illegality. The HA had chosen what it thought to be the most effective methods, from the many at its disposal, for dealing with a pressing problem. The objections raised by the enterprises seemed to be legitimate questions about the wisdom and legality of the HA's choices. The suits brought before the Court raised the classic problem of the unprovided case: the suitability of specific measures to meet unforeseen problems, as tested against the fundamental—but sometimes conflicting —principles of the Coal and Steel Community.

II

The most striking thing about the scrap litigation is its abundance. Successive waves of suits have washed over the Court each year since 1955, reaching a high water mark of nineteen in 1959. It would be impossible within the confines of this study to deal with all of these suits; 62 had been filed through the end of 1960 alone. Fortunately, it will suffice to touch only briefly on many suits while eliminating others altogether. A majority of the cases have not involved significant Community issues, and often a series of suits has raised virtually the same questions. Still, the problem is not simple;

11. Ibid., p. 67. More succinctly, Lister points out (p. 65), "Equalization of scrap prices may be antieconomic insofar as it encourages high-cost producers."

12. Infra, Chapter 14.

each change that the HA made in the scheme tended to alter the pattern of interest involvement. At the outset, however, let us note that virtually all of the scrap compensation measures were subject to the unanimous approval of the Council of Ministers. This prior commitment by the governments tended to drain the politics out of issues before they reached the Court.

While disputes in the Council were heated, assent, once given, foreclosed strong government support of the steelmakers in subsequent disputes. Secondly, it would seem that the governments were more sensitive to the considerable market disequilibrium that faced the HA than were the enterprises which were preoccupied with their particular interests. There were undoubtedly inequities in the various HA programs. However, the governments were aware—through their share in shaping the programs—of the complexity of the problem and the need for a solution. Finally, the various compensation measures introduced formidable technical questions, and the precise impact of these measures was difficult to determine. The result was a complex tangle of constantly changing interests, and it was difficult to ascertain just what was at stake at each moment. Accordingly, opposition to the programs tended to be rather fluid and not conducive to a general and sustained attack.

III

Investment Opinions

The first complaint that the Court disposed of was the significant but somewhat peripheral question of an unfavorable opinion the HA had issued on an investment program submitted by the Société des Usines à Tubes de la Sarre (SUTS). According to Article 54, paragraph 4, the HA may give a "reasoned opinion" on investment projects submitted to it. The enterprise is then to be notified, as is the "government concerned." Finally, a list of such opinions is to be "made public."

What was at issue was the HA's program to discourage scrap consumption. SUTS wanted to build a new electric furnace, and the electric furnace has the highest ratio of scrap consumption. The HA argued that it could not possibly approve a new furnace which could be expected to consume about five thousand tons of scrap per month. Only if order could be restored to the scrap market would long-run steel expansion be possible. Accordingly, the HA denied that its actions were thwarting expansion.[13]

These global views were of only passing interest to SUTS, which claimed that the new furnace was necessary to produce ingots not available on the market. Without these ingots, it was argued, SUTS' production of steel pipes would have to be cut back by 50 per cent. Either the HA was obligated to take steps to deal with the short supply of ingots or else SUTS must be permitted to act independently.[14] While it is clear that the above interests were at the heart of the controversy, the legal issues were considerably narrower. In the first place, the HA questioned the right of the plaintiffs to a Court test of an executive opinion. Secondly, questions were raised about the fairness of the HA's administrative procedures.

The Justiciability of an Executive Opinion

The HA claimed that SUTS was not entitled to ask the Court to annul an opinion, because the opinion was without legal effects. While it is true that an unfavorable opinion on an investment project is not binding, there seems little question that it is a handicap for an enterprise seeking to finance its expansion in the capital market. Moreover, in this instance,

---

13. See mémoire, 1/57 and duplique, 1 & 14/57. For a copy of the HA's letter, see 1 & 14/57, Société des Usines à Tubes de la Sarre (SUTS) v. H.A., 3 Rec. 201, 211 (1957).

14. Réplique, 14/57.

SUTS claimed—and this was not denied by the HA—that one of the HA officials had warned SUTS that those enterprises which went ahead with plans in the face of an unfavorable investment opinion would be subject to disadvantageous treatment under the compensation scheme.[15] Still, Article 33 of the treaty provides for Court appeals only against "decisions and recommendations of the High Authority." What, then, is the legal status of an investment opinion? Are enterprises entitled to attack it before the Court?

The judges said no! Pointing to Article 33, the Court decided that opinions could not be annulled by judicial action. Moreover, the Court held that the opinion in question was not a camouflaged decision, because there was no rule to be applied: no obligation was imposed, nor was the HA committed to any particular line of action, should its opinion not be respected.[16] In the event that SUTS ignored the opinion, the Court held that the HA was barred from direct retaliation. On the other hand, the Court refused to exclude the possibility of unfavorable, but indirect, consequences. According to the judges, the purpose of an opinion is counseling and orientation. Thus, neither the HA nor the enterprise is bound in any way by an opinion. SUTS must, therefore, be prepared to accept the *indirect* consequences of its decision to ignore the opinion, because the HA also remained unfettered.[17]

The Court made no attempt to clarify the distinction between indirect and direct consequences, but Advocate General Lagrange carried the argument a little further in his conclusions. He pointed out that the opinion made known to the enterprises the HA's economic assessment as well as its plans to act. Mr. Lagrange then concluded that the HA remained free to act on the basis of this assessment, but the HA

15. Requête, 1/57.

16. The Court noted that whatever warnings may have been issued by an employee of the HA, they could not be considered as an official action of the HA.

17. 1 & 14/57, SUTS v. H.A., 3 Rec. 201, 223 (1957).

could not, in issuing a regulation, "introduce in this regulation, as a criterion with legal significance, the fact that an enterprise had received an unfavorable opinion." [18]

Administrative Regularity

Having decided that the opinion was not subject to annulment, the judges could have left the other issues unanswered.[19] However, the Court took the opportunity to suggest some administrative standards which it considered appropriate for the HA in the light of an administrative wrangle that had developed over the manner in which the HA had responded to SUTS' investment proposal. The HA had first responded tentatively, indicating that an unfavorable opinion would be issued unless additional supporting information was forwarded. SUTS took this letter as an unfavorable opinion and challenged it before the Court (1/57). The HA denied that the letter was an opinion and issued what it considered to be its official response. In contrast to the first letter, the new letter was forwarded to the government, and its issuance was recorded in a list published by the HA. More particularly, the HA indicated the reasons that compelled an unfavorable response. SUTS promptly attacked this second opinion (14/57), and the two suits were joined by the Court.

SUTS claimed that the HA's first letter was procedurally deficient and should be annulled on these grounds. Particular emphasis was laid on the HA's failure to justify its rejection.[20] On the other hand, if the Court accepted the second letter as the real opinion, annulment was in order because it had been issued too late. SUTS argued that the HA was bound to respond within three months of the original proposal, basing this contention on the HA's regulation which required submission of

18. Ibid., p. 231.
19. This was the approach followed by Advocate General Lagrange in his conclusions.
20. Requête, 1/57.

investment plans three months in advance of the date on which operations were to commence.[21]

The HA argued that the second letter was its real opinion. Indeed, the formal shortcomings of the December letter which SUTS was attacking were proof that this was not the HA's final opinion. The earlier letter did not include a defense of the executive's position, and no copy had been forwarded to the French government because it was not the HA's final word; if it had been, the HA would not have invited further comments from SUTS. The executive denied that its requirement of three months advance notice in any way bound the HA to make its opinion known within that period. Nevertheless, for SUTS' convenience the HA had—in its first letter—informally forwarded its views in advance of the date on which construction was to begin.[22]

Once again, the Court sided with the HA. In discussing the executive's first letter, the Court distinguished between the formal and essential elements of an opinion. If the failure to notify the governments was formal, the requirement of justification was held essential and constitutive. Without justification, there was no opinion.[23] The Court thus extended to opinions what has been a continuing preoccupation: the need for an adequate justification. The requirement has usually been based on the impossibility of Court review if the justification is not present. Since the Court had already decided that opinions could not be tested by the judges, one must assume that justification occupies a key position in its own right.

Since there was no justification attached to the December letter, only the February letter could be considered an opinion of the HA. But what of the charge that the February letter fell outside the three-month deadline? The Court held that

21. Requête, 14/57.
22. Mémoire, 1/57 and duplique, 1 & 14/57.
23. 1 & 14/57, SUTS v. H.A., 3 Rec. 201, 220 (1957).

the HA's request for investment projects three months in advance of the proposed date for beginning construction entailed no obligation to respond within three months. However, it noted that sound principles of administration required the HA to forward its opinion within a reasonable time. The HA, it was concluded, should issue its opinion before the date on which construction is scheduled to begin. Yet, unlike the failure to justify, the failure to respond within a reasonable time was an irregularity which did not affect the nature of the act.[24] It must be assumed, however, that the HA would be responsible for any damages resulting from the irregularity.

In sum, the Court's decision, by defining in detail the role and limitations of the investment opinion, clarified an ambiguous passage of the treaty. Moreover, while refusing to place substantive restrictions on the HA, the Court evidenced a concern for fair administrative procedures. Finally, as a result of the Court's decision, the HA's position was considerably strengthened. One of the executive's limited arsenal of investment weapons, the unfavorable opinion, was freed from the threat of judicial veto. In addition, except for the rather vague distinction between direct and indirect consequences, the Court refused to restrict the HA's actions subsequent to an unfavorable opinion. As for the immediate problem, one barrier to a successful scrap program had been removed; the HA could continue to oppose investment schemes that would aggravate the scrap situation.

IV

The Court issued its investment decision late in 1957. It was not until the early summer of 1958 that the judges came to grips with the more basic questions of the scrap system. On consecutive days, the 12th and 13th of June, four decisions were rendered in suits which challenged the compensation

24. Ibid., pp. 220–21.

scheme in general. Then, on the 21st and 26th of the month, the Court dealt with attacks on the penalty measure. The first four judgments all concerned the compensation principle itself. While covering separate suits, these four judgments can be dealt with in pairs. The suits by two small Italian enterprises, Meroni of Turin (9/56) and Meroni of Erba (10/56) are virtually identical. The same can be said for the two suits by the French pig iron producer, Compagnie des Hauts Fourneaux de Chasse (2 & 15/57).[25] The interesting distinction between the pairs is in their respective strategies. Chasse argued directly against the goals and procedures of the compensation scheme, stressing its own special position. Meroni, on the other hand, emphasized administrative irregularities.

The Compensation Plan: Goals and Methods

Chasse claimed that it used only light scrap, drawn from an isolated market, and subject neither to shortage nor to rising prices. The firm was thus being forced to contribute to a program which was of no value to it. Even worse, it was argued, the program aided Chasse's competitors. In the first place, the compensation scheme lowered the price of scrap. Secondly, Chasse's contribution raised the costs of the pig iron it produced. The result was that it was tougher for the plaintiff to compete against both scrap and imported pig iron.[26] The HA took issue with each claim that Chasse made: the firm had failed to demonstrate that its competitive position was endangered by the levy; the Lyon market was not isolated; and light scrap could not be distinguished from heavy scrap in a manner justifying differential treatment.[27]

In its decision, the Court supported the HA on virtually all

25. Hereafter referred to as Chasse.
26. 15/57, Chasse v. H.A., 4 Rec. 155, 174–76 (1958).
27. Ibid., pp. 174 and 177.

the specific points mentioned above.[28] However, more significant than these "private" issues was the Court's rejection of the Chasse argument that, since the HA was charged with furthering the common interest, it was not entitled to take measures which would modify the relative competitive positions of Community enterprises. The Court held that all HA interventions had such repercussions and that so long as the intervention was necessary the HA was simply obligated "to act with prudence and to intervene only after having carefully weighed the different interests at stake, while limiting —as much as possible—the foreseeable injuries to third parties." [29]

It was in this light that the Court examined the measures taken by the HA, concluding that

> In taking special measures designed to limit the consumption of scrap by the increased utilization of pig iron, the High Authority has proven that it had taken account in a reasonable and considered manner of the interests of the pig iron producers. . . . The legality of

28. See particularly ibid., p. 190. On one significant procedural point, the arguments of the enterprise were accepted. Chasse wished to avoid payment of the levy. However, instead of attacking the order to pay directly, the company argued that earlier decisions setting up the levy system were invalid. For its part, the HA argued that it was too late to attack these 1954 and 1955 decisions. The executive rested its argument on Article 33, paragraph 3: "Appeals . . . must be lodged within one month from the date of notification or publication." The Court held that the enterprises were entitled to base their claim on the earlier decision. As it was put in the judgment (p. 184), if the enterprises were not allowed this leeway, they would have to "analyze every general decision at publication in order to determine that it was not capable of inflicting subsequent injury upon them." (It is important to note the limits of this ruling: the prior decision could not be annulled in such an action. But the decision would obviously be emptied of significance if the Court refused to recognize subsequent decisions based upon it.) The same pronouncement was made by the Court in the other Chasse decision, as well as in the two Meroni decisions.

29. Ibid., pp. 184 and 187.

the High Authority's measures was not subordinated to their absolute efficacy in maintaining the preexisting relationship between scrap and pig iron.[30]

This conclusion rested ultimately on the recognition by the judges that the pursuit of the common interest of the Community might at times require the sacrifice of individual interests.[31] This approach cleared the scrap program of charges of discrimination; more generally, it permitted the Court in its first scrap decision to endorse the goals and methods of the program.

The Compensation Plan: Administration

In its suit, Meroni directed the Court's attention to the operation of the scrap program. The small Italian steel producer held that the program was administered by the big producers and run for their own benefit.[32] The system that Meroni attacked had been set up by the HA, but its operation had been delegated to the steel producers. Specifically, the administrative organ was the Compensation Fund Office (Office Commun des Consommateurs de Ferraille, or OCCF), organized by the producers and supervised by an OCCF Council composed of producers from each country. A permanent representative of the HA was attached to the OCCF and could veto any decision made by the Council.[33]

Meroni had failed to submit the figures necessary to compute its scrap levy. The OCCF, after many requests for these data, had proceeded to assess the levy on the basis of its own computation. Following Meroni's failure to pay, the HA had been called in. As provided by the decisions setting up the

30. Ibid., p. 189.

31. Ibid., p. 190.

32. The efficacy of the compensation measure was also questioned, but the arguments against the administration proved more effective.

33. For a complete description of the structure of the compensation system, see the Conclusions of Advocate General Roemer, 10/56, Meroni: Erba v. H.A., 4 Rec. 51, 92–98 (1958).

scrap scheme, the HA issued a decision ordering Meroni to make payment.[34]

Meroni charged that the HA had never authorized the OCCF to assess the levy on the basis of its own computations.[35] In addition, Meroni challenged the accuracy of the OCCF's figures. Subsidiarily, it was argued that the final levy charges were not made known until after the enterprises had set their steel prices. The provisional figures given out by the OCCF were held to be inadequate. Since the enterprises were obliged to publish exact price schedules, Meroni claimed that they were also entitled to full and precise knowledge of the amount of the scrap levy prior to publication. Finally, Meroni pointed out that the HA had failed to justify its order to pay.

The HA defended its failure to justify by pointing out that the OCCF was an autonomous organization. The HA had merely issued an executory decision resting on the work of the OCCF.[36] As to the procedures followed by the OCCF, the HA alleged that Meroni's failure to forward the figures requested had left no choice but to make the computation on the basis of the available information.[37] Moreover, the HA argued that the provisional figures were adequate for fixing prices. The precise figures were unnecessary because it was normal business practice to allow for deviations in projected costs.[38]

The Court resolved the dispute by a strong denunciation of the administration of the scrap system. The Court's con-

34. See 9/56, Meroni & Co., Industrie Metallurgiche, S.P.A. v. H.A., 4 Rec. 9, 18–22 (1958).

35. Meroni's position is summarized from the requête and réplique, 9/56.

36. For the HA's argument, see mémoire and duplique, 9/56.

37. It would seem that Meroni's production figures—available from the General Levy Division—served as the basis of the OCCF computation. The HA challenged Meroni to offer proof of its charge of incorrect computation.

38. See 9/56, Meroni: Milan v. H.A., 4 Rec. 9, 22–24 (1958).

demnation can be boiled down to two essential points. In the first place, the HA had failed to justify its executory decision ordering Meroni to make payment. The Court noted that the lack of a justification made it impossible for the judges to check the charges made by Meroni; on these grounds alone, the order to pay had to be annulled.[39] While the Court—having found sufficient grounds to annul the decision—might well have stopped at this point, it went on to a general assessment of the administrative apparatus of the scrap system. The judges concluded that the HA had improperly delegated power to the OCCF.

To sum up the Court's position: the HA had used improper methods to delegate too much power. HA decisions had to be justified (Article 15) and published (Article 17); in addition, the HA's decisions and recommendations were subject to review before the Court (Article 33). However, the HA had failed to submit OCCF actions to any of these restrictions. In other words, powers had been delegated to the OCCF which the HA itself did not possess. The HA had also erred in permitting the OCCF—without explicit authorization and control—to make provisional estimates and to assess the levy on the basis of its own determination of Meroni's scrap purchases. Such powers were too easily abused to be given without precise rules governing their application.[40]

The Court concluded with an extensive analysis of the delegation of power issue. Having condemned the HA's administrative abuses, the judges went on to demonstrate that this condemnation was based on a broad and permissive interpretation of HA powers. It was pointed out that Article 53 did not exclude the possibility of delegating the operation of

39. Ibid., pp. 29–31.
40. Ibid., pp. 40–42. One well placed observer suggests that the HA is in sympathetic accord with the Court's determination that the executive must maintain "effective preventative control" when it delegates power. See Louis Sizaret, "Chronique générale de jurisprudence administrative européenne," *L'Actualité juridique, 18* (1962), 163.

financial mechanisms to a "private law organization, endowed with a distinct legal personality and invested with its own powers." [41] What the Court made clear was that power had to be delegated in a manner which allowed the HA to maintain effective control of its authority. The judges noted that the common market was a joint endeavor, with the collective responsibility for its realization shared by the organs of the Community. The Court asserted that the institutional balance of the Community, as spelled out in the treaty, served as a fundamental and mutual guarantee to all the participants—particularly the enterprises. By delegating its discretionary power to the OCCF, the HA had upset this vital equilibrium. [42]

In specifying the implications of this reordering of responsibility, the Court offered an expansive theory of the HA's power to intervene. Since Article 3 specifies several goals which are to some extent contradictory, it is necessary to "accord to one or another of the objectives of Article 3 the preeminence imposed by the facts and economic circumstances on which the decisions have been based." [43] The Court had already indicated that the HA could, after a conscientious balancing, subordinate individual interests to the common interests. [44] Now the Court was saying much the same thing about the fundamental principles. It was sometimes necessary to subordinate certain principles in the service of legitimate objectives being sought. Yet this discretionary power vested in the HA was of such significance that it could not be delegated to others. The OCCF had been given powers which went well beyond accounting operations based on objective standards, and the controls established over the operations of the OCCF were unsatisfactory. The Court had, thus, in the process

41. 9/56, Meroni: Milan v. H.A., 4 Rec. 9, 42 (1958).
42. Ibid., pp. 44, 47.
43. Ibid., p. 43.
44. Supra, p. 114.

of invalidating the action of the HA, reinforced the executive's powers of discretionary intervention in the operation of the market.

With the rendering of the decisions in the Chasse and Meroni cases, the die was cast. The Court had no objections whatsoever to a scrap compensation program. On the other hand, the powers of the OCCF were far out of line and would have to be curbed. There remained one big question: was the HA's penalty mechanism valid?

The Penalty Program

To understand the real significance of the penalty measure, it is necessary to trace the steps leading to its imposition.[45] Throughout 1956 it had been apparent that the pig iron bonus was not sufficient to relieve the scrap shortage. The HA sought permission from the Council of Ministers to take more vigorous action, but the Council was sharply divided as a result of vested interests which had developed directly from previous operations. Let us consider briefly these interests.

Italy, the nation which had profited most from the compensation system in general, joined Germany, which had derived the biggest gains from the bonus, in opposing changes. France, which had been called upon to make the most substantial contributions wanted direct and effective limitations on scrap purchases.[46] The HA kept trying to negotiate a change, and at the beginning of 1957 the executive finally managed to get the penalty proposal accepted.[47] The real heart of the scheme was an attempt to tie the penalty to the structural changes necessary to end the scrap shortage. To force sharp cutbacks in the use of scrap before there

45. Recall the earlier discussion, supra, pp. 101–05.
46. *Europe CECA,* 23 April 1956, p. 2.
47. Ibid., 1 January 1957, p. 2.

was pig iron available to replace it would be to treat the symptoms while the disease was gathering strength.

Since time was required to create the productive capacity necessary to fill the Community's pig iron gap, application of the penalty was delayed for seven months. Moreover, it was to begin at 5 per cent of the regular compensation charge and rise over the next year to 100 per cent.[48] Thus, the full force of the penalty would not be felt until pig iron capacity had a chance to rise. However, if the Community was to stay ahead of the game, new facilities which would increase pressure on scrap supplies had to be discouraged. Accordingly, equipment put into operation after January 31, 1958, was given no base period, meaning of course that the penalty would be automatically applicable to *all* scrap purchased.[49]

While the plan had thus been carefully worked out by the HA and accepted by the member governments, the Community's steelmakers had practical reasons for opposing the penalty. Essentially two interests were involved. Firms that used steelmaking processes in which it was difficult, if not impossible, to economize on scrap faced the unpleasant alternatives of not expanding production to meet the rising demand or of paying a stiff penalty on their increased purchases of scrap. On the other hand, because the HA had allowed no base period for productive equipment put into operation after 31 January 1958, firms with plans to expand their capacity had to count on a penalty added to their regular compensation levy.

The steel firms wasted no time in carrying their grievances to the Court of Justice. During the five days between the 9th and 13th of March, suits were brought by the French,

---

48. On the other hand, reduced scrap purchases were to be rewarded by a bonus which could eliminate the penalty entirely.

49. HA 2/57, *J.O.C.E.C.A., 6* (28 January 1957). See also HA, *Fifth General Report* (1957), pp. 96–98.

Belgian, and German steel associations in addition to individual suits by two French steelmakers and a regional French steel association. Altogether, six suits were filed against the penalty, and the Court's decisions—together with the Meroni and Chasse cases—take up the entire fourth volume of the Court Reports.[50]

The enterprises attacked the necessity, efficacy, and fairness of the penalty plan. The rigor of the new program was *unnecessary* because Community reserves had risen as a result of the bonus program. Moreover, present business conditions were exceptionally good and scrap consumption very high; it would, then, be unrealistic to base long-range standards on such exceptional circumstances. As for imports, they were less than those of both coal and iron ore; only a U.S. embargo could create really serious problems.[51] It was also argued that the penalty plan would be *ineffective* because it could not hope to save scrap; it would merely redistribute the available scrap or freeze the existing distribution. Consequently, the program was *unfair:* firms which had economized in the past would be hit harder than those which had squandered and, accordingly, had a considerable margin for economy.[52]

---

50. Since the six attacks were all seeking roughly the same goal, the arguments used by the plaintiffs tend to differ only in emphasis. By the same token, the HA was represented by the same member of its legal service in five of the six cases, and its responses were even more uniform than the charges made in the various suits. Accordingly, the arguments on both sides will be grouped and the Court's decisions will be treated as a single assessment of the HA's program and powers.

51. Réplique, 13/57.

52. 9/57, Chambre Syndicale de la Sidérurgie Française v. H.A., 4 Rec. 363, 376 (1958). Additionally, it was claimed that to use any given date as the basis of distribution was an arbitrary procedure without economic justification. (See memorandum by Mannesmann, intervening in 13/57.) The enterprises were given considerable leeway in establishing their base period. They could choose any six months within any consecutive seven months between 1 January 1953 and 31 January 1957. HA, *Fifth General Report* (1957), p. 97. Of course, 31 January 1958 was the single date established for penalizing new equipment.

The legal arguments developed from these complaints tended to focus on the alleged violation of certain fundamental principles. The HA was charged with interfering with the expansion of productive capacity [Articles 3(d) & (g)]; with discriminatory treatment of those producers whom the HA knew could not cut down their proportion of scrap used [Article 4(d)]; and with failure to advance the common interest [Article 3], that is, with disregarding the interests of large groups of Community steel producers.[53] Finally, the HA was attacked for having improperly used Article 53 to establish measures that in effect allocated the short supply of scrap and influenced the course of investment. Articles 54 and 59 provided measures for dealing with each of these problems. It was claimed that the HA had turned to Article 53 in order to escape the restrictions imposed on the exercise of the other articles.[54]

The HA responded that repercussions on investment plans or the allocation of resources did not indicate a misuse of financial mechanisms or, more specifically, rob financial mechanisms of their indirect character. The nature of indirect action was to achieve concrete results, though by way of indirect *means*.[55] The compensation plan worked through prices and was thus quite different from direct measures that leave the enterprises no choice whatsoever.[56]

There remained more basic issues, and the HA staked its defense on the dual aims of the scrap program, firmly

53. Réplique, 13/57.
54. 8/57, Groupement des Hauts Fourneaux et Aciéries v. H.A., 4 Rec. 223, 235, 237, and 239 (1958).
55. Mémoire, 13/57.
56. See 12/57, Syndicat de la Sidérurgie du Centre-Midi v. H.A., 4 Rec. 471, 486 (1958), and 8/57, Groupement des Hauts Fourneaux v. H.A., 4 Rec. 223, 236 (1958). The enterprises contended that the HA had employed direct measures indirectly. In support of this position they had argued that the enterprises were not, in fact, free to disregard the indirect pressures of a heavy penalty which would price them out of the market. Mannesmann intervention, 13/57.

anchored in Article 3: regular supply of the scrap market at low prices. Among the numerous and sometimes contradictory goals of this article, the HA argued that it had to choose, according to the situation, which goals were paramount. In this instance, an adequately supplied scrap market had been deemed the prerequisite to long-term expansion of steel production.

Although some enterprises found themselves disadvantaged, the common interest that the HA was charged with pursuing could not properly be equated with each of the particular interests.[57] By the same token, the HA defended itself against charges of discrimination, pointing out that general measures taken by the HA would always fall with different weight upon individual enterprises. What mattered was that the penalty mechanism was in line with the goals of the scrap program.[58]

The Court's decision combined an interesting and far-ranging discussion of indirect market control by the HA with a resolution of the immediate issue, the scrap penalty plan. The Court, it should be noted at the outset, declined to challenge the HA's assessment of the economic situation—the shortage of scrap on the Community market, the increasing difficulty of obtaining imports, and the ever rising cost of these imports.[59] Moreover, the Court accepted the HA's contention that it had been led to try the penalty tax by the shortcomings of the previous system.[60]

The decision went on to defend both the methods used and the goals pursued by the HA and opened a rather remarkable degree of latitude to the HA in both respects. Extending its argument in the Meroni decision, the Court pointed out that

57. Mémoire, 13/57.
58. 8/57, Groupement des Hauts Fourneaux v. H.A., 4 Rec. 223, 248 (1958).
59. 13/57, W.E.S. v. H.A., 4 Rec. 261, 290–91 (1958).
60. Ibid., p. 289.

insofar as Article 53 financial mechanisms required fulfill-
ment of the objectives of Article 3, the other articles setting
out the fundamental goals of the Community must be respected, that is to say, Articles 2, 4, and 5. All these articles
must be considered in their totality and applied simultaneously. Yet, in practice, the Court conceded that "it will be
necessary to proceed to a certain conciliation between the
diverse objectives of Article 3, for it is manifestly impossible
to realize all of them at the same time, and each to the maximum." [61] The HA was charged with seeking permanent
reconciliations, but if those could not be realized the Court
permitted the HA to grant "temporary preeminence" to those
objectives which were crucial—given the economic circumstances—to achieving its mission.[62]

The Court's interpretation of the "common interest,"
which Article 3 obligated the HA to respect, followed the
same lines: "Far from limiting itself to the sum of the particular interests of the enterprises or of categories of enterprises under the jurisdiction of the Community, the concept
of the common interest [clearly] surpasses the circle of these
interests." [63]

Given this sort of analysis, claims by enterprises or associations of enterprises that raised particular injuries or pointed
to violations of individual facets of Article 3 were easily turned
aside by the Court.[64] The HA had properly given preeminence
to the regular supply of the market, specified in Article 3(a),
and had sought to insure rational use of scrap. The Court
admitted that the measures did not fall upon all enterprises
with equal force. Yet there was no discrimination so long as
the rules were based upon the objectives of the regulation
and were generally applicable. It was neither improper nor

61. Ibid., p. 288.
62. Ibid., p. 290.
63. Ibid., p. 294.
64. See, for example, 8/57, Groupement des Hauts Fourneaux v. H.A.,
4 Rec. 223, 243 (1958).

surprising that enterprises using great quantities of scrap were forced to pay a greater surcharge.[65]

There still remained the charge that the HA had applied direct means indirectly; this claim was also rejected. The Court pointed out that indirect measures cannot be distinguished by their results, which can be "powerful and effective." The HA's compensation scheme affected prices by changing costs and thereby influenced market behavior, including, for example, the distribution of resources. Consequently, these indirect measures prompted the enterprises to act according to the HA's conception of the common interest. In contrast, direct measures impose such actions.[66] The HA had induced the enterprises to cut down their use of scrap and to expand production through the creation of new pig iron capacity, rather than through additional scrap consumption.[67] The judgment also noted with approval the measures added by the HA to ease the adjustment, including the progressive increase of the tax, the delay in its application, the opportunity to escape the penalty, etc.[68]

V

In approving the penalty plan, the Court had cleared up the last doubts about the scrap compensation system. Yet, although the compensation program had been approved in its entirety, it should be remembered that the Court had in the Meroni decision thoroughly discredited the administration of the scheme. It was abundantly clear that the powers of

65. 13/57, W.E.S. v. H.A., 4 Rec. 261, 297 (1958).

66. Ibid., pp. 287 and 296. In his incisive conclusions, Mr. Lagrange treated the question somewhat differently, while arriving at the same result. He pointed out that to act directly on prices is considered by the treaty as indirect action on production. While the conditions of competition are modified, the play of competition is not eliminated as it is by direct intervention. See 13/57, W.E.S. v. H.A., 4 Rec. 261, 297 (1958).

67. 8/57, Groupement des Hauts Fourneaux v. H.A., 4 Rec. 223, 236 (1958).

68. 13/57, W.E.S. v. H.A., 4 Rec. 261, 297 (1958).

the occf had to be curbed. Accordingly, the HA, with the approval of the Council, took over interim operation of the program in July 1958.

The HA then attempted to convince the Council of Ministers to accept a kind of contingency program: a compensation system which was to be used only when market conditions required HA intervention. The compensation levy was to decrease progressively and end definitely 27 months after its reintroduction. Moreover, while a pig iron bonus was to be employed, the penalty was to be eliminated.[69] However, the HA was unable to sell its plan. The improved conditions of the scrap market—due largely to the general business slump [70]—reduced the immediate pressure for a program of control. Consequently, particular national interests assumed increasing importance and, with Germany, Italy, and Luxembourg voting in the negative, the Council rejected the HA's proposal.[71] The scrap market was freed on December 1, 1958, and has remained so.

With the scrap compensation plan ended, the HA turned its attention to closing out the old program. The HA set out initially to compute and bill the enterprises for back assessments due on the penalty plan.[72] The process has, however, turned into a nightmare of litigation as enterprise after enterprise has challenged the methods employed by the HA and the prior exemptions accorded by the occf. In addition to this administrative hassle, fraud that turned up in the opera-

69. HA, *Seventh General Report* (1959), p. 93.

70. Ibid., p. 86.

71. *Europe CECA*, 25 November 1958, p. 1–2.

72. The occf had successfully avoided assessment of the penalty levy. Not one penny had been paid in at the time the HA took over operation of the compensation plan in July 1958, although the progressive penalty was to have hit its 100 per cent ceiling by May 1 of that year. The HA had apparently concurred in this passive resistance to the penalty, pending the Court's decision on its legality. Nonetheless, the situation highlights the autonomy enjoyed by the occf and bears out the Court's condemnation. See *Europe CECA*, 30 May 1958, p. 1 and 9 June 1958, p. 2.

tion of the compensation plan led to still further litigation. The story is too voluminous, complex, and peripheral to deal with in this study; only its broad outlines need be mentioned.

Closing Out the Program

There are, in fact, two lines of cases growing out of the final demise of the scrap plan. Many disputes have boiled up over just which categories of Community scrap were subject to the levy. The major problem concerned the exemptions allowed circulating scrap, i.e. scrap reclaimed from the production process and then returned to the production cycle. This exemption was extended to two enterprises which—though legally distinct corporations—were *locally integrated*. That is to say, the two plants were adjacent and their production processes were integrally linked. Conversely, an exemption was denied to so-called *group scrap:* transfers between enterprises which—though legally distinct—were closely connected by financial ties. Various facets of this issue have been raised in a series of suits.[73]

Running parallel to the exemption question was another line of litigation growing directly out of the Meroni decisions. Attempts have been made to capitalize on the Court's condemnation of the administrative shortcomings of the program in order to gain exoneration from the levy.[74] Once the Authority took over the program, additional suits grew out of the HA order to pay.[75] The latter suits sought a declaration of official fault against the HA for its ineffectual control of the OCCF.

73. 32 & 33/58, S.N.U.P.A.T. v. H.A., 5 Rec. 275 (1959); and 42/58 and 49/59, S.N.U.P.A.T. v. H.A., 7 Rec. 101 (1961).

74. 36–38, 40, & 41/58, Società Industriale Metallurgiche di Napoli v. H.A., 5 Rec. 331 (1959).

75. 5, 7, & 8/60, Meroni & Co., FERAM, SIMET v. H.A., 7 Rec. 201 (1961); and 14, 16, 17, 20, 24, 26, & 27/60 and 1/61, Meroni et al. v. H.A., 7 Rec. 319 (1961).

Major questions remain to be resolved in both series of suits. On the one hand, Court decisions led the HA retroactively to withdraw exemptions which had been granted by the OCCF. This withdrawal raised questions about the rights of enterprises subjected to retroactive withdrawal, in addition to giving rise to disputes over the complicated problems of redistributing the fruits of withdrawal. On the other hand, the Court has indicated that enterprises which can prove injury attributable to the laxity of HA administration of the scrap program will find a sympathetic ear at the Court of Justice. The beginning of 1962 thus found the Court faced with two significant avenues for continued scrap litigation, and throughout that year and 1963 the Court has been inundated with suits.

VI

The detail, complexity, and seemingly open-ended character of the scrap litigation should not obscure—and, indeed, should underline—the fact that scrap litigation has been one of the most highly legalized aspects of the Court's work. Political issues have been muted, and the Court has been under constant pressure to establish rules and provide remedies for those parties who have been confused and inconvenienced by the operations of a highly intricate mechanism. The Court has responded with broad and forthright assessments of issues. Its extended discussions have gone beyond the confines of the immediate question and, in so doing, have illuminated the supports on which the response to the narrow issue rested. Moreover the Court adopted a functional technique for laying the normative foundation for rules it has developed.

Symptomatic of the Court's functional approach was its ordering of the docket. Although the Chasse suit (2 & 15/57) was filed more than two months after the Meroni appeal (9/56), the decisions were rendered on the same day. By reading the Chasse suit first, the Court gave its endorsement to the goals and methods of the scrap plan before its vigorous denunciation of the administrative failings. Moreover, by presenting the remainder of the decisions before the end of the month, the Court was able to offer a systematic and definitive assessment of the entire scrap plan rather than a series of random responses. While all this required some manipulation, it was made possible by the concentrated fashion in which the suits testing various aspects of the scrap system were filed. Since the Court held all the reins in its hands, it consequently could act with considerable freedom.

As to the rules set forth by the Court, their significance extends well beyond the boundaries of the scrap program. The textual restrictions applied to the HA's discretion in the Monnet Margin cases and loosened in the Belgian coal judgment were broadened still further.[76] In allowing the HA to pick and choose among the goals of Article 3 according to the economic circumstances, the Court recognized the right to subordinate temporarily one or more of the fundamental principles of the treaty. Since only under exceptional circumstances is judicial review of the executive's economic assessment possible, the latitude opened to the HA was considerable. The Court's unexpressed premise seemed to be that indirect management of the market is a complex process. Consequently, when the HA properly undertakes such action, it must be allowed the flexibility necessary for success. Although this power is not unlimited, neither the interests of individual enterprises or groups of enterprises, nor particular provisions of the treaty can pose an absolute bar to action.

By the same token, the Court refused to restrict narrowly the HA's use of powers provided by the treaty. Thus, the power to institute financial mechanisms (Article 53) could be wielded to influence investments, even though it was Article 54 that specified the HA's investment competence. Given

76. For a similar analysis, see *Europe CECA,* 26 June 1958, p. 1.

the rather limited potency of Article 54, the use of indirect measures could certainly enhance the effectiveness of the HA.

In more general terms, it would seem that the Court's reading tends to give the powers of the HA a life of their own. They are not to be strictly confined to instrumental use in the service of the objectives of those articles in which they are specified. Instead the capabilities of the HA take on a more general applicability, thus increasing the HA's alternatives for action. This development is merely a tendency suggested by the Court's words, not an accomplished fact.

Finally, it should be noted that in the measure that the HA's discretion is broadened the opportunities for the enterprises to obtain judicial relief are narrowed. Yet at the same time the Court has evidenced a sensitivity to, and a willingness to curb, administrative abuses. In other words, the judges have asserted a firm control over procedures while allowing the HA great substantive leeway in its management of the market. The role assumed by the Court, in these cases, has been that of the classic administrative tribunal.[77]

77. For a similar conclusion, see Louis Sizaret, "Chronique générale de jurisprudence administrative européenne," *L'Actualité juridique, 18* (1962), 163.

4 PARTIAL INTEGRATION

INTRODUCTION

In Part Three, we learned that the Court's policy of testing HA programs according to functional standards proved workable for two ambitious financial schemes undertaken by the Community executive. In both instances, the Court evidenced a willingness to allow the HA considerable discretion in its use of methods. The propriety of these methods was judged by the needs of the program, but set against the general orientation of the Community. By the same token, the Court refused to allow enterprises or member governments to raise particular interests or individual principles of the treaty as barriers to effective action.

This new approach was possible only because the Court turned away from the idea that specific provisions of the treaty must be taken as imperatives,[1] requiring no other justification for application than their relevance to the issue at hand. In other words, the Court rejected the false security of absolute certainty for the more realistic and workable goal of operative, but variable, standards of guidance.[2] Yet, the precondition to this flexible mode of judicial review was a determination by the Court in each case that the objective of the program was supported by the treaty, and that the methods chosen were appropriate for pursuing this objective. Insofar as the Belgian coal suit was concerned, there was no real issue. Both the objective of the program—integration of the

1. Supra, pp. 64–65.
2. See H. L. A. Hart, *The Concept of Law* (Oxford, Oxford University Press, 1961), Chapter 7.

Belgian coal industry—and the appropriate mechanism—a compensation scheme—were directed by the Convention.

The problem was somewhat more difficult in the scrap cases, because both the objective—economizing scrap—and the choice of a compensation mechanism were open to question. Accordingly, in the latter instance, the Court had to decide whether the HA had made a strong enough case for the need to economize scrap, and whether the indirect measures were appropriate. The scrap shortage was both obvious and critical, but the judges had to come to grips with the legal suitability and operational limits of indirect market action. In the course of this investigation, relevant legal norms were sketched out, and certain provisions of the treaty were clarified and made more meaningful.

It must be borne in mind that the starting point for even this flexible form of judicial review is the treaty. The goals and methods set forth in the treaty must be the anchor for any effective and stable system of norms. We now turn to a series of disputes in which the incomplete and partial character of the Coal and Steel Community becomes an issue. But it is important not to think of partial integration as a fixed quantity; it is a variable factor, which can enter into disputes in either a central or a derivative manner. Accordingly, the possibilities for positive judicial action will tend to vary with the relative significance of this area of "no guidance" in the dispute in question. To the degree possible, the four chapters that follow will be presented in sequence, on the basis of the increasing centrality of the partial integration issue.

7

THE INTEGRATION OF TRANSPORT:

SPECIAL RAIL RATES

I

The long term goal of Community transport policy is the harmonization of transport rates. The precise meaning of the term harmonization is not clear, but it seems to call for an integrated rate structure—the acceptance by each nation of the same principles for establishing transport rates.[1] Because it is such a complex and extensive task, the HA has tended to defer harmonization and concentrate on the more limited problem of discrimination. The executive has acted with considerable vigor against discriminatory rates and various other discriminatory practices. In distinguishing the obligation of the governments to eliminate discrimination from their pledge to seek harmonization, Louis Lister writes: "The former concerns the relationship of rates in comparable transactions; the latter concerns rate levels." [2]

When the Community commenced operation in 1953, there existed in France and Germany a confusing maze of rail rates governing the shipment of coal and iron ore between mine and factory.[3] Although general rate structures existed,

1. Diebold, *The Schuman Plan*, pp. 186–91.
2. *Europe's Coal and Steel Community*, p. 361.
3. Litigation on rail rates was limited to France and Germany. In its *Seventh General Report* (1959), the HA indicated that some special Italian

they tended to be illusory because of the multiplicity of exceptions or *special rates*. The exact dimensions of these systems need not concern us. What is important is that the result was to alter the relative costs of steel production, according to whether one received the benefits of special rates or operated under the general rates.[4]

Article 70, paragraph 2, unequivocally forbids discriminatory rates based on "the country of origin or of destination." However, this uncompromising prohibition of national discrimination is in practice softened by the Community's basic commitment to national autonomy in transport matters.[5] Presumably in recognition of the fact that coal and steel account for only a portion of national transport, the treaty respects the traditionally intimate relationship between transport and public policy.[6] According to Article 70, paragraph 5:

> The fixing and modification of rates and conditions of transport of any type, as well as the arrangement of transport prices required to assure the financial equilibrium of the transport enterprises themselves, remains subject to the legislative or administrative provisions of each of the member States; the same is true for the measures of co-ordination or competition among different types of transport or among different routes.

Unfortunately, as we shall see, the results of national policy designed to regulate competition within the transport industry are, at times, very hard to distinguish from the discrimination forbidden by Article 70, paragraph 2.

---

rail rates would be investigated, but no further action was reported. See p. 165.

4. See Diebold, Chapter 7, particularly pp. 173–77 for further detail.

5. Cf. Maurice Lagrange, "The Role of the Court of Justice of the European Communities as Seen through Its Case Law," *Law and Contemporary Problems*, 26 (1961), 413–14.

6. Lister, pp. 360–61.

The textual link between these two provisions seems to be Article 70, paragraph 4, which provides that "special domestic tariff measures" must accord with "the principles of the Treaty." It is the HA's responsibility to sort out the legal from the illegal. Therefore, special rates must be approved by the HA before application. But in some ways Article 70, paragraph 4, just adds to the confusion. Is the HA, for example, required to review special measures regulating competition within the transport industry—in other words, measures falling within the area reserved to the member states? Are the principles in question the fundamental principles of the treaty—it would seem a priori that all special rates would distort competition and hamper rationalization—or just those singled out in Article 70, paragraphs 1 and 2, i.e. equal treatment and no national discrimination?

It is clear that behind all of these particular questions is the general problem of partial integration of the transport industry. In this instance the partial integration issue has a dual character. In the first place, it is clear that only shipments of coal and steel come under the provisions of the treaty. Secondly, even for these two products, complete integration is not required by the treaty. Equal treatment is prescribed and harmonization is sought, but the rights left to the national governments seem to preclude a Community-wide integrated rate structure under the treaty.

Thus, it would seem that the relationship of transport to the Coal and Steel Community is instrumental rather than primary. Given this peripheral connection, it could be argued that a stable system of Community norms for transport is out of the question. Yet, the treaty does, as we have seen, set forth jurisdictional rules, albeit rules fraught with ambiguity. In a series of suits brought by French and German steel concerns and by the two national governments, the Court was handed the difficult job of drawing the line between sovereign right and Community authority, and of an-

choring this distinction in a meaningful and durable interpretation of the treaty.

II

Just after the opening of the Community, the HA, in
accordance with Section 10 of the Convention, appointed a
commission to make a complete study of the transport market
for coal and steel. The report of this commission was to provide guidance for the application of Article 70, the transport
article. On the basis of this report the HA sent a number of
letters to the German and French governments, accepting
certain of the special rates for transport of coal and steel
while ordering the suppression or revision of others.[7] The
response to these decisions was general dissatisfaction. The
French were unhappy because the HA had been too rigorous
in eliminating special rates in France but not sufficiently
rigorous in eliminating German rates. The Germans, on the
other hand, objected to the orders for suppression or revision
of some of their special rates.[8]

Twenty-four suits resulted from the HA's decisions; the
Court, by grouping, cut the number to four, and for purposes
of this examination there are in reality only two problems to
be considered. The French steel and mining firms that had
benefited from the special French rates objected to their
elimination, and the interest of the firms was immediate and
direct. They were not, however, able to interest the French
government in their plight and were forced to fight the battle
alone. Substantively, the position of these French enterprises
(27–29/56) was no different from that of the German enterprises whose low transport rates were under attack (3–18, 25,
& 26/58). The only distinction was that the German enterprises had the direct support not only of the German government (19/58), but also of six German states which intervened

7. *J.O.C.E.C.A.*, 7 (3 March 1958), 105–31.
8. Lister, pp. 228–29.

on their behalf. The second problem involved the major French industrial interests. They were not engaged in the attack on the elimination of the French rates, but in the German rate question (24 & 34/59). Moreover, these firms— Lorraine steelmakers—were not so much interested in doing away with the special German rates as sharing in their benefits. The Lorraine concerns draw upon the Ruhr for much of their coal. Consequently, a considerable saving was in prospect if the reduced rates applied to shipments to German steel firms outside the Ruhr were extended to coal destined for France.[9]

A puzzling aspect of these cases is the limited involvement of the French and German governments. Because in both countries the railways are government owned, each government automatically had a stake in the dispute. However, the degree of engagement remains in question. It is argued in some quarters that the German state governments intervened only because they had doubts about the enthusiasm with which the Federal Republic was pursuing its claims. The French government's commitment was limited to intervention in the Lorraine case; no suit was brought in its own name. Moreover, there is no evidence that either government pursued the case very vigorously in the Council of Ministers, the Community institution in which the really crucial questions are thrashed out.

III

The Limits of National Autonomy

Since the French enterprises which were attacking the HA's suppression of special French rail rates (27–29/58) and all of the German interests were in much the same position, they

---

9. The importance of costs to the French steel industry is underscored by the tight rein the government has kept on steel prices and the consequently low profit margins. Lister, pp. 228–29.

made virtually the same arguments before the Court.[10] As relatively small and isolated enterprises, they defended their right to special treatment. Specifically, it was claimed that the favored treatment could be justified as contributing to programs of regional development and economic decentralization. What all the firms were requesting was an exceedingly limited application of the treaty's provisions which prohibit discrimination. Examined from a different perspective, German and French firms stressed provisions that would enable them to shield national enterprises from the impact of the common market. Taken in context, the emphasis was on stability and autarchy.[11]

The HA's position, which ran directly counter to that of the enterprises, was based upon those treaty principles which emphasize rationalization through free market forces. This could, of course, result in some unemployment or a rise in prices previously held artificially low through subsidies. While prepared to ease the burden of these developments, the HA claimed that it could not accept measures which served the purpose of Community autarchy or national protection. Even regional development schemes were rejected unequivocally. In short, the HA argued that where the goal of special rates was to alter competitive positions by compensating for *natural* disadvantages, these rates must be rejected.

The Court responded to the suits with a series of forthright decisions which supported and, in fact, extended and clarified the position taken by the HA. Both sets of suits were rejected and the executive's large-scale crackdown on special rates was upheld. More significantly, a major portion of the ambiguity of Article 70 was eliminated. A diffuse article of the treaty was given a considerable measure of unity by the judgments.

In the first place, the Court cleared up the question of

10. The integrated argument presented here has been gleaned from the dossiers of the suits in question.

11. If the Community protected weak enterprises, it would never be expected to adopt a liberal commercial policy. Among the Community goals, Article 3(f) specifies "the development of international trade."

which special rates had to be submitted to the HA, by a declaration that all rates which benefited one or several enterprises were subject to HA approval.[12] Accordingly, even if the rates were motivated by a desire to maintain the financial equilibrium of the transport enterprises—a power reserved by Article 70, paragraph 5, to the member states—they had to be cleared by the HA. The Court thus avoided the hazards of attempting to draw a general and definite distinction between Community powers and the private preserve of the member states. Instead, the judges held that all special rates —even those which were established under the autonomous transport powers of the member governments—had to conform to the principles of the treaty.[13] It remained for the judges to determine just which treaty principles were supposed to be used by the HA in testing special rates. The Court held that the principles in question are those included in the transport article itself, specifically its first paragraph: "the application of such rates for coal and steel as will make possible comparable price conditions to consumers in comparable positions." [14] But what are the guide lines offered by this provision?

The key to the Court's analysis is its emphasis on, and

12. 19/58, Germany v. H.A., 6 Rec. 469, 491 (1960).

13. Recall that Article 70, paragraph 4, charges the HA with ensuring that special rates "are in accordance with the principles of this Treaty," supra, p. 137.

14. In order to make this first paragraph of Article 70 a solid foundation for its decisions, it was necessary to clear the transport article of the charge that it was merely programmatic and without binding force. To this end, the Court simply pointed out that paragraphs 2, 3, and 4 of Article 70 all contained words which unambiguously signaled their immediate applicability. 3–18, 25 & 26/58, Barbara Erzbergbau AG v. H.A., 6 Rec. 367, 402 (1960). Advocate General Lagrange agreed with this interpretation, ibid., p. 430. By the same token, it was held that the HA could act directly against those rates which interfered with the accomplishment of valid Community goals. Unlike Article 67, which permitted the executive to deal only with the *consequences* of actions that hamper the realization of Community goals, Article 70 allows direct—but limited—action against the objectionable measure. 27–29/58, Compagnie des Hauts-fourneaux et Fonderies de Givors et al. v. H.A., 6 Rec. 501, 525–26 (1960).

interpretation of, the factor of comparability. By defining comparability to exclude all non-transport considerations, the Court took the first step toward a free market approach to transport questions. The free market implications are pointed up by the Court's analysis of the only transport sub-sidies it was willing to accept in Germany. These subsidies aided enterprises "temporarily" cut off from their natural markets by the fall of the iron curtain. It was a *political* calamity that distinguished these subsidies from those denied to enterprises in Germany and France which labored under *economic* hardships.[15] On the other hand, by excluding all non-transport factors, the Court could reject claims to special rates based upon the location of the enterprise or the quality of its coal or iron ore beds.[16] Although the member states retain general control of their transport policies, these poli-cies cannot be used to shield their industries from the forces of the free Community market.

The Limits of Community Authority

The judges thus made clear their support for vigorous and purposeful supranational supervision of special rates, but in rejecting the suit of the Lorraine steel enterprises (24 & 34/58), the Court specified the limits on this power. Let us recall that the Lorraine firms were challenging the HA's ac-ceptance of certain of the German special rates. With the French government in support, the enterprises objected to the HA's practice of considering special rates separately. Whatever the justification offered by the Germans for indus-trial rates, the general result was that the steel producers of Lorraine and Luxembourg were paying more for their coal

15. 19/58, Germany v. H.A., 6 Rec. 469, 494 (1960). The Court could hardly have involved itself in the dispute about the durability of the iron curtain, but steps were taken to keep the situation somewhat fluid. Emphasis was placed on the *need* of the enterprises, and the HA was given discretion to refuse or reduce the subsidy in the measure that the enterprise had been able to adjust to the new conditions.

16. Ibid., 489–90.

than German enterprises at equal distances from the Ruhr mines. The French contended that the HA's examination of the trees was obscuring the discriminatory shape of the forest. Directing the Court's attention to the history of the rates, the plaintiffs pointed out that Lorraine—while part of Germany —had received the benefits of special rates; only in 1946 were they denied to the Saar, Luxembourg, and Lorraine.[17] All told, it was argued, the German rates disclosed systematic discrimination based on the country of destination—a practice specifically prohibited by Article 70, paragraph 2.

That the winds of political controversy were blowing was made particularly clear to the Court at the conclusion of the oral hearings. The French held that the HA could not ignore obvious discrimination and Professor Paul Reuter, the "father" of the ECSC Treaty, concluded his argument for the French government with the following warning: "After this decision of the Court, the French Government will know what it is necessary to understand by the term 'Community.'"[18] The French went on to demand a generally applicable rate for full trainloads, special rates for non-German traffic, or some other way of ending the discrimination. Of course, as has already been pointed out, the French were not simply interested in ending the discriminatory rates. This would not have reduced their costs and would have benefited them only to the extent that they were in competition with German produced steel—a point open to considerable debate.[19]

Most significantly, the logic of the French position led it to an expansive interpretation of Article 70, which would have increased the powers of the HA even beyond its own goals.

17. *Exposé des Experts Français à propos des Tarifs Allemands,* included in the dossier, 24 & 34/58. See also Werner Feld, "The Significance of the Court of Justice of the European Communities," *North Dakota Law Review, 39* (1963), 46.

18. Public hearings, 8 March 1960.

19. See Advocate General Roemer, 24 & 34/58, Chambre syndicale de la sidérurgie de l'est de la France et al. v. H.A., 6 Rec. 573, 622 (1960).

The HA was content to consider each rate subjectively, i.e. according to whether or not it was given in the interest of protecting the railroad in question from competitive types of transport. The French, on the other hand, wanted the HA to wipe out the whole system because of its consequences. They even asked the HA to impose a general rate.

In essence, the French were arguing that national transport autonomy had to be limited in order to protect Community interests. The supranational implications of this uncharacteristic French position were not lost on Professor Van Hecke, the attorney for the HA, who stated to the Court: "Gentlemen, I hope that in the reading of your decision the French Government will understand that sometimes supranationalism is a good thing, because if there were more supranationalism in the Treaty in transport questions, the HA would have done what the plaintiffs asked it to do." [20]

The Court rejected the French suit, holding invalid the argument that the HA should be forced to extend the special German rates to the Lorraine and Luxembourg steelmakers. The German steel firms—unlike the French or the Luxembourg—had water routes available to them. Consequently, when setting rates the Bundesbahn had always to consider the possibility of a loss of traffic should the German enterprises decide to utilize water transport. Accordingly, the situations were not comparable. The test of comparability, the Court held, was not restricted to the distance from the Ruhr, but extended to the availability of alternative means of transport.

The judges were thus unwilling to accept the sweeping interpretation of treaty powers put forth by the French. However, the Court's approach did lay the foundation for a significant consolidation of Community authority. Specifically, limitations were provided for the rather open-ended autonomy guaranteed to the member states by Article 70, paragraph 5, i.e. the right to coordinate competition among

20. Public hearing, 9 March 1960.

the different modes of transport. In exercising this reserved power, each member state was enjoined by the Court to make certain that other Community transporters comparably situated were treated equally. This restriction of national authority was, of course, based squarely on the fundamental requirement of Article 70: the application of equal transport rates to consumers in comparable conditions. In this instance the French—without any alternative means of transport— were not really in a situation comparable to the Germans.[21] However, the fact remains that when the member governments adjust national transport rates, they are bound by the Court's ruling to extend any special favors to all Community enterprises comparably situated.

As shaped by the Court of Justice, Article 70 thus emerges as a surprisingly effective instrument of supranational action. More specifically, the Court developed the dynamic, free market implications of the article. The plaintiffs in the first cases discussed (19/58 and 27–29/58) stressed those provisions based on stability—continuity of employment, indiscriminate maintenance and expansion of existing Community production, and low prices. For its part, the Court put itself on the side of rationalization and change, even at the cost of some unemployment and the loss of unprofitable Community resources. It was held that the HA was obligated to maintain the natural conditions of competition, although it could relieve some of the consequences of rationalization.[22]

The limits of free enterprise are found in the right of national governments to adjust relations among their transport industries, provided only that these adjustments do not stop at national borders. It is certainly true that the results can be

21. Viewed from this perspective, the question of comparability becomes essentially a technical question. Accordingly, the Court simply accepted the report of its expert. See *Expertise* ordered by the Court, dossier 24 & 34/58.

22. 3–18, 25 & 26/58, Barbara Erzbergbau AG v. H.A., 6 Rec. 367, 407 (1960). Note, for example, the references to the transitional dispositions Convention, Section 10, paragraph 7, and Section 23. Cf. Lagrange, "Role of the Court of Justice," p. 415, note 44.

disadvantageous for some parties, as they were in this case for France. Nevertheless, without complete control over transport it is hard to see how the judges could have gone any further. In addition, the criteria established by the Court clearly limit the extent of discrimination and open an avenue of relief to those disadvantaged.[23]

IV

As it happens, the whole Lorraine problem became academic when the Germans decided in July 1960 to replace the special rates with a new trainload rate, applicable generally to traffic within the Community.[24] It is difficult to assess the role of the Court in this solution, which satisfied the French demand and most certainly advanced the ultimate goal of Community harmonization of transport rates. As influential a French newspaper as *Le Monde* attributed the new law to the Court decisions rejecting the appeals of the German government and the enterprises.[25]

The HA contended that the Bundesbahn was not eager to maintain subsidy rates which cut into its profits.[26] My own interviews indicate that the government itself was not anxious to maintain these rates.[27] Almost immediately after the Court's May 10th invalidation of the special German rates, it was reported that the government intended to introduce the trainload rates.[28] Presumably, all those who had

23. Presumably, completion of the Mosel Canal has made the situation of the Lorraine "comparable" to that of South German industry served by the Rhine.

24. *Europe CECA*, 25 July 1960, p. 2.

25. 30 July 1960. See also *Combat* (Paris), 30 July 1960.

26. Duplique, 19/58.

27. Moreover, as was noted earlier, it would seem that the lukewarm attitude of the Federal Government is reflected in the intervention by six state governments, supra, pp. 138–39.

28. *Europe CECA*, 12 May 1960, pp. 2–3.

been denied the benefits of the old rates would now support the government's measure. All told, it can be argued that the Court action validating the HA's suppression of the German rates was the catalyst that brought the final change.

The significance of the Court decision in the political process is perhaps further attested to by the unsuccessful last minute attempt made by the French to withdraw their suit.[29] The German decision to introduce the trainload rates seemed firm, and the French chances of winning their suit were slim indeed, after the expert's report. In these circumstances, no Court action at all was obviously preferable to a judgment which, by supporting a few of the special rules, might weaken German resolve to overhaul the system. However, the Court was unwilling to accept the withdrawal, since the oral procedure had been completed and the conclusions of the Advocate General had been given. Consequently, the Court rendered its adverse decision, but the new rates were introduced anyway.

V

By any measure, the Court's work on the problem of special transport rates must be judged productive and successful. Practically speaking, the HA had for some time been seeking the application of trainload rates, which it considered "an important advance towards harmonization." [30] Judicial action supported the efforts of the HA and yielded an additional dividend when the trainload rates were introduced. If harmonization remains a rather distant goal, its realization has

29. Ibid., 12 July 1960, p. 1.

30. HA, *Ninth General Report* (1961), p. 183. Advocate General Lagrange comments: "This solution had at all times been championed by the High Authority which could, however, not impose it. Thus, a problem had been solved *in a field where the powers of the High Authority are especially limited*—a problem in regard to which responsible governments, due to the divided opinions of their experts, had always been powerless." "Role of the Court of Justice," pp. 415–16.

been appreciably furthered by the decisions of the Court.

Just as critical in terms of this study was the Court's clear and unified interpretation of Article 70, which now stands as a fine foundation for future integrative steps. While limitations were imposed on the HA, they are consistent with the spirit of the article and the general problem of partial integration. Instead of proposing a rule for distinguishing rates of Community concern from the province of the member states, the Court delegated the job to the HA. All special rates are to be tested by the executive, and they are to be judged individually according to standards laid down by the Court.

The Court's reading of the provisions authorizing member governments to coordinate competition within the transport industry calls for Community-wide measures of comparability. Moreover, the justification for special treatment—a noncomparable position—is not to stem from a weak competitive situation, but only from transport problems per se, or from political difficulties. This interpretation, based upon the Court's construction of Articles 2 and 3, is of course in keeping with the Community's goals of growth and rationalization.

The judges can, however, be criticized for their flat rejection of special transport rates for regional development schemes.[31] The Common Market Treaty explicitly authorizes such assistance,[32] and sooner or later the two treaties will have to be harmonized. It is unthinkable that special transport rates for regional development would be allowed for all industries except coal and steel. Both advocates offered alternative solutions to the Court, although neither of them accepted transport subsidies for regional development as a

31. 27–29/58, Compagnie des Hauts-fourneaux v. H.A., 6 Rec. 501, 527 (1960).

32. Article 92, paragraph 3.

general remedy.[33] They recognized that if regions were in serious economic difficulty, and if the measures were only temporary, approval would be possible. Only Mr. Roemer dealt specifically with the special French rates (27–29/58), and he rejected them. Nevertheless, both he and Mr. Lagrange showed an awareness of the long-range problem and indicated possible solutions. It was not at all certain that the French rates were, in fact, either temporary or intended for regional development. Under the circumstances, it would seem that the Court should have awaited a more appropriate situation to take a stand.

However, regardless of this minor shortcoming, the fact remains that the Court was able to grapple successfully with the rail rate problem. The judges disposed of the claims for special protection and still managed to respect the restrictions imposed by partial integration. This was possible because the judgment sidestepped the question of harmonization of rail rates. In making this adroit maneuver, the Court displayed an impressive syntactical skill along with an alert grasp of the substantive issues.

The judges took full advantage of an opportunity to limit the confining effects of partial integration, but the opportunity was presented only because partial integration was not central to the problem of special rail rates. In the litigation covered in subsequent chapters the partial character of the Coal and Steel Community becomes increasingly central, thus narrowing—but never eliminating—the normative opportunities of the judicial process.

33. 3–18, 25 & 26/58, Barbara Erzbergbau AG v. H.A., 6 Rec. 367, 446–50 (1960) and 27–29/58, Compagnie des Hauts-fourneaux v. H.A., 6 Rec. 501, 565–68 (1960).

8

THE INTEGRATION OF TRANSPORT:

COMPETITION AMONG TRUCKERS

I

Article 70, paragraph 3, provides that transport rates "shall be published or brought to the knowledge of the High Authority." No litigation has resulted from this provision in connection with rail traffic, but the HA's attempt to apply it to road transport has raised a substantial question: Is there a meaningful distinction between publication of rates and their communication to the HA? If the HA makes the rate schedules public, or available to Community enterprises, this distinction is without significance. On the other hand, the competitive value of keeping the information secret is apparent. The article itself is ambiguous as to both the public character of the rates and the authority to decide which of the alternatives is to be followed. Is it all a matter of HA discretion or can a definitive answer be teased from the treaty?

The issues are similar to those already dealt with in connection with the publication of steel prices.[1] Publication is not only a bar to discrimination but since transport costs are a factor in steel prices, it could be argued that publication of trucking rates is indispensable to price alignment.[2] On the

1. Supra, Chapters 3 and 4.
2. Truckers account for a small but increasing share of steel shipments.

other hand, the trucking industry is characterized by intense competition. Publication, of course, sacrifices competition on the altar of fair trade.

The similarity with earlier cases should not, however, obscure the distinction. As a part of the transport industry, trucking is only partially integrated into the Community. If, as Lister claims: "Truck haulage increases the propensity of steel producers to give secret price rebates," [3] the grounds for HA action are clear, but the scope of HA power remains uncertain. Moreover, there seems to be no evidence that variations in trucking rates "are based on the country of origin or of destination of the products in question." [4] On the contrary, it would seem that reductions are aimed at the competitively praiseworthy goal of maximizing business. Accordingly, the case for intervention would be proportionally weakened.

The HA's response to this delicate situation was to seek a negotiated settlement. Since the truckers were not community enterprises,[5] the HA could not deal with them directly but had to work through the member governments. On the basis of a 1956 report by the Experts' Committee on Transport, negotiations were conducted, at first, through a committee of governmental representatives and then by direct negotiation in the Council of Ministers.[6] In early 1958 an agreement seemed at hand, but it foundered on detail after the principle of prior publication of maximum and minimum rates had been accepted.[7]

Lister, *Europe's Coal and Steel Community*, pp. 374–75. See also, Diebold, *The Schuman Plan*, p. 185.

3. Lister, p. 375.

4. Article 70, paragraph 2.

5. Article 80 provides, "The term enterprise, as used in this Treaty, refers to any enterprise engaged in production in the field of coal and steel within the territories" of the member states.

6. HA, *Sixth General Report* (1958), 2, 82–83.

7. HA, *Seventh General Report* (1959), p. 169.

II

The halting progress of political negotiation finally led to litigation. Because publication of trucking rates was already required in Germany, the German steel industry saw general publication of trucking rates as the prerequisite to equal competitive conditions. Accordingly, the HA, which had been willing to negotiate patiently for two years, was finally prodded to action in the summer of 1958 by the German steel association, Wirtschaftsvereinigung Eisen und Stahlindustrie (WES).

Responding immediately to a July letter from WES demanding action, the HA took steps to end the deadlock. In August the HA offered the member states three choices for fulfilling the obligations of Article 70, paragraph 3. Two possibilities involved prior publication of trucking rates. The third permitted forwarding to the HA rates already applied and offered two grounds for WES dissatisfaction.[8] Subsequent communication of rates, rather than prior publication, would not permit effective alignment. Reinforcing this deficiency was the likelihood that the rates would not be made public, but would be confined to internal administrative use, i.e. checking for discriminatory practices. WES expressed its dissatisfaction with these half-measures by filing suit in September (39/58).[9] By December, the French government had added its voice to the opposition to post-contract forwarding of rates.[10]

Seemingly in response to this mounting opposition, the HA sent to all the governments a new letter which eliminated the third choice.[11] In the interim, however, the Dutch government wrote to the HA accepting the third possibility, and

8. HA, *Seventh General Report* (1959), p. 169.
9. *J.O.C.E.*, *1* (15 September 1958), 424–25.
10. Mémoire, 25/59.
11. HA 18/59, *J.O.C.E.*, *2* (7 March 1959), 287–91.

at the same time issued an official decree requiring truckers to forward rates after the conclusion of transport contracts. In its letter to the HA, the government expressed its assumption that the HA would keep the rate information secret and, accordingly, promised the Dutch truckers that any information forwarded would be kept confidential.[12] In withdrawing the third choice, the HA declared that the responses to its first letter had been unsatisfactory and constituted a failure to fulfill a treaty obligation.

Both the Dutch and Italian governments were as unhappy with the HA's revised decision as WES had been with the initial letter. Although given until 30 June 1960 to take the necessary action, the two governments filed suit well before the deadline—Italy on 4 April 1959 (20/59), and Holland on 24 April (25/59). In November, five Dutch enterprises intervened on the side of their government. Of course, with the third alternative eliminated and the new suits filed, German steel withdrew its suit.

Despite the fact that the Dutch and Italians filed almost identical suits, their respective reasons for opposing the HA measure were significantly and portentously distinct. Italy's objection to published prices was clearly at cross purposes with the treaty. The Italian steel industry, which produces primarily for the home market,[13] gets added bargaining power from unpublished trucking rates. By permitting secret rebates, the confidential rates give added leverage in the battle for markets. Specifically, the opportunity for foreign competitors to align on Italian prices is eliminated as long as

---

12. 25/59, Netherlands v. H.A., 6 Rec. 723, 732 (1960). The government also noted its belief that obligations imposed by Article 70, paragraph 3, were in the service of avoiding the discriminatory action prohibited in the first two paragraphs of Article 70. For this reason, the Dutch held that the HA was not entitled to draw transport obligations from Article 60, which governed only price policy. The Dutch, of course, wished to prevent the HA from basing a decision to make rates public on the alignment requirements of Article 60.

13. Lister, p. 47.

transport costs remain unknown. The Italians were, thus, directly in conflict with the significant treaty goal of market interpenetration, and with the HA which—under strong pressure from the German steel industry—was trying to clear away the obstacles to alignment.

From Lister we learn that Holland, too, "as a permanent steel importing country . . . is the beneficiary of uncoordinated rates." [14] Yet it is immediately clear that the Dutch were interested in increasing, rather than suppressing, the flow of intra-Community trade. In fact, the Dutch interest in trade and in unpublished prices extends well beyond the problem of steel pricing. Dutch transporters have been fierce competitors and the Dutch economy is heavily dependent on the foreign exchange earned by the transport industry. Prior publication would limit the transporters' flexibility and cut down their bargaining power.

The conflict with the Dutch was thus primarily over methods: if the competitive power of the Dutch transporters could be protected, compromise was possible. However, it was difficult to see how this was possible, except within the context of a wider settlement of the full range of transport questions. The dispute with the Dutch also extended to rail rates, with this controversy over trucking being little more than a pilot problem. The Dutch government had been willing to forward rail rates to the HA but only on condition that the HA would keep them secret. France had used an agreement between the HA and the Dutch on this matter to justify French refusal to let the Bundesbahn know French rail rates. [15] Consequently, it is clear that the conflict over publication of trucking rates was really a prelude involving principles that had significance for the entire transport question. [16]

14. Ibid., p. 375.
15. See *Europe CECA,* 20 January 1959, p. 1.
16. See HA, *Eighth General Report* (1960), pp. 208–09.

With transport at the periphery of the treaty, there was reason to wonder whether the issue could be settled within the framework of the Coal and Steel Community. The Dutch wanted the larger question of transport coordination and harmonization dealt with and were unwilling to give up their competitive advantages until they were assured a broader settlement.[17] Consequently, one could wonder whether the issue might not be dealt with most effectively within the broader reaches of the Common Market. At any rate, the partial character of the Coal and Steel Community was squarely in the background of the Dutch suit.

III

The dispute, as it was presented to the Court, was one step removed from the complicated legal and economic issues spelled out in the preceding section. The HA had acted under Article 88 of the treaty, which empowers the Community executive to take action against a member state that fails to fulfill an obligation imposed by the treaty. The question for the Court to resolve was whether the treaty—and specifically Article 70, paragraph 3—required prior publication. Obviously, if there was no such obligation, the refusal of the Dutch to go beyond subsequent and confidential notification could not be faulted.[18] There would then have been no failure to fulfill a treaty obligation, and Article 88 would not have been an appropriate tool of executive action.

The Dutch position rested on the generally limited Com-

17. Somewhat later, the Dutch government published a full presentation of this position. Ministry of Transport and *Waterstaat, Memorandum Concerning the Common Transport Policy in the European Economic Community* (The Hague, 1961).

18. Supra, pp. 152–53. Because the Dutch had accepted this third alternative offered in the HA's first letter, their case was somewhat stronger than that of the Italian government. Accordingly, citations from the Dutch suit (25/59) will predominate in the following presentation.

munity authority over transport. The inference drawn by the Dutch was that this power had been purposefully withheld: transport was to remain essentially a national matter until the question could be dealt with in its entirety. Such a settlement could only be contemplated within the context of the Common Market, or through joint action by the two Communities.[19] Given the marginal relation of transport to the Coal and Steel Community, the Dutch proposed a narrow construction of Article 70.

The argument of the plaintiffs centered on the alternative methods provided in Article 70, paragraph 3, for eliminating discriminatory practices. Since the provision presented a choice of publication or forwarding to the HA, the executive had no right to make one of these obligatory. Moreover, the phrasing of this passage was held indicative of the intent of the framers. The use of the past tense, "prices . . . applied," made it clear to the Dutch that the provision aimed at subsequent rather than prior notification.[20] In support of their textual position the plaintiffs contended, on practical grounds, that the HA's regulation was *unnecessary* and *ineffectual*.[21] Communication of rates—even without making figures generally available—would still permit the HA to prevent discrimination.[22] Moreover, alignment was also possible without publication: it was clear from the many fluctuations in transport rates and the relative permanency of steel price lists that steel companies used average transport costs for alignment, and these were, of course, available without prior

19. Réplique 25/59.
20. Ibid.
21. Additionally, the Dutch and the Italians agreed that prior publication would be positively harmful because it would interfere with the free movement of prices and the free choice of a transporter. The result would be a more rigid transport market, less sensitive to the needs of the Community. See 20/59, Italy v. H.A., 6 Rec. 663, 680 (1960) and réplique, 25/59. The HA denied these allegations of market inflexibility, pointing to the leeway allowed under the new regulations. See duplique, 25/59.
22. 25/59, Netherlands v. H.A., 6 Rec. 723, 745 (1960).

publication.[23] The argument of ineffectuality was based on the number of transactions that would be left uncovered: those cases where the producer or purchaser provided his own transport as well as third-country shipments.[24]

So far as the HA was concerned the Dutch argument led to a dead end: either the *all* of a complete solution, or the *nothing* of partial integration. The HA, for its part, argued programmatically for the power necessary to piece together a successful operation.[25] Article 70 was seen as an executory part of the treaty. The failure of the governments to reach agreement during the transitional period should not, it was argued, immobilize the executive.[26]

In order to insure the "comparable price conditions" which Article 70, paragraph 1, sought for all "consumers in comparable positions," the HA argued that secret rebates had to be eliminated. Yet, with thousands of contracts concluded, the executive held it would be impossible to set up an effective check for illegal rebating—at least, not without an enormous administrative apparatus. However, once the rates were published, each user would become a potential policeman. Finally, the HA sought to demonstrate that prior publication of transport rates was indispensable to the right of alignment guaranteed by Article 60. In other words, the HA claimed that one of the reasons transport had been included in the Community was its vital connection to price policies agreed upon by the framers. The Court had, of course, recognized in its

23. Ibid., p. 753.

24. Réplique, 25/59.

25. In developing its position, the HA took note of Article 232 of the Common Market Treaty, which provides that "the provisions of this treaty shall not affect those of the Treaty establishing the European Coal and Steel Community, in particular in regard to . . . the rules laid down by the said Treaty for the functioning of the common market for coal and steel." See mémoire, 25/59. Except where otherwise indicated, the following arguments are taken from the duplique, 25/59.

26. Section 10 of the Convention provided procedures for dealing with the transport question.

very first judgment that publication of prices was indis-pensable to alignment.[27] The HA contended that since trans-port costs are a significant pricing factor, to allow such costs to remain secret would be tantamount to interfering with the competitive right of alignment.

In sum, the HA contended that prior publication was a necessary step toward the objectives of Article 70. The article might not permit the executive to impose this step directly on the member states. But the HA was required by Article 88 to take note of the failure of the national governments to ful-fill treaty obligations. In specifying prior publication, the HA had merely sought to indicate with some precision the under-lying goals of Article 70. How could the executive make cer-tain that the member states lived up to their treaty obliga-tions unless it were free to indicate the nature of these commitments? [28]

Interestingly enough, the Court accepted the HA's practical approach but not its methods. At the outset the Court noted that the HA enjoyed no regulatory powers under Article 70, paragraph 3. It further pointed out that where—as in the parallel provision of Article 60—the treaty authorized regula-tory power for the HA, the wording was quite explicit: "price lists . . . shall be published to the extent and in the form prescribed by the High Authority." [29]

Although neither the words of Article 70, paragraph 3, nor the analogy with Article 60 could justify regulatory power for the HA, the Court was willing to see whether such power was implied: "Doctrine and *jurisprudence* are in agreement in

27. See 1/54, France v. H.A., 1 Rec., 7, 24–27 (1954), as cited in mémoire, 25/59. Supra, Chapters 3 and 4.

28. Mémoire, 25/59. The Court was also invited to look at the extended history of the dispute. The HA sought to convince the judges that the Dutch government was well aware that prior publication was crucial insofar as the executive was concerned.

29. Article 60, paragraph 2(a). See 25/59, Netherlands v. H.A., 6 Rec. 723, 757 (1960).

admitting that rules established by a treaty imply the norms without which these rules cannot be applied usefully, or reasonably." [30] The Court's search for implied powers was based on two arguments made by the HA:

1. Publication of transport rates was the logical extension of Article 60, for without it the right of alignment would be ineffective.
2. Publication of transport rates was necessary in order to avoid the discriminatory practices prohibited by Article 70.

Both claims were rejected, but one is left with the impression that the Court never really dealt with either of them. Perhaps the reason is that the Court's search was textual rather than economic. Without dealing with the question of whether alignment is, *in fact,* possible without knowledge of transport costs, the Court wrote:

it is incorrect that the terms "price" and "conditions of sale" in Article 60 include those of goods and transport; that in effect the seller can only be required to publish his own and not the prices applied by a transport enterprise;
that to the extent that it would be incumbent on the seller to pay the freight to the transporter, it would be an element of the net costs of the seller;
that the seller is not required to make public the elements of his net costs; [31]

---

30. Ibid., pp. 757–58. The Court was presumably distinguishing the *executory* character of Article 70, which it had established two months earlier from the *regulatory* powers with which it dealt here. See 3–18, 25 & 26/58, Barbara Erzbergbau AG et al. v. H.A., 6 Rec. 367, 402 (1960). However, it is rather hard to square the Court's approval of the HA's elimination of special German rail rates with its pronouncement here that "in the realm of transport, the text of the treaty refuses all power of executory decision to the High Authority."

31. 25/59, Netherlands v. H.A., 6 Rec. 723, 758 (1960).

In support of its position, the Court noted that the HA had never called for publication of transport rates in any of its decisions prescribing publication of prices. To the extent that the HA had taken notice of transport costs in these decisions, it had only been in connection with alignment on prices, actually disbursed. Accordingly, *subsequent* control, rather than prior publication was in order.[32]

The Court also rejected the possibility that implied regulatory power might flow from the HA's obligation to control discrimination. While Article 70 includes repressive action by the HA against discrimination, "one cannot deduce . . . a capacity . . . to exercise a prior control by prescribing disclosure of *barèmes* or of prices, such competence being exceptional and subordinated to a renunciation by the member states which in this instance the treaty authorizes neither expressly nor implicitly."[33] There is, somehow, a circular quality to this search for implied powers, because once again the Court avoids facing the issue as to whether publication is in fact necessary to avoid discrimination.

With the hardest part of the job behind it, the Court went on to test the HA's application of Article 88. The relevant passage of the article reads as follows: "If the High Authority considers that a state has failed in one of the obligations incumbent upon it by virtue of this Treaty, it shall, after permitting the State in question to present its views, take note of the failure in a reasoned decision accompanied by a justification." As applied by the Court, the article raised two questions about the actions of the HA. First, there was an administrative issue: had the member governments been permitted to present their views? More significantly, the Court explored the substantive issue: had the Dutch and Italian governments failed to fulfill an obligation imposed by the treaty?

On the administrative problem, the judges held that the

32. Ibid., p. 759.
33. Ibid.

HA had not really sought the observations of the governments. The Court took note of the lengthy Dutch reply to the HA's August 1958 letter and the executory decree issued by the Dutch government,[34] and held that it could not be concluded "that every point of view contrary, expressed by a government whose opinion diverges from that of the High Authority as to the proper means for attaining the goal that the High Authority pursues, must be considered as automatically constituting the observations sought by Article 88, paragraph 1, and as exhausting its arguments as to the determination of the obligations which actually or supposedly would flow from the Treaty." [35] The Court thus interpreted the call for observations as a requirement for extended negotiations. It is patently clear that this judicial stand is based on a desire to avoid the use of Article 88 wherever possible. Negotiation rather than coercion is the key to the Court's position.

The same conclusion can be drawn from the judicial treatment of the second and more central problem, the applicability of Article 88. The Court concluded that the HA had attempted to use its Article 88 decision to assert a nonexistent regulatory power.[36] The member states were obligated only to seek the *goals* of Article 70, paragraph 3. Accordingly, the HA was incorrect in holding that there had been a failure to fulfill a treaty obligation merely because of a failure to accept unconditionally one of the choices offered by the HA in the August 1958 letter.[37] In short, the Court concluded that since the HA had no regulatory power to execute the provisions of Article 70, paragraph 3, the use of Article 88 had been improper. The executive was entitled to seek only the goals of Article 70. Accordingly, a *recommendation* was in order, but

34. Supra, pp. 152–53.
35. 25/59, Netherlands v. H.A., 6 Rec. 723, 764 (1960).
36. The Court's support for this charge was drawn from the text of the decision and need not detain us.
37. 25/59, Netherlands v. H.A., 6 Rec. 723, 764–65 (1960).

not a *decision* which prescribed the methods necessary to attain the goals.[38]

IV

The HA did not respond very quickly to its legal setback, but before long irresistible pressure began to mount. Opposition to the HA's inaction and to the unsettled question of publication began in November 1960, when WES—the German steel association which had previously prodded the executive into action with a suit (39/58)—asked the HA to issue the recommendation authorized by the Court.[39] Following the failure of the November Council of Ministers meeting to arrive at a compromise solution, WES gained the support of the government and the German trucking association.[40] The pressure on the HA was not limited to the Germans but reportedly came from numerous other sources, including a majority of the member governments.[41]

Yet much more important than the amount of pressure were the lines pursued by the opposition. There seems to have been a movement afoot to settle the whole question through bilateral agreements on publication which would exclude the Dutch and Italians.[42] There was, of course, a dual danger: the anarchy of internecine solutions to Community problems and the collapse of the entire transport program.

The problem of ensuring that price and conditions of carriage were made known was not confined purely to the road-haulage sector. . . . An increasing propor-

38. Ibid., p. 760.

39. *Europe CECA,* 15 November 1960, p. 2.

40. Ibid., 4 January 1961, p. 1 and 27 January 1961, p. 2. The German truckers complained that their own published rates resulted in a loss of business *on German roads.*

41. Ibid., 28 February 1961, p. 2.

42. Ibid., 4 January 1961, p. 1, and 16 February 1961, pp. 1–2.

tion of rail traffic in certain Community countries is being effected under unpublished contracts: in the case of the Netherlands, indeed, this has latterly been so for most consignments. Furthermore, the High Authority has been unable to secure a satisfactory position with regard to international transport on the Rhine and on waterways west of the Rhine.[43]

The HA met the crisis with a sweeping recommendation that differed from the earlier decision on a number of critical points.[44] First, the action undertaken was, in accordance with the judgment, in the form of a recommendation rather than a decision. Accordingly, it set forth the goals to be pursued, leaving to the states the choice of methods consistent with these goals. Among the goals specified were not only those mentioned in Article 70 itself but also alignment, specified in Article 60, and international through-rates and harmonization as provided in Section 10 of the Convention. Moreover, the recommendation extended to the entire transport industry, not merely trucking. Finally, the recommendation was based on Article 70, whereas the earlier decision had been taken under the precipitous provisions of Article 88.

Both the Dutch and Italian governments quickly filed suit (9 & 11/61, respectively). However, negotiations reopened and dragged on while the written procedure was going forward before the Court. No settlement with the Dutch and Italians proved possible, although by early in February 1962 it was reported that only details remained to be resolved with the other four governments, all of which indicated a willingness to comply with the HA's interpretation of Article 70, paragraph 3.[45]

43. HA, *Tenth General Report* (1962), p. 223.
44. HA Recommendation 1/61, *J.O.C.E., 4* (9 March 1961), 469–71.
45. *Europe CECA*, 8 February 1962, pp. 1–2.

V

The HA had softened its stand considerably by retreating from Article 88 and by substituting a recommendation for its earlier decision. Nonetheless, it was clear to the Dutch and Italians that only unpalatable measures would allow realization of the broad goals set forth in the recommendation. The Dutch government argued in a manner consistent with its earlier all-or-nothing stand, which had as its ostensible goal blocking any action until a general solution to the transport problem could be worked out.[46]

In the first place, the Dutch held that the HA was without power to issue a recommendation, since a recommendation, like a decision, was obligatory.[47] As the Dutch saw it, a recommendation entailed an exercise of regulatory power in matters reserved by Article 70, paragraph 5, to the member states. In accord with its attempt to restrict as much as possible the exercise of Article 70, the Dutch went on to contest the HA's attempt to base its Article 70 recommendation on other portions of the treaty. They contended that, even assuming the authority to deal with the discrimination forbidden by Article 70, the HA was not entitled to pursue such additional goals as alignment and harmonization. It was, of course, in the service of these latter goals that the HA claimed the right to make generally available the rates submitted to it by the member governments.

The Dutch claimed that their objections would be met by a proper limitation of HA powers in the transport field. The choice of publication or communication of rates to the HA would be left to the member states. Secondly, the competitive character of the transport market would be protected rather

46. Again, attention will be devoted to the Dutch suit, 9/61, Netherlands v. H.A., 8 Rec. 413 (1962). The Italian suit (12/61) was withdrawn without a judgment in September 1962.

47. For the arguments of the parties, see ibid., pp. 425–46.

than being devitalized by publication. Finally, the solution to transport problems would be left to agreement by the member governments as provided in the Convention. It was, in sum, a static conception of partial integration that the Dutch offered: the boundaries of integration set forth in the treaty would have been protected not only from direct assault but also from erosion by way of other provisions of the treaty. Not surprisingly, the HA's defense of its recommendation was founded on a more dynamic conception of the limits of partial integration—a conception that made the recommendation the ideal instrument of action. The HA's position was consistent with its immediate purposes as well as its traditionally goal-oriented view of the treaty. A little more surprising was the fact that the executive was supported in this stand by the nationalized coal industry of France, which has maintained the most consistent opposition to extensions of Community authority.

Essentially, two points had to be argued: the executive's right to pursue the broad range of goals which it sought, and the appropriateness of a recommendation for achieving these goals. In defense of its pursuit of goals extending beyond Article 70, the HA argued that the various provisions of the treaty which called for making rates public must be considered as a whole. Moreover, reference was made to Article 70, paragraph 5, which both guarantees and limits national transport autonomy. Specifically, autonomy is subjected "to the provisions of this article, as well as to the other provisions of this Treaty." As interpreted by the HA, this passage meant that although the member governments retained rights with regard to transport, these rights could not be raised against the implementation of the treaty. In other words, the obligations of the states cannot be avoided by pleading the limits of partial integration.

On the other hand, because the HA was without regulatory power, the member states were free to choose any methods which would permit the realization of the goals in question. Accordingly, it was concluded that the recommendation which sets forth goals, but permitted freedom of means, was the proper instrument with which to proceed.[48] This part of the argument was, of course, in accord with the previous Court decisions to which it constantly referred: Article 70 was executory but the HA was without decision-making power.

The judgment added a new dimension to the problem of partial integration and at the same time cleared up some of the uncertainties raised by the initial decisions. Without reference to these earlier efforts, the Court began by reiterating its holding that Article 70 is a "concrete and obligatory rule" of the treaty.[49] This left the question of how much authority and responsibility the HA had for making certain that the obligations were fulfilled.

The Court had already decided that the HA was without decision-making power, but had suggested as an alternative the recommendation: "In the case where this regulatory power is refused and remains reserved to the States, the HA, if it desires to recall to the States their obligations, can only have recourse to a recommendation." [50] Again, the Court followed the path already charted in the earlier judgments, concluding that the recommendation was the permissible, necessary, and appropriate way to proceed in a situation where the HA was denied regulatory power to implement an obligatory provision of the treaty.

48. Article 14 reads as follows: "Recommendations shall be binding with respect to the objectives which they specify but shall leave to those to whom they are directed the choice of appropriate means for obtaining these objectives."

49. 9/61, Netherlands v. H.A., 8 Rec. 413, 447–48 (1962). For the statement of this position in the earlier decisions, see 25/59, Netherlands v. H.A., 6 Rec. 723, 756 (1960). See also 3–18, 25 & 26/58, Barbara Erzbergbau AG et al. v. H.A., 6 Rec. 367, 402 (1960).

50. 25/59, Netherlands v. H.A., 6 Rec. 723, 760 (1960).

But what of the HA's interpretation of Article 70, paragraph 3? Just what obligations did this provision impose on the member states? The Court concluded that, both in substance and in form, the HA's recommendation was valid. Without elaboration, the Court rejected the plaintiff's charge that the recommendation did not leave the states free to choose means. With this formal question out of the way, the Court moved on to more important issues. The ensuing portions of the judgment are interesting, not only in connection with the immediate problem of transport but also for the light shed upon the question of partial integration.

The Court rejected the static conception put forth by the Dutch, accepting in its stead the dynamic and functional argument of the HA. The key to the Court's holding lies in the fundamental unity or integrity attributed to the treaty. In itself, this conception excluded the Dutch argument that certain provisions of the treaty must be considered in isolation. "The dispositions of the Treaty form a whole, and complement and supplement each other reciprocally." Accordingly, each provision of the treaty is of potential service to the others, and the HA is entitled to make such indirect use of them as is necessary—including those provisions which are in some ways hobbled by the limitations of partial integration. Since Article 70 does not stand by itself, it was proper for the HA to use it to make certain that such other objectives as alignment and harmonization were realized.[51]

Most significant for the immediate issue, the Court agreed with the HA that knowledge of transport costs was essential to alignment. Along the same functional lines, the Court accepted the HA's requirement that the states set up some method of control for insuring that objectives of the recommendation were achieved. Rather than an improper interference with the sovereignty of the member states, such measures were held necessary, because "in the absence of a control

51. 9/61, Netherlands v. H.A., 8 Rec. 413, 453–54 (1962).

of their execution or of coercive sanctions, the recommendation would run the risk of remaining without effect." [52]

At any rate, it is clear that the HA's recommendation was accepted in toto by the Court of Justice. After a political and legal battle which lasted five years, the Dutch and Italian governments found themselves faced with the unequivocal obligation of prior "publication" of transport rates. It is hardly to be expected that the two nations will give in easily to this obligation. It is reasonable to assume that the Dutch, at least, will renew efforts to arrive at a general solution to transport matters which will allow them to maintain some portion of their competitive advantage. But the legal obligation has been clearly defined, and community attention has been directed to the problem of compliance.[53]

VI

There remains the problem of reconciling the two decisions of the Court. At first glance there are numerous inconsistencies, which can be summed up in the contrast between the seemingly illusory functionalism of the first judgments and the real functionalism of the latter cases.[54] However, upon closer inspection these inconsistencies are, in fact, more apparent than real. The tentative and ambiguous character of the earlier decisions is both resolved and explained by a careful consideration of the two sets of cases.

The Court's conclusion in the first decision that the HA had improperly used Article 88 can be explained, in part, by a continuing preoccupation with equitable administrative pro-

52. Ibid., p. 455.

53. At the time of this writing the final returns are not yet in, but it is clear that a serious problem of compliance faces the HA. The executive had set a December 1, 1963 deadline for compliance with its recommendation, but that date passed unheeded. *Europe CECA* reported that the HA was ready to turn to Article 88 to gain the required measure of publication. 9 December 1963, p. 2.

54. Supra, p. 159.

cedures. Certainly, the HA could be condemned on procedural grounds—as Advocate General Roemer noted—for failing to stick to the letter of Article 88 where the Dutch were concerned and to justify sufficiently its Article 88 decision. Yet, as has been pointed out, the entire judgment is characterized by textual caution which harkens back to the Monnet Margin cases.

A full understanding must begin with an awareness of the difficult position in which the Court found itself. A significant Community dispute was marking time in anticipation of the Court's decision. It had proven impossible to resolve this dispute in the Council of Ministers, and action had shifted to the courtroom. Litigation was based on Article 88 which, according to the Court, "opens ways of execution and constitutes the ultima ratio permitting the interests of the Community, as authorized by the Treaty, to prevail over the inertia and against the resistance of the member states." [55] Given the scope and extent of the power involved, the Court concluded that the article should be interpreted strictly. The whole decision bespeaks a desire to restrict the utilization of Article 88: meticulous observance of its procedural requirements and a reluctance to see it used to support a particularly liberal construction of the HA's power to intervene.

In this context, what I have termed the illusory functionalism and textualism of the first decisions is easily understood. The Court was not attempting to ascertain whether publication was necessary to avoid discrimination or permit alignment. It merely was trying to determine whether the HA had the regulatory power to seek these goals by way of decision, or whether this decision-making power was implied in the text of the articles. In the latter decisions, with the HA on sound ground procedurally, the Court returned to its functional techniques for dealing with the substantive issues.

On the other hand, it might seem that an understandably

55. 25/59, Netherlands v. H.A., 6 Rec. 723, 761 (1960).

cautious Court could have stayed entirely clear of substantive issues in the first two judgments by confining itself to a denunciation of the use of Article 88. However, if the Court had not gone beyond the procedural problems, another suit on exactly the same issue was in prospect. The judgments, of course, did lead to more litigation, but the Court had at least directed the HA along approved paths. The dispute had been moved off dead-center, and the new suit offered the Court an opportunity to define fresh approaches to the problem of partial integration. By the Court's own formulation the issue was central rather than peripheral, as it had been in the rail rates cases. Accordingly, it is understandable that the judges were reluctant to see Article 88 used to deal with the problem. The recommendation, on the other hand, seemed to be a particularly appropriate tool, leaving the member states considerable freedom without allowing them to put an insurmountable obstacle on the road to integration.[56]

Finally, in addition to defining an appropriate instrument for dealing with partial integration, the Court has offered a dynamic and expansive treatment of the general problem. For those partially integrated sectors which are included in

---

56. 9/61, Netherlands v. H.A., 8 Rec. 413, 435 (1962). However, if the distinction between a decision and a recommendation is to retain significance, the Court will have to deal with another question. The parties had contended that the wording of the recommendation was so vague as to make it impossible to distinguish means from ends. The result of this ambiguity, it was held, was to put the states under pressure to accept both the means and ends chosen by the HA. The Court, it will be recalled, held that the member states had not been denied the choice of means, but a real question is left unanswered: what if the combination of goals set forth by the HA so limited the options open to the enterprises as to make illusory the freedom of choice which the recommendation is designed to protect? Insofar as the publication problem is concerned, if the HA had not been permitted to protect the right of alignment, the freedom open to the member states would have been critically broader; it was principally the needs of alignment that justified making public the rates forwarded to the HA. Given the wide variety of ends the Court has decided it is proper for the executive to pursue, the distinction between a decision and a recommendation could in practice become blurred.

executory provisions of the treaty, the needs of the Community have first call. National autonomy will not be permitted to block the general operations of the Community. Although the motives for inclusion of a partially integrated sector may be narrow and specific, still, authority can be exercised over that sector if such authority proves necessary for the realization of broader Community goals.

9

SOCIAL AND FISCAL AUTONOMY:

THE MINERS' BONUS

I

The boundaries between Community authority and the reserved powers of the member states are often poorly defined. The national governments have, in general, retained control over their own financial affairs, including, of course, their system of taxation. Similarly, the governments are left with considerable independent power over wage policy and social benefits. However, the limits of this social and fiscal autonomy are not clearly specified in the treaty. This chapter will explore the manner in which the institutions of the Community dealt with this thorny problem as it materialized in a dispute over a shift bonus paid to underground miners in Germany.

Prior to the opening of the Coal and Steel Community, governments had maintained ceiling prices for coal. In order to avoid disturbances, these ceilings had been continued by the HA. However, by the end of 1955 only the Ruhr prices remained under HA control.[1] The coal industry was pressing the HA for price increases, indeed, for elimination of ceilings altogether.[2]

1. Except where otherwise noted, the information in this section is drawn from Diebold, *Schuman Plan*, pp. 242–51.
2. HA, *Fourth General Report* (1956), p. 170.

Although, legally, the decision was the HA's alone, the German government was strongly opposed to any price increases, let alone to the 6 DM per ton requested by the Ruhr. In February 1956 the mine owners and the government worked out a compromise, and in April the HA eliminated its price ceilings. The agreement, duly forwarded to the HA, contained the following provisions:

> 1. tax concessions on write-off of underground installations
> 2. assumption by the government of a portion of the employers' contribution to the miners' insurance fund
> 3. payment by the government of a shift bonus for underground miners [3]

These changes resulted in a reduction in costs for the mining companies totaling roughly 4 DM per ton. When added to the 2 DM increase in prices accepted by the government, the net effect was equivalent to the 6 DM price rise requested by the coal firms.

The settlement was not, however, acceptable to the HA, which held that the miners' bonus constituted illegal government assistance to the coal mining companies. Negotiation with the German government produced another compromise. The government agreed to discontinue paying its increased share of the insurance fund contribution. This discontinuation resulted in an increase in the costs of the mining firms which was slightly larger than the government's bonus payments, so the HA accepted this compensatory arrangement.

Although the settlement satisfied the HA, the Dutch coal association, De Gezamenlijke Steenkolenmijnen, objected. The association claimed that regardless of the compensation the publicly financed bonus remained an illegal subsidy, and the Court of Justice was asked to invalidate the measure

3. Ibid., p. 169.

(17/57).[4] The Dutch suit presented the judges with a significant problem stemming directly from the partial character of the Community. Was the miners' bonus to be considered an exercise of the power over labor policy retained by the national governments? Article 68 #1 defines this reserved power as follows: "The methods of fixing wages and social benefits in force in the various member States shall not be affected, as regards the coal and steel industries, by the application of this Treaty." It is true that, in the long run, the HA is pledged by Article 3(e) to harmonize the "living and working conditions of the labour force . . . in an upward direction." However, in the short run, the competitive inequities inherent in this reservation of sovereignty are accepted.

There are two exceptions to this general rule. In the first place, the Community is committed to holding the line against unfavorable changes in an already unsatisfactory status quo. As Lister comments: "The treaty rests on the proposition that a common market can be reconciled with State sovereignty over transport rates, taxes . . . *wages and social benefits,* immigration and mobility of capital. Though many of these factors affect competitive conditions, the status quo was for the most part accepted with the proviso that subsequent distortions be avoided." [5] Secondly, Article 4(c) forbids "subsidies or state assistance, or special charges imposed by the state, in any form whatsoever." Both of these provisions limit national autonomy but there are important differences between them which must now be examined.

The Community's commitment to the social status quo is provisional and indirect. Article 67, the instrument of execu-

4. In February 1959, this suit was rejected by the Court on a technicality. 17/57, De Gezamenlijke Steenkolenmijnen v. H.A., 5 Rec. 9 (1959). But the following June a new suit was filed (30/59). It is with the latter that we shall be concerned.

5. See p. 383; italics supplied.

tive action, authorizes the HA to act only in case of "appreciable repercussions on the conditions of competition." Moreover, the executive must act indirectly, by way of recommendation: the undesirable consequences of the measure in question may be neutralized, but the measure itself is not subject to the control of the HA. In contrast, the prohibition of subsidies is unconditional and direct; they can be immediately suppressed.

The distinction between subsidies and social measures is, therefore, important but it is often difficult to make. As a rule, general legislative enactments directed at coal or steel enterprises are not considered subsidies.[6] In this instance, the HA settled for a compensatory arrangement, appropriate to Article 67, but seeming to fall short of the immediate and unconditional prohibition of Article 4(c). In other words, one of the basic issues facing the Court was to decide whether the miners' bonus was a *special* subsidy measure, subject to direct suppression, or a *general* legislative enactment, subject only to Article 67.

Beneath the dispute over the miners' bonus lay the more fundamental matter: the scope of Community authority in problems bearing on the reserved power of the member states in the area of social policy. As we shall see, the Court's position in this judgment bore a marked resemblance to its solution of the problem of partial integration in the road transport cases.

II

The bonus had been instituted by the German government as a device to ward off the inflationary pressures of a booming Germany economy. Whatever may have been the intent, its result was to confer a distinct cost advantage on German mining interests. The Dutch coal association which

6. See Paul Reuter, *La Communauté Européenne du Charbon et de l'Acier* (Paris, Librairie Générale de Droit et de Jurisprudence, 1953), pp. 194–95.

filed suit viewed the public assistance as a threat to its competitive position vis-à-vis Ruhr coal. The Dutch were unable to gain the support of their own government, which presumably preferred not to join in a suit that sought a restrictive interpretation of provisions of the treaty guaranteeing an area of independent action to the member states in social matters.

The HA was in the middle. On the one hand, it had agreed to the compromise that the Dutch were protesting. Yet, the issue as presented by the Dutch bore directly on the executive's meager powers to work toward social integration of the Community. The ambiguous nature of the HA's position was to become apparent in its reaction to the arguments made by the German government, which intervened. While ostensibly on the side of the HA, the government's sweeping claims to national social autonomy were clearly distasteful to the executive, which questioned several of the demands of its immoderate ally.

III

The Dutch understandably took the position that the miners' bonus was an illegal subsidy, unconditionally prohibited by Article 4(c). The HA's obligation was to eliminate the bonus, not to compensate for its illegal effects.[7] Moreover, the Dutch charged that both the miners' bonus and the insurance fund contribution which had been withdrawn by way of compensation were illegal subsidies. Of course, under no circumstances could it be proper to compensate for the effects of one illegal subsidy by withdrawing the benefits of another, equally illegal. The Dutch attributed the HA's questionable tactics to the prolonged pressure applied by the German government—including the personal intervention of Chancellor Adenauer.

7. The Dutch argument is taken from the requête and the réplique.

The HA's defense [8] of its compensation arrangement was staked principally on the claim that the miners' bonus was not a subsidy.[9] The HA noted that the miners' bonus was directed at avoiding the continual departure of underground miners to more appealing lines of work. Public financing was important, because this made clear the government's continuing interest in the underground miners and attested to the importance of the economic contribution being made by the miners to the German recovery.[10] The HA claimed that, given its purposes, it would be unwise and unfair to treat the bonus as a subsidy. Accordingly, the executive's sole obligation was to avoid the undesirable effects of the measure. The compensation measure could be counted on to achieve this objective by maintaining unchanged the market position of the German coal mines. Moreover, since the insurance fund contribution was a social matter left by the treaty to the member governments, there was no reason why it should not be the instrument of compensation.

The HA refrained from characterizing the miners' bonus as a social measure outside the jurisdiction of the Community, holding simply that it was not a subsidy. The German government went considerably beyond this limited argument. The government did not deny that the miners' bonus was a subsidy, although it did point out that the measure was general—applying to all underground miners—not a special measure directed at those miners digging coal. However, the basic claim of the German government was that the bonus, as

8. See mémoire and duplique, 30/59.

9. Of course the HA denied that it had given way before government pressure. On the contrary, the HA claimed that initially the compensation idea had been opposed by the German government; it was the government which had retreated.

10. In its *Fifth General Report* (1957), the HA noted that the labor situation had improved in the first year following the institution of the bonus (see p. 116).

a social measure, was not subject to HA suppression. It was held that in areas where the member governments retain their sovereignty the prohibition of subsidies was not absolute. Only where competitive conditions were distorted or the realization of Community goals hindered could the HA act directly against subsidies. Otherwise, the executive was limited to Article 67 which prescribed only indirect action.

Since the claims of the German government would have sharply restricted HA action, it is hardly surprising that the Community executive joined the Dutch coal association in opposition.[11] The Dutch held that the treaty prohibition of subsidies was absolute and denied that there was a need to demonstrate an impact on the market. The HA, while not going quite this far, also rejected the German government's permissive interpretation of Article 4(c).[12] Finally, both the Dutch and the HA agreed that the bonus was neither *general* nor *social*. The competitive position of the mines that benefited from the bonus was improved; and it was intended, above all, for the *coal miners,* who received 89 per cent of the benefits of the measure.

It is not entirely clear from the judgment which party's argument the Court found most convincing. It agreed with the Dutch that the miners' bonus was a subsidy. Based primarily on a February 1956 letter from the German Economics Minister, the Court decided that the miners' bonus

11. One commentator notes that the German government ended as the HA's "principal adversary." Roger Chevallier, "L'Arrêt 30/59 de la Cour de justice des Communautés Européennes," *Revue générale de droit international public, 66* (1962), 567. An interesting legal problem was raised by this rather odd turn of events, because limitations are imposed on the introduction of new arguments by the intervening party. For a critical discussion of the manner in which the Court coped with this problem, see ibid., pp. 565–68.

12. The German argument was based on the fact that the treaty permitted the HA itself to grant subsidies in some cases. The HA held that while exceptions to the rule of Article 4(c) exist, they are stated explicitly in the treaty and confirm, rather than weaken, the general prohibition; they are, in other words, the exceptions which prove the rule.

was an attempt to avoid a price rise, "the coal industry retaining the profit without supporting the cost." [13] The Court did not deny that the bonus was a "sort of decoration for an extremely hard profession," but concluded that it remained an increase in salary "with which the Treaty would not be concerned if it were paid by the coal industry [but] it becomes evident that it is a subsidy since it is tantamount to a salary increase paid from public funds by the Government of the Federal Republic." [14]

The Court also accepted the Dutch distinction between the absolute character of the prohibition of Article 4(c) and the conditional powers granted by Article 67 #3. Having decided that subsidies and state assistance—as defined in Article 4(c)—are unconditionally prohibited and that the miners' bonus fell within these categories, the Court had pretty well disposed of the case presented by the German government. There remained the HA's contention that competition was not distorted by the miners' bonus because of the compensating withdrawal of the government's insurance contribution.

At first glance it might appear that the Court again agreed with the Dutch, "considering that the abolition and prohibition established by Article 4(c), having a general and absolute character, cannot in any case be annulled by the utilization of an approximate and uncertain compensation procedure." Certainly the Dutch had won the battle: as it stood, the miners' bonus was illegal. However, the last part of the above citation indicates that the Court has not rejected the

---

13. 30/59, De Gezamenlijke Steenkolenmijnen, 7 Rec. 51 (1959). This determination was based on the earlier conclusion that, despite the failure of the treaty to define subsidy, general usage provided a guide. Since both subsidies and state assistance were prohibited by Article 4(c), the Court decided that the prohibition "includes not only such positive payments as subsidies themselves, but equally interventions which, under diverse forms, lighten the charges that normally burden the budget of an enterprise, and which . . . without being subsidies in the strict sense of the word, are of the same nature and have identical effects." Ibid., p. 39.

14. Ibid., p. 52.

principle of compensation, but merely its application. Since, in this instance, the compensation was "approximate and uncertain" and not "in any fashion a reversal, equal at every moment" to the bonus, there was no need to render a decision on the matter of principle.[15]

IV

While the miners' bonus was thus invalidated, there seemed to be several possibilities for transforming it into a legal measure. In the first place, an acceptable sort of compensation scheme seemed possible. Moreover, it is significant that the Court took pains to indicate that the absolute character of Article 4(c) was applicable *only within the domain of the treaty*. Conversely, Article 67, it was pointed out, represented an attempt to deal with the problems of partial integration—to protect the independence of the member states with respect to social policy while at the same time permitting the HA to cope with the prejudicial effects of this autonomy. The Court noted a similar independence in fiscal matters.[16] In other words, an alternative open to the German government would be a social or fiscal measure to which the HA could respond only under the restricted provisions of Article 67.

The decision of the Court was rendered in February 1961, and the German government seemed convinced that it offered the possibility of satisfactory alternatives.[17] However, the search for an alternative proved much more difficult than anticipated. At first the government wished to delay introducing a new measure into the parliament until after the fall elections.[18] But the elections came and went with no action.

---

15. Ibid., p. 55.
16. Ibid., pp. 43, 44–45.
17. I gained this impression from interviews with responsible government officials in May 1961.
18. See *Europe CECA,* 15 December 1961, p. 1.

The government continued to assure the HA it intended to act,[19] but by the summer of 1962, after almost a year and a half, the judgment remained unsatisfied. It was at this time that the HA finally decided to use Article 88 against the Germans, who were given until 31 October to formulate acceptable propositions. However, before the expiration of the deadline the German government asked for and obtained the HA's agreement to set up a joint committee to iron out a final solution.[20]

It is not entirely clear why a satisfactory compromise has proved so difficult, but it is possible to piece together an explanation from the available information. *Europe CECA* speculated that the Federal Republic was seeking to satisfy the Court ruling by a fiscal measure which, in line with the Court's suggestion, could be considered an exercise of the government's reserved power.[21] The HA, for its part, accepted and publicly acknowledged that it was politically impossible to adopt a solution resulting in a reduction in the pay of the miners.[22] The solution the HA seemed to prefer was one based upon precise compensation, i.e. the mining companies would be required to repay directly to the government the exact sums that had been publicly expended for the bonus.

In the end, the HA made its point. In January 1964 the German government notified the HA that the parliament of the Federal Republic had accepted a solution calling for compensation. The new law required reimbursement of the entire bonus plus an additional 10 per cent to balance the tax exemption from which the miners' bonus benefited.[23] This resolution of the dispute was somewhat surprising; my own

19. See, for example, ibid., 30 June 1962, p. 2.
20. Ibid., 8 November 1962, p. 2. See also HA, *Eleventh General Report* (1963), pp. 266–67.
21. *Europe CECA*, 15 December 1961, p. 1.
22. Ibid., 15 November 1962, p. 2.
23. See HA Document No. 134/64 f (mimeo., dated 8 January 1964).

interviews, in accord with the report of *Europe CECA*, indicated that the government preferred a fiscal or social measure. Certainly the German officials would have had greater leeway and, of course, the Court seemed to be beckoning toward this more inviting path.

V

The decision rendered by the Court had invalidated the miners' bonus, but it was to be close to three years before that decision was executed. In no other instance has the common law of the Community come so close to foundering. One is naturally tempted to reconsider the judgment in order to find some clues to the source of noncompliance. Is it possible that the Court is responsible for this legal pause?

Certainly the terms of the judgment were ambiguous and seemed to offer alternatives to strict compliance. The Federal Republic was encouraged by the decision to bargain hard, and the HA was put on notice that the simple elimination of the miners' bonus was not the only legal solution. However, the ensuing negotiations would seem to indicate that the HA was amply aware of the political obstacles to elimination of the bonus and, even without the judgment, would have been unlikely to push this radical solution. If anything, the Court's decision strengthened the HA's resolve to resist the most questionable of the alternatives. The Court did, in the first place, offer an all-inclusive definition of subsidy [24] and, secondly, agreed with the Dutch that such measures were unconditionally prohibited by the treaty. While the HA was free to compromise on the political issue, the compensation possibilities offered by the judges were so restricted that the economic significance of the concession was nil. The path opened by the Court thus represented an economically impeccable and politically sage alternative.[25]

24. For details, see Chevallier, p. 570.
25. Cf. ibid., p. 579.

The other avenue suggested by the judgment was more significant and less easily disposed of. While setting itself in firm and effective opposition to subsidies "within the domain of the Treaty," [26] the Court explicitly recognized and extensively explored the limitations imposed on the Community by the problem of partial integration. According to the Court, in those areas remaining under the control of the member states, Community action was restricted to Article 67 and was limited in the following ways:

> 1. The HA could act only where the "effective execution of the Treaty is greatly impaired" or its "ultimate goals seriously compromised."
>
> 2. Executive action was limited to the power of recommendation, i.e. only the ends could be specified by the HA, the member states retained the right to select the means.
>
> 3. This free choice remained, even if the means chosen were not altogether consistent with the ultimate goals of the Community.[27]

The Court termed these pitfalls the "necessary and legitimate consequences of the partial character of the integration consented to in the Treaty." [28] Besides indicating that the member states remained responsible for their general economic policy, the Court singled out three specific sectors of national autonomy: commercial policy (Article 26), social policy (Article 68 #1), and fiscal policy.[29]

We have already seen that the Federal Republic's first effort was directed at taking advantage of these latter loopholes—fiscal and social autonomy. The government seemed to hope that it could use its general economic powers

26. See supra, p. 180.
27. 30/59, De Gezamenlijke Steenkolenmijnen, 7 Rec. 51, 46 (1959).
28. Ibid.
29. Ibid., pp. 44, 45.

to hold on to the political benefits of the levy, without making the economic changes called for under the compensation formula suggested by the Court. Viewed from one angle, this might all seem like a pointless game of financial musical chairs. However, the failure of the government to arrive at a satisfactory compromise underscores the very real inroads made by the Community into the authority of member states in these vital matters.

The critical point, however, is that the loopholes are not of the Court's making. It might, of course, be said that the Court should not have gone out of its way to specify the available loopholes. But by fully and sensibly exploring the problem of partial integration presented by the case, the Court offered considerable and effective guidance to the parties. Had the decision been significantly less illuminating, additional time-consuming litigation would have been needed to clarify the ambiguities. If a by-product of the Court's guidance was a long period of hard bargaining, the results indicate that the Federal Republic has, in the end, been nudged toward the most desirable Community solution.

10

THE CUSTOMS UNION ISSUE

I

Among the lacunae in the Coal and Steel Community Treaty, one of the most worrisome is the absence of a common external tariff barrier. According to Article 71 the member states retain responsibility for their trade policy, or "commercial policy" as it is referred to in the article. It was clear from the outset that the irregular character of the Community's external tariffs would invite diversion of trade. In other words, goods would tend to flow into the Community at the point where the barrier was lowest and then move toward markets across unprotected national frontiers. The resultant Community dilemma is obvious. If member states are to retain effective control of their commercial policy, trade diversion must be prevented. On the other hand, if this control is protected by intra-Community obstacles to trade, the common market concept is undermined.

In practice, the major trade diversion problem has concerned coal. Not surprisingly, the problem arose out of the 1958 coal crisis and centered on France, more specifically on its import cartel, l'Association technique de l'importation charbonnière (ATIC).[1] The first tack pursued by ATIC was an

[1] A general treatment of the application of the treaty's cartel regulations to ATIC is reserved for Chapter 13.

effort to convince the Community to adopt a common import policy, which would have eliminated the problem of trade diversion. Having failed in this endeavor, ATIC simply sealed off France; [2] third country coal was not allowed to enter France via the low tariff Benelux nations. While the French action was an economic success, it raised a number of serious legal problems.

National Protection

Was it proper to respond to the threat of trade diversion by suspending the free circulation of coal within the Community? Section 15 of the Convention does authorize a "protectionist" method for dealing with the problem. According to this provision, the Benelux countries were to be allowed to continue their low tariff policies, but only for imports required for domestic consumption. To protect the other member states, quantities beyond domestic needs were to be subjected to higher duties.[3] However, these arrangements were to apply *only to steel,* because at the time coal duties were "negligible." [4]

Perhaps more significant was the apparently temporary nature of this procedure. In the long run, it was assumed that customs duties would be sufficiently harmonized to make trade diversion unprofitable.[5] Following the transitional period, diversion of trade would no longer be considered a justification for restricting the flow of trade within the Community. This certainly was the understanding of the French delegation to the conference which drafted the treaty. In its

2. Lister, *Europe's Coal and Steel Community,* p. 327.

3. Moreover, Belgian importers were to be entitled to the low rates only if they agreed not to reexport to the rest of the Community.

4. Ministère des Affaires étrangères, *La Communauté européenne du charbon et de l'acier. Rapport de la Délégation Française sur le Traité et la Convention signés à Paris le 18 avril 1951* (Paris, Imprimerie nationale, 1951), p. 146.

5. Section 15, paragraph 7.

report the delegation pointed out that it was in the self-interest of high tariff members of the Community to lower their duties. If they failed to do so "the imports originating in third countries will reach them indirectly by passing through the territory of another member state with lower protective barriers." [6]

The HA took a similar stand, first in 1953 and again in 1956. As summarized in its *Fourth General Report,* the HA's position on the question of free circulation was as follows:

> The primary principle of the Common Market, that of free circulation of products, applies equally to coal and iron and steel products of third countries imported *in the normal way* into any country of the Community. Once these products have been imported, no member State has the right unilaterally to block free circulation of such products within the Common Market, either by Customs duties or by a quantitative restriction. [7]

Mutual Consultation

However, by 1960 the HA was ready to admit that there were substantial obstacles to harmonization. In discussing its interest in a low-tariff Community that would equitably balance common market and third-country objectives, the HA noted: "Endeavors to establish this balance would no doubt be facilitated if the Paris Treaty provided for a genuine commercial policy, or if the High Authority at least possessed

6. *Rapport de la Délégation Française,* p. 144. The major reason for not setting up specific procedures and beginning an immediate push toward harmonization seems to have been tactical. Since harmonization was expected to result in generally lower tariffs, the Community was determined not to make these reductions until corresponding concessions had been gained from third countries—particularly Great Britain. Ibid., pp. 145–46.

7. See p. 133 (italics supplied). Just what the HA meant by imports "in the normal way" is not clear but, as we shall see, it became a crucial issue in the course of litigation over the question.

greater powers to ensure harmonization of the commercial policy measures taken by the member States." [8]

Without the power to force a policy of free circulation upon the Community, the HA turned to the Council. However, the ministers rejected the executive's program for concerted Community action. Only one possibility remained; the HA sought to implement the procedures provided in the treaty for cooperative solutions to disputes over commercial policy.[9] While there was no possibility that this approach would result in free circulation, it would at least head off the spread of the type of unilateral protection of national frontiers undertaken by the French. Moreover, a semblance of Community control over developments would be maintained.

According to the HA, the cooperative solution decided upon was not to be left to the discretion of member states. "On the contrary, if the conditions specified in the Treaty as prerequisite for such assistance are considered by the High Authority to exist, the Government wishing for assistance is entitled to obtain it from the other member States concerned." [10] In this instance, the HA authorized Germany, Belgium, and Holland to suspend the free circulation rule for third-country imports.[11] Of course, the distinction between these suspensions and the barriers raised in France is that the

8. HA, *Eighth General Report* (1960), p. 49.

9. See Article 71, paragraph 3: "The governments of the member states will lend each other the necessary assistance. . . . The High Authority is empowered to propose to the member States concerned the methods by which this cooperation shall be undertaken." Of course, if a coordinated energy could have been agreed upon for the three European Communities the trade diversion problem could probably have been resolved at the same time. However, at best this project would take a great deal of time, and the coal surplus called for prompt action. See HA, *Eighth General Report* (1960), pp. 49–50 and 96–100.

10. HA, *Fourth General Report* (1956), p. 134.

11. See 9 & 12/60, Antoine Vloeberghs S.A. v. H.A., 7 Rec. 391, 401 (1961). It is not altogether clear that Holland was included in this authorization, but there is no question as to Germany and Belgium. See HA, *Eighth General Report* (1960), pp. 49–56, and Lister, pp. 326–32.

former were effected with the permission of the HA and followed requests to the executive for assistance. In contrast, the French government, by taking matters into its own hands, had thwarted the policy of "mutual consultation." This "no compromise" attitude not only contravened the provisions of Article 71, but was out of character with the Community's generally cooperative method of decision making. Understandably, the measures adopted by ATIC led ultimately to litigation.

II

The immediate source of litigation was the denial by ATIC of an import license to French firms wishing to purchase coal from a Belgian firm, the Antoine Vloeberghs Company. Vloeberghs had in 1957 imported American coal into Belgium, but ATIC's refusal to allow the coal into France left Vloeberghs with a considerable quantity of coal and no buyers. For three years the company tried without success to gain the support of the HA or, alternatively, to get permission directly from ATIC. Finally, in 1960, Vloeberghs brought two suits to the Court. The first (9/60) sought monetary compensation for damages suffered as a result of the HA's failure to take action. The second suit (12/60) asked that the Court annul the HA's decision refusing to put an end to ATIC's interference with coal imports.

III

The heart of Vloeberghs' argument was that the HA had itself accepted the principle that third-country coal, properly imported into one of the Community countries, should be allowed to circulate freely. Consequently the HA was obligated by its own interpretation of the rules to prevent France from interfering with Vloeberghs' sales to its French customers.[12] The HA answered that Vloeberghs was not a Community enterprise according to the terms of Article 80 and

12. Requête, 12/60.

had no right to sue for annulment of an HA decision. The Authority claimed that Vloeberghs would be entitled to damages only if HA negligence could be demonstrated.[13] The executive denied that it had been negligent. It had, for example, continually pressed France to accept the principle of free circulation. However, both before and after the 1958 constitutional changes brought President de Gaulle to power, France had rejected free circulation unless accompanied by a common Community commercial policy.

The HA also contended that by the time Vloeberghs got around to raising the question of free circulation, in May 1959, the Community was well into the coal crisis. The HA had already agreed to barriers against free circulation in Belgium, Germany, and the Netherlands. Could it, therefore, be considered an official fault that the HA had failed to force France to eliminate barriers which had been accepted in three member nations? [14]

The hole in this argument was, of course, that—regardless of the year in which Vloeberghs had raised the issue—the HA had since 1959 failed to force France to comply with the executive's interpretation of the treaty. While Germany, Belgium, and the Netherlands had all raised barriers to the circulation of third country products, this had been done with permission of the HA and in "mutual cooperation" with the other member states, in accordance with Article 71, paragraph 3, and the ruling contained in the HA's 28 May 1955 letter [15] to all the governments.

---

13. Mémoire, 9/60. It was also argued that for the same reason that Vloeberghs was not eligible to sue for annulment, he could not question the legality of the HA's refusal to force ATIC to allow importation of Vloeberghs' coal. In other words, if Vloeberghs was not entitled to question the legality of the HA's decision directly, the same question could not be raised in a suit for damages.

14. Oral Argument, 9 & 12/60. Mr. Gerard Olivier for the HA, pp. 42–51 (mimeo).

15. See 9 & 12/60, Antoine Vloeberghs S.A. v. H.A., 7 Rec. 391, 428 (1961).

It came as a considerable surprise—not least of all to the legal staff of the HA—when the Court on 14 July 1961 not only refused to accept the appeal to annul, but also refused Vloeberghs the damages sought under Article 40.[16] The Court's opinion was rather hard to follow. While it accepted the principle of "free circulation" as defined in the HA's letter and Vloeberghs' right to appeal for damages under Article 40, the Court concluded that Vloeberghs was not in fact entitled to these damages. The Court held that Vloeberghs was not an ordinary importer, but the agent of an American firm, the Hudson Coal Company of Scranton, Pennsylvania.[17]

The Court ruled that the right of free circulation was not adopted for the sake of either third-country products or their producers. It was simply feared that obstacles established for third country products might also interfere with the circulation of Community products. In this instance, the products were clearly for French buyers. There never had been any intention to offer them on the Belgian market, and the Court pointed out that Article 73 reserves the granting of import licenses to the government "on whose territory is situated . . . the point of destination of imports," in this case, France.[18]

The judges concluded that "even if" the mutual cooperation prescribed by Article 71 could deal with attempts to escape the barriers raised against third-country imports, this article certainly could not be invoked in the interest of third country products or producers.[19] The Court's reasoning here

16. The Advocate General concluded that while Vloeberghs was not entitled to demand annulment it was entitled to damages. Ibid., p. 478.

17. There was ample proof in the dossier of the case that this was in fact true. In one letter Vloeberghs was referred to as Hudson's European distributor and on the same page reference was made to the "groupe Hudson–Vloeberghs." The attorney who wrote the letter referred to himself as the attorney for both Hudson and Vloeberghs. See documents 29 & 30, dossier 9 & 12/60.

18. 9 & 12/60, Antoine Vloeberghs S.A. v. H.A., 7 Rec. 391, 429 (1961).

19. Ibid., p. 430.

is somewhat obscure. What it seems to say is that those who have attempted to evade the regulations of member states should not be allowed to tell the Community how to deal with the problem. The paradoxical result was that Vloeberghs, although entitled to bring his suit, was not eligible to win it.

IV

The immediate result of the Court's decision was to permit ATIC to continue its unilateral protection of the French market. However, because the judgment was, in part, based on the irregularity of Vloeberghs' import into Belgium, the Belgian government asked the Court to review its ruling.[20] The Belgians contended that the judgment had both misconceived their import regulations and infringed upon their sovereignty over trade questions. Specifically, they claimed that according to Belgian law the Vloeberghs coal had been properly imported into Belgium.[21]

In its judgment the Court never reached the merits of the question, deciding instead on procedural grounds. The Court pointed out that "in the interest of good administration of the law and of security of legal relationships," it was important that those with an interest in a judgment intervene *in the suit itself* wherever possible.[22] On this issue, the Court accepted the Belgian position, noting that there was no way in which the Belgian government could have known that Vloeberghs' suit would have raised questions about its cus-

20. Article 36 of the *Protocol on the Code of the Court of Justice* permits the Court to review judgments when requested to do so by a party whose rights were affected by the judgment, but who were not heard in the case. See Werner Feld, "The Court of Justice of the European Communities: Emerging Political Power? An Examination of Selected Decisions of the Court's 1961–1962 Term," *Tulane Law Review, 38* (1963), 77. The Protocol designates the review procedure *tierce opposition*.

21. 9 & 12/60, *Belgium v. Antoine Vloeberghs S.A. and H.A., tierce opposition*, 8 Rec. 331, 347–49.

22. Ibid., pp. 353–54.

toms regulations. However, the judges denied that the original judgment in any way prejudiced the rights of the Belgian government.

The Court noted that the judgment did not hold Belgian regulations contrary to the treaty, it merely took note of the effects of the Belgian rules on free circulation. Not only was Belgian sovereignty unencumbered by the decision, the Court denied that its earlier decision impugned the motives of the Belgian government. The judges had not considered the absence of duties as a deliberate invitation to divert trade, but merely a factual condition which made such diversion possible. It was Vloeberghs, not the Belgian government, which had tried to make the operation look like a Belgian import although it was manifestly an indirect delivery of American coal to France.[23] Accordingly, the Court dismissed the Belgian appeal.[24]

V

The Court's first decision was criticized for leaving the crucial questions unanswered,[25] and its rejection of the Belgian government suit can hardly be expected to have cleared the air. Yet have not a number of important issues been resolved? For Vloeberghs the case is, indeed, a total loss, but for the Community a significant point is established: the principle of free circulation of third-country products has been unequivocally accepted.[26] The judges reserve only the right to determine whether there has been a valid importation, or only an attempt to "use" the principle for improper ends.[27]

23. Ibid., pp. 356, 357–58.
24. For a discussion of this ruling and the review procedure in general, see Feld, pp. 77–78.
25. See report, *Europe CECA*, 19 July 1961, p. 2.
26. 9 & 12/60, Antoine Vloeberghs S.A. v. H.A., 7 Rec. 391, 428 (1961).
27. Recall that from the beginning the HA had called for free circulation of only those goods imported in "the normal way." Supra, p. 187. However, the subjective nature of the Court's standard of normalcy might be difficult

In this instance, there was substantial evidence that Vloe-berghs' entire purpose was to circumvent French commercial policy. Vloeberghs not only fails to qualify as a Community enterprise according to the terms of Article 80, it is, in fact, virtually an American coal company. Vloeberghs–Hudson hardly seems the proper agent for effecting the substantial changes in basic Community policy which were involved in this case. Consequently, the Court was probably wise to re-fuse Vloeberghs' claim for damages. An order to pay damages would have put the French government under heavy indirect pressure to revise its commercial policy.

There remains an obvious question: under what conditions would the Court be justified in applying such pressure? *Europe CECA* has speculated that the Court awaits only a suit by a member state which raises a Community interest to speak its mind.[28] This is not an unappealing approach. The failure of any state to challenge the French government in court, either on this issue or the general question of ATIC,[29] evidences at least a minimum degree of satisfaction with the situation as it stands. The HA too has shown reserve in deal-ing with France on these questions. Consequently the situa-tion is relatively stable, if slightly tainted.

Let it be understood that the Court, even under the best of circumstances, cannot entirely clear up the difficulties. France argues that the treaty preserves the right of each member state to an independent commercial policy, and that this right is meaningless without the right to control trade diversion. Consequently, until the erection of a general tariff wall, the French government claims the right to effective control of third-country imports. The coal crisis has only

---

to apply. See Pierre-Henri Teitgen, "Jurisprudence récente en matière de droit économique et professionnel: Organisation du commerce du charbon dans la C.E.C.A.," *Droit Social, 24* (1961), 529–30.

28. *Europe CECA,* 19 July 1961, p. 2.

29. Infra, Chapter 13.

strengthened France's resolve to maintain this control, to which ATIC attributes its success in reducing the impact of the crisis.[30]

Up to a point, the French argument is irreproachable. It is true that harmonization was to be compelled by the threat of trade diversion and that the kind of unilateral protection undertaken by ATIC was ruled out. Certainly, this was the argument made in the *Report of the French Delegation.*[31] However, the provisions of the treaty are ambiguous and evidence only a weak resolve to harmonize rates. Even more to the point has been the constant French pressure for a harmonized commercial policy. Of course the French have not been seeking the downward adjustment suggested by the Convention, but neither has the Community, in general, considered free trade as an appropriate response to the coal crisis. Insofar as the treaty goal of harmonization of commercial policy is concerned, France has been on the side of the angels.

Given the antisupranational preferences of President de Gaulle, the motives of the French government are automatically suspect. In this case, however, France seems to be supporting a marked advance in the scope of the Community. However, the treaty does unambiguously call for cooperation in solving problems.[32] France has continually defied HA efforts to reach a compromise. The issue is *not* whether France has created obstacles to "free circulation" similar to those imposed by other member countries. The point is that

30. See statement by ATIC President Picard to the Community's Consultative Committee. *Europe CECA,* 9 April 1960, p. 2.

31. It is difficult to know just what to make of the position adopted by the French delegation, supra p. 187. Legally, this indication of French intent is certainly non-negotiable currency. Practically, it seems arguable that the French have retreated from their position. It might be possible to attribute this retreat to the constitutional and governmental changes of 1958, although France's uncooperative attitude on ATIC has certainly predated the presidency of General de Gaulle.

32. Article 71, paragraph 3.

the other three nations established these barriers with the permission of the HA and within a framework of mutual cooperation. Under the proper conditions, the Court certainly has an obligation to call France to task for this cavalier disregard of Community rules.[33]

Still, it is important to be aware of the limitations of a policy of mutual cooperation. For the enterprises the situation would hardly be improved at all. By enforcing this *secondary* rule, the Court would not necessarily be promoting a stable system of *primary* rules upon which the enterprises could count.[34] While one might hope and even expect that continued mutual cooperation would lead toward harmonization and, accordingly, toward stable primary rules, the process could well be fluid and erratic. However, this rather contingent state of affairs is a direct result of partial integration. To expect the Court of Justice to close the political gap is to require of it an uncharacteristic and not necessarily salutary measure of judicial activism.

33. Cf. Teitgen, p. 531. Here it is suggested that the terms of the judgment allow for unilateral action against imports where there is reason to believe that the shipment represents a diversion of trade. Presumably, relief could be obtained subsequently through executive or judicial action if it turned out that there had been, in fact, no trade diversion. However, according to this interpretation, unilateral action would not, in itself, be improper.

34. For this distinction between primary and secondary rules, see reference to H. L. A. Hart, *The Concept of Law,* supra, pp. 12–13.

5 CHANGE

INTRODUCTION

The Court's opportunities for building a normative system are clearly restricted by the partial character of integration. The issue has been germane to a number of suits but its relevance varies markedly from case to case. Certainly the problem of partial integration has not been posed squarely in each instance. Accordingly, the judicial process was not immobilized. Opportunities for functional interpretation remained, and a premium was placed on judicial strategy. However, in the end, the partial nature of the integrative commitment must be recognized as a legitimate restriction on the judicial process. Where vital decisions have not been made or where national autonomy has been written into the treaty, the Court must respect its political mandate.

Paralleling, and to some extent intertwined with, the problem of partial integration is the incomplete and tentative character of the Community's institutions. As with the former, the latter deficiency imposes significant limitations on the judicial process. It has been pointed out that the Community's political institutions tend to be inflexible and ill-adapted to deal with dynamic and fluid conditions which are endemic to regional integration.[1] Instead of majority rule, the Community's decision making process is oriented toward compromise and concession. The unanimity required to amend the treaty is particularly awkward as well as politically explosive—involving, as it does, a return to the national parliaments. While it may be true that the contrast with veto-

1. Supra, pp. 13–16.

type international organizations is greater than the similarity, the resultant problems for the judicial process are remarkably alike.

The process of implementing the provisions of the treaty is likely to be slow and sometimes will be based on compromises that veer away from the path of the law. Parties whose rights are imperiled by the delays or the legal shortcuts may often decide to press their claims before the Court. If these political settlements are in step with the changing patterns of integration, the Court's assertion of treaty norms may inhibit, rather than promote, the cause of integration. But such bargaining may also result in integrative retreats, thus offering compelling reasons for the Court of Justice to assume a positive role.

For the judges the situation is delicate because a failure to apply norms tends to undermine their legal position, while a vigorous defense of treaty rules may lead to hazardous conflict with the political authorities. Morover, the problem is complicated by additional variables. For example, political settlements sometimes reflect the considered and unanimous decision of all the member states, and at other times are only expediential bargains struck between individual states, with the majority of the Community in disagreement. Clearly, the Court's task is difficult and the stakes are high. In the ensuing chapters we shall review the judges' experience with problems of political change in search of reliable guides for proper action.

11

THE COAL CRISIS: SOCIAL RESPONSIBILITY

I

The transitional period (1953–58) was supposed to provide the time necessary to integrate the Belgian coal industry into the common market. To that end, a series of secial measures was authorized by the Convention. In addition to the subsidy program which we have already reviewed,[1] the HA was empowered to grant Community financed readaptation allowances to workers injured by dislocation incident to the introduction of the common market.[2] Symptomatic of the failure of this entire program were the figures on readaptation payments made by the HA. If marginal mines had been closed as planned, the number of workers in need of readaptation assistance would certainly have been sizable. However, as of February 1958—the close of the transitional period—while assistance had been given to a total of 18,600 Community workers, only "about 60" were helped in Belgium! [3]

Although the compensation plan was to end with the transitional period, the Convention authorized an additional two years of both readaptation assistance and Belgian govern-

1. Supra, Chapter 5.
2. *Convention Containing the Transitional Provisions*, section 23.
3. HA, *Sixth General Report*, 2 (1958), p. 187.

ment subsidies. The HA could grant these extensions only with the approval of the Council. The coal glut which began to develop in 1958 hit the high cost Belgian mines first and hardest. As a result, the Council agreed to extend assistance during the grace period, but the extension was conditioned on vigorous Belgian pursuit of rationalization, including a stepped-up closing of marginal mines.[4] Under the excess supply conditions, the government was somewhat more willing to force closures and, accordingly, Belgium became a better customer for readaptation aid.[5]

By the summer of 1959, with the grace period scheduled to run out the following February, it seemed clear that the need for readaptation assistance would continue. While Article 56 of the treaty itself also authorized readaptation payments, assistance could be granted only to deal with problems resulting from "the introduction of technical processes or new equipment." [6] Since the problems of the coal industry were considered to be not technological but structural—resulting from long-run changes in demand patterns [7]—Article 56 could not be used to deal with pressing readaptation needs flowing from the coal crisis.[8] Consequently, in July of 1959, the HA proposed to the Council that Article 56 be revised.

The treaty offered two possibilities for amendment, the *petite revision* of Article 95, paragraphs 3 and 4, and the *grande revision* of Article 96. The HA chose the former because its procedures were much simpler. Specifically, there was no need either for unanimity or for time-consuming and

4. HA, *Eighth General Report* (1960), pp. 143–44 and 149.
5. HA, *Ninth General Report* (1961), pp. 276 and 279.
6. Article 56, paragraph 1.
7. See HA, *Eighth General Report* (1960), pp. 110–11.
8. Ibid., p. 289. The HA also objected to the fact that Article 56 was restricted to area-wide problems of "exceptionally large" dimensions and could not, therefore, be tendered to individual enterprises. *Europe CECA,* 9 July 1959, p. 2.

potentially troublesome ratification by national parliaments. Let us note that Article 95 provided a less cumbersome method of change, and the more it could be utilized the more flexible the treaty would become.

Yet, because of its simpler procedural requirements, Article 95 was hedged with substantive restrictions. The Court was included in the amendment process to make certain that the limitations were observed. After the HA and the Council— "acting by five-sixths majority"—had agreed on the proposed change, it was necessary to submit it to the Court. If approved by the Court, the proposal came into force following acceptance by the Parliamentary Assembly. It is thus clear that, to a significant degree, the flexibility of the treaty depended upon the Court's interpretation of the key provisions of Article 95. As to the substantive restrictions, the Court was called upon to make certain that amendments were demanded by "unforeseen difficulties" or a "profound change in the economic or technical conditions." Moreover, the amendments were not to "modify the provisions of Articles 2, 3, and 4," the articles setting out the fundamental principles of the Community, or the power relationships among the Community's institutions. Because it was mindful of these restrictions when it drew up its amendment proposal, the HA was very reluctant to accept the alterations demanded by the Council of Ministers, particularly by the Germans.

The Germans wanted the program limited to two years and argued that only the coal industry should be covered. These arguments raised some obvious questions. The powers delegated to the Community by the member governments were granted for the life of the treaty, 50 years. Was it, therefore, proper to restrict the HA's authority under Article 56 to two-year periods, renewable at the discretion of the Council of Ministers? Secondly, the change would guarantee additional readaptation protection to the coal miners only. Could it not be argued that this amounted to discriminatory treatment of the steel worker?

II

If these issues seem rather academic, ideological and financial questions of some magnitude were in the background. The German government, it was reported in *Europe CECA*, feared that extension of readaptation assistance to steel might provoke similar requests from other industries and lead ultimately to a commitment to public assumption of the burden of structural unemployment. The government was also under pressure from the German steel industry, which opposed the extension but for different—and to some extent contradictory—reasons. It is, after all, the enterprises that support the Coal and Steel Community through the levy assessed on their production, and the steel firms objected to assuming the burden of readaptation.[9]   At any rate, what was at stake was an extension of the HA's power to implement a Community social policy.

Negotiations in the Council of Ministers verged on deadlock. Germany was virtually isolated, but continued to hold out for the restrictive form of amendment. Italy gave the Germans some support, but it would seem that the Italian role was more one of attempted conciliation than of direct encouragement of the German position.[10] Still, Germany eventually won its battle in the Council, compromising only to the extent of settling for three-year extensions rather than the two-year grants requested initially. The Court was thus called upon to legalize this political "compromise."

9. *Europe CECA*, 18 November 1959, p. 2. Although the grants were on a matching basis—thus obligating the member states to pay half the costs—the German steel firms pointed out that industries covered by the Common Market Treaty escaped the costs of readaptation entirely, because the Common Market is supported directly by the member governments.

10. *Europe CECA*, 17 November 1959, pp. 1 and 3.

III

The opinion bore out the HA's reservations about the changes inserted by the Germans. The Court admitted that the problems which had led to the demand for the change had arisen only in coal mining. Nonetheless, to exclude the steel industry from the benefits of the change was judged contrary to the fundamental principles of the treaty and particularly to Article 4(b), which prohibits practices "discriminating among producers." [11]

The Court also objected because the change was not to run for the full 50-year life of the treaty. The judges held that the three-year limitation indicated an inclination to extend the transitional period, rather than a commitment to change the treaty itself. Moreover, the Court noted that the first line of the proposal, "if profound changes in the condition *d' écoulement,*" was broad enough to include almost any revisions, not excluding those resulting from the opening of the common market.[12] Such changes were, of course, among those to be effected during the transitional period.

But why did the Court object to an extension of the transitional period? Legally, its position rested on the opening lines of Article 95, paragraph 3: "If, after the period of transition provided for in the Convention containing the transitional provisions. . . ." The Court concluded that if Article 95 was available only after the transitional period, it would be improper to use it to reopen or extend this period.[13] This rather narrow textual interpretation provided an authoritative solution to what could have become a problem of some magnitude. There was widespread feeling at the time that the Community had been spared the shock of adjustment to the common market—particularly in coal—by

11. Avis, 5 Rec. 551, 561 (1959).
12. Ibid., p. 560.
13. Ibid., p. 555.

the good business conditions prevailing during most of the transitional period. The transition had been postponed, and the coal crisis was now forcing the coal producers to come to grips with the common market. What was Belgium's problem today would be a Community problem before long.[14]

While an extension of the transitional period might have seemed the logical response to this situation, the Court was understandably opposed to this regressive step. The Convention was replete with qualifications and hedges against the common market; the argument was strong for making a definitive break with this conditional regime. Accordingly, the Court rooted out all facets of the amendment proposal which suggested an extension of the transitional period.

The Court's criticism of the methods chosen was balanced by its acceptance of the need for a change and the propriety of a petite revision. The judges recognized that there had been the profound change in economic conditions required as a prerequisite to the application of Article 95. Specifically, the Court took note of such structural changes in the coal market as the increasingly heavy competition from petroleum and low priced American coal.[15]

Even more important was the judicial acceptance of Article 95 as an appropriate agent for extending readaptation aid to cover unemployment problems resulting from the above structural changes. According to its own provisions, the article was restricted to changes in the "rules for exercise by the High Authority of the powers conferred upon it." In other words, new powers could not be attributed to the HA by way of this article. However, the Court concluded that the proposed amendment merely modified the means for exercising a power.[16]

14. See the report of German and French attitudes expressed in the Council. *Europe CECA*, 1 August 1959, p. 2. See also HA, *Sixth General Report*, 2 (1958), p. 187.

15. Avis, 5 Rec. 551, 559 (1959).

16. Ibid., p. 557–58.

The amendment was, thus, rejected but it was clear that the Court would be receptive to a new proposal relieved of the objectionable features. However, since most of the changes required by the Court ran directly counter to the wishes of the German government, there was some doubt whether the HA would be able to get the amendment through the Council in an acceptable form. Even assuming Council acceptance, the Court's rejection had been issued on 17 December 1959, and it seemed unlikely that there would be time to make the changes before the permission to grant readaptation assistance under the Convention ran out the following February. With the distinct possibility that the opportunities for readaptation assistance would be greatly limited after the February deadline, the HA was flooded with requests for aid.[17]

IV

The HA, which was trying to decide whether or not to offer a legally acceptable version of the amendment proposal to the Council, was bolstered by a unanimous resolution of the Parliamentary Assembly in the middle of January, calling for an extension of readaptation aid.[18] When on January 26th the HA offered a new proposal, the Council accepted it and it was sent on to the Court. As the Court was to note in its opinion, the revised plan satisfied all of the objections raised by the judges to the initial proposal. The Court's suggestions were accepted in total. However, the Germans prevailed upon the Council to include an annex which was forwarded with the following rather noncommittal words: "The High Authority and the Council are lastly agreed to bring to the

17. *Europe CECA,* 8 January 1960, p. 2.
18. HA, *Eighth General Report* (1960), p. 292. The joint trade union federation of miners and steel workers also voiced support of the change. *Europe CECA,* 9 January 1960, p. 1.

Court's attention certain legal considerations, which have
been formulated in the course of the session of the Council,
whose terms appear in the annex." [19]

Then, in this unsigned annex, obviously prepared by the
German government, there followed a complete denunciation of the suggested amendment. The heart of the argument
was that readaptation powers had been authorized under two
very specific circumstances: the introduction of the common
market and technological changes. The proposed change
would, on the other hand, allow the HA to exercise this power
under different circumstances—to deal with structural adjustments: "The Federal Government considers, then, that the
establishment of new conditions in which certain powers can
be exercised . . . creates entirely new powers." [20] Since
Article 95 authorizes only changes in the "rules for the exercise by the High Authority of the powers conferred upon it,"
the German government concluded that the change sought
could only be made under Article 96, the grande revision.
Subsidiarily, the annex argued that the power to grant such
readaptation assistance was restricted to the member states,
and thus the amendment altered the balance of Community
power. Arguments were also included concerning the potential rise in the general levy and the interference with
competition. [21]

The submission of the annex put the Court in a rather
strange position. The official proposal conformed exactly to
its specification, and it had been approved by the necessary
five-sixths majority of the Council. Moreover, as the Court
pointed out, the main contention of the German government
had already been rejected by the Court in its initial opinion:
the change in Article 56 was an adaptation of powers already
conferred on the HA and, therefore, appropriate to a petite

19. Avis 1/60, 6 Rec. 93, 100 (1960).
20. Ibid., p. 103.
21. Ibid., 104–05.

revision.[22] The judges, nevertheless, felt called upon to deal with the objections raised in the annex.

The Court first pointed out that the interpretation of Article 95 suggested by the Germans would restrict its use to procedures and forms, and would hardly enable it to deal with the "profound changes in economic or technical conditions" mentioned in its first paragraph. The judges agreed that the HA was not authorized to grant readaptation assistance to help cope with the structural changes wracking the coal market. However, it was to deal with just such "profound economic changes" that the petite revision was included in the treaty.[23] The Court also rejected the other arguments raised in the annex:

1. There was no change in the balance of Community powers, because the powers of the member states were not restricted by the revision, i.e. they remained free to grant readaptation assistance.

2. The HA's intervention was in the service of a healthier market.

3. The *possibility* of an eventual increase in the levy involved a political, not a legal appraisal.[24]

Judicial approval cleared the way for submission to the Parliamentary Assembly where the amendment was accepted by an overwhelming majority, 114 to 2.[25] As a result of the Court's insistence, an important social measure had been made a permanent part of the Coal and Steel Community Treaty.[26] The judges had also shown their willingness to

22. Ibid., p. 112.
23. Ibid., pp. 113 and 114.
24. Ibid., pp. 115–16. This is not a direct quotation.
25. HA, *Ninth General Report* (1961), p. 278. The required vote was either two thirds of the total membership, 94, or three fourths of those voting, 87.
26. Perhaps this action will serve as a precedent for a similar extension of readaptation assistance under Article 126 of the Common Market Treaty which leaves open the question of readaptation after the transition period.

accept the petite revision as a significant instrument of substantive change, thus adding measurably to the flexibility of
the treaty.[27]

In pressing its interpretation in the face of the demonstra-
bly questionable political agreement arrived at in the Council of Ministers, the Court had risked stalling the Community
machinery. In order to gauge this victory of the normative
over the political, it is important to note that, in this instance,
the German government was isolated in the Council of Ministers. Moreover, the speed with which the amended change
got through the Council, and German willingness to stake its
interests on the Court's interpretation of an argument it was
almost bound to reject, demonstrate clearly that this was not
a highly charged issue. While it might appear at first glance
that the Court had successfully asserted its authority over the
Council of Ministers, the truth of the matter is that the Court
of Justice was marching in step with the HA and five out of six
of the member states.

27. Cf. Hans Jürgen Lambers, "Les Clauses de révision des traités instituant les communautés européennes," *Annuaire français de droit international,* 7 (1961), 593–631.

12

THE COAL CRISIS:

BELGIUM LEAVES THE COMMON MARKET

I

Even more troublesome than the readaptation issue were the chaotic conditions that the coal crisis imposed on the common market. The crisis was not limited to Belgium, but because of its vulnerability the Belgian industry was hit earlier and harder than its Community counterparts. Moreover, when both the German and Dutch mining firms—experiencing selling difficulties—invaded Belgian markets with relatively low-priced products, the weaker Belgian companies were unable to defend themselves.

From the outset, the HA had argued that the coal crisis was a Community problem. According to the HA, boom conditions during the transitional period had delayed the inevitable adjustments to the common market. Given the sellers' market which prevailed during the initial years of the Community, the coal industry had not been subjected to competitive pressures.[1] The Council of Ministers, however, rejected this argument and in May 1959 refused to authorize the Community-wide crisis program presented by the HA. In place of a systematic program, the HA turned to "a series of

1. HA, *Sixth General Report* (1958), p. 187.

measures, of necessity temporary and incomplete." [2] Consequently, it is not surprising that coal stocks continued to
mount at an alarming rate in Belgium. The flow of competitive coal from Germany was cut to manageable proportions
through a bilateral agreement with Bonn, but coal continued
to stream in from the Netherlands. Belgium demanded help
from the HA and threatened to take unilateral action; the
Dutch promised to retaliate.[3] With uncontrolled measures of
self-help threatening to replace Community rules, it began to
appear that the common market might crumble.

The most obvious response to the emergency would have
been to impose quantitative restrictions on imports and, at
the same time, prohibit the mines from flooding the market
with their increasing stocks. However, it was difficult to find
an appropriate legal base for thus taking Belgium out of the
common market. The application of Article 58 was premised
on a "manifest crisis"—something of Community-wide proportions. But in rejecting the HA's crisis program in May—a
program based on Article 58—the Council had evidenced its
belief that the coal problem was limited to Belgium.

As for Article 95, it was excluded because the petite revision prescribed respect for Articles 2 to 4, and cutting off
Belgium from the common market could hardly be squared
with the fundamental principles of the treaty. Finally, it was
decided to utilize Article 37, an emergency provision designed to deal with "fundamental and persistent disturbances
in the economy" of a member state:

> If a member State considers that in a given case an
> action of the High Authority, or a failure to act, is of
> such a nature as to provoke fundamental and persistent
> disturbances in the economy of said State, it may bring
> the matter to the attention of the High Authority.

2. HA, *Eighth General Report* (1960), pp. 129–30.
3. *Europe CECA,* 4 November 1959, pp. 2–3.

The High Authority, after consulting the Council, shall if it is appropriate recognize the existence of such a situation, and decide on the measures to be taken, under the terms of the present Treaty, to correct such a situation while at the same time safeguarding the essential interests of the Community.

Article 37 was particularly attractive because the approval of the Council of Ministers was not required; it had only to be consulted. Nor were there requirements for consultation with any other Community organs, although action taken under the article could, of course, be challenged in court. There was, however, one clear obstacle: it was generally assumed that Article 37 was for use only against those "disturbances" which had been caused by an action of the HA, or by its failure to act.[4] The coal crisis could hardly be attributed to the HA, nor could it be argued that the HA had a prior duty to cut off the Belgian market. Nonetheless, it was decided to go ahead on the basis of Article 37.

What is particularly interesting about this decision is the light that it sheds on the HA's operational attitude toward the treaty. The investigation of legality and the testing of procedures against the treaty is a serious endeavor at the High Authority. Conducted by men who over the years have become experts on the treaty, the goal is to turn up a procedure that will solve the problem at hand and also be properly legal. However, a decision that no legal solution is possible would seem just as unlikely as a resort to patently illegal

---

4. Ibid., 12 November 1959, pp. 1–2, and 14 November 1959, pp. 1–2. For an authoritative presentation of this position, see Paul Reuter, *La Communauté Européenne du Charbon et de l'Acier*, pp. 246–47. Professor Reuter's analysis is a little ambiguous: he considers but seems to reject an interpretation which would permit the HA to "suppress the common market" in case of "fundamental and persistent disturbances." At any rate, he holds unambiguously that the intention of the framers of the article was simply to force the HA to reexamine the position under attack.

action.[5] In this instance, steps *had* to be taken and the lesser of the legal evils was chosen.

Once the HA decided to use Article 37 procedure, a round of informal discussions began. They resulted in a proposal which met the Belgian demands but bound the Belgian government to more vigorous rationalization measures. A quantitative limit was set on imports of coal into Belgium, and quotas were assigned to France, Germany, and Holland. In return, the Belgian government was required to control the liquidation of stocks on hand and—more significantly— was called upon to increase the tempo and extent of its closure program for marginal mines.[6] After the Council gave its unanimous approval, the HA issued a decision on 23 December 1959 putting the program into operation.[7]

II

The HA's action did not go long unchallenged. In February 1960 two German coal mining companies, Niederrheinische Bergwerks-Aktiengesellschaft (2/60) and the Unternehmens- verband des Aachener Steinkohlenbergbaues (3/60), both traditional suppliers of the Belgian market, filed suits against the HA's quantitative barriers. It should be noted that these enterprises represented only a small portion of the German

5. The grande revision is unlikely to be seriously considered a workable solution to a pressing problem. It seems certain that the HA would ultimately make a choice offering a better chance of rapid results.

6. Total closures were to rise from the previous figure of 5.5 million tons to 9.5 million tons. These totals were broken down into yearly figures and the government was required to submit a detailed reorganization plan by 1 May 1960. Belgian exports to other Community countries were to be held at a constant level and the inflow of coal from outside the Community—third country coal—was to be limited to 600,000 tons. See *Europe CECA*, 3 December 1959, p. 1, and HA, *Eighth General Report* (1960), pp. 152–57.

7. HA 46/59, *J.O.C.E.*, 2 (23 December 1959). It was reported that President Malvestiti of the HA, in response to warnings by Germany and France as to the extraordinary degree of power involved in this action, promised that he would act in accord with the member governments. *Europe CECA*, 15 December 1959, pp. 1–2.

coal industry and that the government did not support them. The decision they were attacking was, of course, taken to avoid unilateral actions by the member governments which would have threatened the Community. Certainly, the suing companies were swimming upstream against this emergency measure.

III

Naturally, the enterprises did not hesitate to turn the HA's earlier stand against the executive organ. It was held that the coal problem was Community-wide and could not properly be dealt with on an isolated basis. The appropriate avenue for action was Article 58, and the Council of Ministers had blocked this path. The German firms thought it unlikely that Article 37 was designed as an easy shortcut, with sweeping powers.[8]

So far as the mining companies were concerned, Article 37 was simply an assurance to the member states that the HA would act as required by the treaty. The enterprises pointed out that of course the disturbances, in this instance, were not by any means the result of the HA's failure to act. Moreover, it was held that Article 37 called for action "under the terms of the present Treaty." These terms, spelled out in Articles 2 through 4, could in no way be squared with measures which distorted the normal conditions of competition in favor of the weaker competitors, the Germans contended.[9] The HA, for its part, stressed the serious dimensions of the problem [10] —both for the Belgian coal industry and the entire Belgian economy.[11] Since the right to take action under Article 58 had been denied, because France and Germany saw the crisis

8. Requête, 2 & 3/60.

9. Mémoire, 2 & 3/60.

10. The HA arguments are drawn from the mémoire and duplique, 2 & 3/60.

11. The plaintiffs had argued that only the coal sector had been struck and that the remainder of the economy was healthy. Requête, 2 & 3/60.

as a Belgian phenomenon, emergency action under Article 37 offered the only opportunity to deal with this pressing problem.[12]

Of particular interest for this study was the assumption on which the plaintiffs' case ultimately rested. Making reference to the 1954 Monnet Margin cases, the two firms argued that the Community was based upon a written treaty, and the existence of a problem did not create the power to solve it.[13] The HA, on the other hand, referred to the Court's first Belgian coal decision and appealed for a teleological assessment of the HA's actions under Article 37. It is not by accident, and certainly is symptomatic of the positions assumed, that the German firms cited as precedent the Court's most narrowly textual decision, while the HA directed the Court's attention to the decision which this study has characterized as the first functional judgment.[14]

The HA denied that the words "under the terms of the present Treaty," used in Article 37, bound the HA to respect the restrictions of Articles 2–4. On the contrary, in this emergency the usual restrictions had to be loosened to allow the HA to suspend temporarily the normal rules of competition in the interest of a long-run reestablishment of a healthy market. Finally, the HA denied that Article 37 would give it unlimited executive authority: measures had to be chosen which were least likely to upset the market, and executive action could be only as broad as required by the material, chronological, and geographical objectives.

There was one other issue of more than just passing interest. The HA flatly denied the enterprises' right to a judicial hearing: the question was not justiciable. Action under Arti-

---

12. The HA pointed out the problems mentioned earlier (supra, p. 212 and note 5) with regard to both the petite and grande revision.

13. Réplique, 2 & 3/60.

14. Supra, Chapters 3 and 5, respectively.

cle 37, it was held, was "political arbitration" to safeguard the "essential interests of the Community." Put in context, it must be assumed that the HA meant to convey by its use of the term "political arbitration" the idea of action not subject to the normal substantive legal rules. At any rate, the HA assimilated action under Article 37 to the French administrative law category, *acte de gouvernement,* traditionally protected from judicial inquiry.[15] In response, the enterprises simply held that the importance of the measures in question to the German firms entitled them to their day in court. As for the HA's defense, only in those instances when the public law obligations of the Community and the member states were called into question could the enterprises be denied access to the Court.[16]

The Court, in its judgment, accepted the HA's argument on justiciability: only member states could appeal decisions made under the authority of Article 37.[17] The judges pointed out that Article 37 required a reconciliation of the interests of the member states hit by economic disturbances with the general interest of the Community. It was, according to the Court, the states—as members of the Council—which were charged with safeguarding Community interests. Moreover, in a suit dealing with the application of Article 37 the issues would inevitably center on the political responsibilities of the member states. Accordingly, the Court deemed it inappropriate for enterprises or enterprise associations to

15. See again mémoire and duplique, 2 & 3/60.

16. Réplique, 2 & 3/60.

17. 2 & 3/60, Niederrheinische Bergwerks-Aktiengesellschaft Unternehmensverband des Aachener Steinkohlenbergbaues v. H.A., 7 Rec. 261, 289 (1961). It was, of course, clear from the text that only member states could ask the HA to take the emergency action authorized by Article 37. Accordingly, the Court saw no reason to doubt that, if the HA should refuse to act, or should act with insufficient vigor, only the state in question would be entitled to bring the issue before the Court of Justice.

raise such questions. Besides, only the member states could furnish the facts and figures necessary to resolve the dispute.[18]

Of course, since the companies were not entitled to bring the suit, there was no reason for the Court to deal with any other issues. The judges simply decided that it was unnecessary to examine the substantive complaints raised by the plaintiffs and thereby avoided the economic assessment provided for in Article 37.[19] On the other hand, fully aware of the power potential of Article 37, the Court did explore at some length its legal limits.

By and large the judgment accepted the functional argument, attributing "to the High Authority, under control of the Court, special powers permitting it to deal with the consequences resulting from the application of the clauses of the Treaty not ordinarily concerned with the existence or the threat of fundamental and persistent troubles." [20] In other words, the Court decided that Article 37 could be used as an emergency procedure to deal with the existence or threat of fundamental and persistent disturbances resulting from the normal application of the treaty. This decision entailed rejection of the narrower interpretation according to which action under Article 37 was proper only when the disturbances resulted from the HA's failure to take some action required by the treaty. It was precisely in situations in which the HA could not otherwise act that Article 37 was to be used.[21]

18. Ibid., pp. 288, 289–90.

19. While according to Article 33 the Court is ordinarily not permitted to review "the HA's evaluation of the situation based on economic facts and circumstances," Article 37 obligates the Court to review the "cogency" of the executive decision.

20. 2 & 3/60, Niederrheinische Bergwerks-AG v. H.A., 7 Rec. 261, 286 (1961).

21. Advocate General Lagrange, who in his conclusions dealt with the substance of the case, developed this argument in some detail. Article 37, he pointed out, is directed at a situation "where the normal play of the common market, desired and organized by the Treaty, brings on troubles in the econ-

As to the limitations on these special powers the Court held that they "must be *necessary* and *opportune,* and must thus on the one hand constitute a *remedy suitable* for dealing with troublesome predicaments provoked by its action or its failure to act and on the other hand safeguard the *essential interests* of the Community." [22] It was, of course, the role of the Court to ascertain whether the HA's actions were within these limits. And since the power involved was great and the HA did not require the approval of the Council to implement the emergency measures, the Court held that any member state which did not share the HA's evaluation of the situation was entitled to bring suit.[23]

IV

The judgment of the Court was handed down on 13 July 1961 and paved the way for continued isolation of the Belgian market. But there were indications that the Community's three-pronged attack—subsidies, closures, and isolation—had made at least some progress. Accordingly, Belgian import quotas were raised each year and finally abandoned at the end of 1962.[24] However, at the same time that it was being decided to end import restrictions, the Belgian government was pressing the HA for additional emergency action under Article 37.[25]

The HA, wielding its discretionary power to apply Article

---

omy of a member state. Thus the real cause of the troubles is the *common market itself,* that is to say, the integration realized by the Treaty. When Article 37 speaks of an action or a failure to act by the High Authority, that signifies that the HA is not in a position to prevent this regular functioning from provoking threats of troubles in the economy of a state . . . because of an 'action' or an 'abstention' imposed on it by the normal application of the Treaty." 2 & 3/60, Niederrheinische Bergwerks-AG v. H.A., 7 Rec. 261, 315 (1961).

22. Ibid., p. 288. Italics in original.
23. Ibid., pp. 289–90.
24. HA, *Eleventh General Report* (1963), p. 260.
25. *Europe CECA,* 17 September 1962, p. 2.

37 as a lever, bargained hard with the Belgian government. The executive refused to retreat from its 31 December 1962 deadline on halting import restrictions. The HA also conditioned the application of additional emergency relief on the successful completion of Belgium's first program of closures and on the adoption of a new program. The target date for the first program was 31 January 1962, and the goals of the second program were to be achieved by the end of 1966. The Belgians were specifically after salary subsidies—that is, payments which would allow the mines to meet the wage increases then being demanded by the miners. The government claimed, and the HA agreed, that the enterprises could not support increased salary costs, nor was a price rise possible. Since the inflationary pressures were Community-wide, there was considerable opposition among the other member states to special help for Belgium.[26]

However, the HA maintained that only the Belgians were actively engaged in a program of rationalization and closing. The problems of the other member states would have to be considered separately.[27] Accordingly, Article 37 was used for a second time in circumstances much less critical than the precipitous situation when it was first invoked.[28] Moreover, it was used in the face of objections from the Council, again in contrast with its initial employment. Since none of the opposing states took their grievances to the Court of Justice, it would seem that their objections were not particularly strong. The wisdom of the new measures is, of course, still an open question; neither the political nor the economic ramifications of the second application of Article 37 offer

26. See report of the attitudes voiced in the Council of Ministers, ibid., 17 November 1962, pp. 1–2. Of course, under the provisions of Article 37, the HA had only to consult with the Council. Disapproval by the ministers could not affect the executive's right to proceed.

27. HA, *Eleventh General Report* (1963), pp. 260–63.

28. *Europe CECA*, 21 February 1963, p. 1.

very fertile ground for analysis. However, the constitutional issues raised are of real interest and stem directly from the judgment of the Court which led to the renewed application of Article 37.

V

Given the generally awkward character of the Community's mechanisms for political change, the Court's interpretation of Article 37 must be considered a significant contribution to the building of a viable political system. However, in order to understand the full significance of this judgment it is necessary to see Article 37 in context, that is, in comparison to the other mechanisms of change, Articles 95 and 96.

The grande revision (Article 96) is both time-consuming and inflexible, requiring unanimity; it is also likely to be diffuse rather than well-focused. By forcing issues back into the national parliaments for ratification, the immediate question is exposed to the entire range of domestic politics. In other words, the issue is likely to become enmeshed in both irrelevant national political considerations and only slightly more pertinent questions about the general utility of the Community. For reasons of time, flexibility, and effectiveness, the grande revision is, therefore, a procedure of very limited utility.

In contrast, the petite revision (Article 95) would seem to offer a useful procedure for change. Practically speaking, the suitability of Article 95 stems from its methods: the Council of Ministers, which represents the interests of the member states and is also the Community organ of final political authority, is put under pressure to resolve the problem. The pressure is applied in terms of a HA proposal which, it can be taken for granted, will attempt to reconcile Community interests with the individual interests of the member governments. Article 95 thus focuses the attention of the member

government on a constructive solution within the cooperative setting of the Council of Ministers.

In more general terms, it can be said that the petite revision is particularly appropriate for dealing with many of the
problems likely to be thrown up by the fluid process of
regional integration. Article 95 is specifically directed to
situations in which changing conditions require a reevaluation of Community methods in terms of Community values
and goals: "Appropriate amendments may be made provided
they do not modify the provisions of Articles 2, 3, and 4, or
the relationship between the powers of the High Authority
and those of the Community." [29] A redefinition of means
within a framework of stable ends is thereby encouraged,
holding out the appealing possibility of ordered change.

Finally, we come to emergency action under Article 37,
which opens the widest range of action. It permits the Community to deal with problems which cannot be handled
within the essentially conservative confines of the petite revision. In the first place, there is no requirement that the action taken be consistent with Articles 2 to 4. Moreover, the
HA is not obliged to gain the approval of the Council of
Ministers.

According to the Court's reading, expeditious executive
action at the moment of crisis would seem to be the goal of
Article 37. There can thus be no question but that the
Court's interpretation of Article 37 has given a new measure
of flexibility to the treaty. However, the second application of
this emergency provision suggests that the Court may perhaps
have done the Community something of a disservice by not
extending its obiter dicta remarks to an exploration of that
key phrase, "fundamental and persistent disturbances in the
economy of the said State." [30] If the normative framework
which is developing is going to rest on something more than

29. Article 95, paragraph 3.
30. Article 37, paragraph 1.

the assessments of the HA and faith in judicial review, then it is particularly important to know just *when* the HA is entitled to operate outside the normal limits of the treaty.

It is, of course, understandable that the Court was reluctant to engage in the economic analysis that an elucidation of the concept of "fundamental and persistent disturbances" would have required. However, it is absolutely essential that this idea should take on significant dimensions. Given the broad area of substantive freedom and the minimum of procedural restraints, it would seem that its use should be limited to real emergencies. The Court neither emphasized nor clarified this point, and the rather casual way in which the Belgian government asked for a second invocation of Article 37 is evidence of the need for stabilization.

13

THE CARTEL TANGLE

I

Article 65 of the Treaty of the European Coal and Steel Community provides for an ambitious program of cartel control.[1] The rigorous character of the Coal and Steel Community's commitment to antitrust operations stands in sharp contrast to European regulation at the national level, which has been exceedingly moderate. National patterns vary too widely to be satisfactorily summarized here.[2] Only a few salient points need be considered.

In some of the member states, cartels are prohibited, in

1. Cartels are defined as "agreements among enterprises . . . decisions of associations of enterprises, and all concerted practices tending directly or indirectly, to prevent, restrict or distort normal operation of competition within the common market." In addition to cartels, other types of anti-competitive practices proscribed include concentrations (Article 66), and discriminatory pricing practices (Article 60). For a discussion of problems stemming from the "fluid boundaries" between these categories see Stefan Riesenfeld, "Protection of Competition," in Eric Stein and Thomas L. Nicholson, eds., *American Enterprise in the European Common Market: A Legal Profile* (Ann Arbor, University of Michigan Law School, 1960) , 2, 301–02: "There is no escape from the conclusion that the Treaty has not followed sharply defined and consistent criteria of classification, but has approached the protection of competition in a pragmatic and rather unsystematic way, leaving it to practice and theory to weld the dispersed provisions into a coherent and workable scheme."

2. For an extended treatment of national cartel legislation among the European Six, see Riesenfeld, ibid., pp. 216 ff. (Germany), 244 ff. (France), 261 ff. (Netherlands), 275 ff. (Belgium), 287 (Italy), and 292 ff. (Luxembourg)

others they are not. But even where the legislation in force begins with a blanket prohibition, exceptions are made for those cartel operations which are deemed salutary. In France, rationalization cartels are both accepted and supported by the legislation in force.[3] In Germany, there is a broad range of cartel arrangements that are considered either salutary or innocuous with respect to competition.[4]

Article 65, which opens with a general prohibition of cartel arrangements, also approves of salutary cartel operations. The second section of the article accepts cartels which "contribute to a substantial improvement in the production of the products in question." However, not all beneficial cartels escape the ban. All agreements which are "capable of giving the interested enterprises the power to determine prices, or to control or limit production of a substantial part of the products in question within the common market, or of protecting them from effective competition by other enterprises within the common market," are unequivocally rejected.[5] It is at this point that the exceptional rigor of the Coal and Steel Community regime emerges. The treaty rejects without exception all cartels capable of wielding an unacceptable measure of market power. In other words, if the potential power for violation exists the cartel is prohibited. The actual behavior of the cartel is beside the point, as is its otherwise salutary character.

In contrast, national authorities within the Community are more concerned with preventing cartels from engaging in impermissible activities. In general, it can be said that operations at the national level are policing actions to make certain that cartels do not use their market power in an abusive fashion.[6] Accordingly, the vital distinction is largely one of

3. Ibid., p. 246.
4. Ibid., pp. 218–21.
5. Article 65 #2(c).
6. See ibid., pp. 207–94. The concern for abuse of market power recurs constantly in these pages.

timing. The treaty is not limited to ex post facto proscription of unacceptable behavior; there is an obligation to eliminate it at the source. Obviously, this preventive market maintenance implies an aggressive program of control. More specifically, since size is the most readily apparent measure of potential market power, it is reasonable to assume that there is considerable concern about the problem of size per se.

The origin of this surprisingly tough attitude toward cartels is not altogether clear. Given the limited amount of European experience, it is understandable that United States antitrust practices seem to have attracted the drafters of the Coal and Steel Community Treaty.[7] But there are more revealing explanations for the choice of restrictive American-style methods. In part, this choice can be traced to the ideological root of the American experience. When the Sherman Act was passed, it was not simply concentrated economic power which was to be feared. The United States was faced with an incipient plutocracy; the "new feudalism" of the "robber barons" was a political as well as an economic threat. Certainly, plutocracy was not an issue in Europe in 1950. However, no one was unaware of the connections between German industrialists of the Ruhr and the Nazi juggernaut that had rolled across Europe; these considerations were not far from the surface in the planning of the Coal and Steel Community.

Specifically, the building of the Coal and Steel Community was a precondition to the relinquishing of Allied controls of German industry, controls which included an ambitious program of deconcentration in the Ruhr.[8] While the restora-

7. Norbert Lang has written: "The antitrust . . . provisions of the Treaty are in many respects similar to those in the American antitrust law and go considerably farther than national legislation in the member states." "Trade Regulation in the Treaty Establishing the European Coal and Steel Community," *Northwestern University Law Review, 52* (1957–58), 772.

8. William N. Parker, "The Schuman Plan—A Preliminary Prediction," *International Organization, 6* (August 1952), 385–86.

tion of German industrial sovereignty was hardly to be expected a bare five years after World War II, a transfer of
control to the supranational organs of the Coal and Steel
Community—in which Germany would have a voice—was a
desirable expedient.[9] Still, it is hardly surprising that the
transfer involved a Community commitment to vigorous controls over German industry. It can thus be assumed that
while the prestige of, and respect for, American antitrust experience is considerable in Europe, the influence of the U.S.
government on Community policy was a direct result of its
crucial position as an occupying power. However, it would be
incorrect to think of Article 65 as imposed American policy.
There can be no doubt that the distrust of German industrial
potential was not limited to the United States. Indeed, Euro-
peans were equally uneasy, and the whole idea of the Community was to prevent permanently the harnessing of Ruhr
industrial might to national purposes; the Community was to
mesh irretrievably the coal and steel industries of the member states.

It is thus patently clear that the attraction of a vigorous
supranational antitrust policy does not rest on a social purpose which unites the member states across national boundaries. On the contrary, it rests on a disruptive sort of distrust
that the Community must seek to eradicate if it is ever to
fulfill its goals. Moreover, it is not even a general and mutual
distrust which might induce the reciprocal support of all the
nations. Rather, it is a reflection of the questions in the minds
of five member states about the reliability of the sixth—an
atmosphere hardly likely to reinforce the initial bonds of
European unity.

Let us recall, at this point, that the foregoing applies not to
cartel control in general, but merely to the surprising rigor of
the Community commitment. Certainly cartels and trusts
could not be left unchecked. As William Diebold has com-

9. William F. Diebold, *The Schuman Plan*, Chapters 2 and 3.

mented, "It would have done little good to abolish governmental trade barriers if private trade restrictions could take
their place." [10] In other words, if goods were to flow freely
across national boundaries and if an integrated market was to
be established, cartels would have to be controlled. While the
regulation of cartels was thus tied directly to the logic of
integration, the form it took in Article 65 was associated with
latent hostility for Germany. Given the moderation which
characterizes anti-cartel action at the national level, it was
hardly likely that the member states were prepared to accept
the stringent controls called for by Article 65.

II

In fact, litigation on cartel questions has been limited to
the coal market. At the time the treaty became operative, the
coal market was highly cartellized along two lines: according
to function and according to control. In both France and
Luxembourg there were government-controlled cartels
which functioned as import monopolies. Sales cartels existed
in Germany and Belgium. The two German cartels, Ge-
meinschaftsorganisation Ruhrkohle (GEORG) and Oberrheinische Kohlenunion (OKU), were private, while the
Belgian organization, Comptoir Belge de Charbon (Cobechar), was a government agency. In Italy the market was
free, and the Dutch cartel was dissolved voluntarily.

It seemed clear from the outset that this web of cartels was
contrary to Article 65. Section 12 of the Convention containing the transitional provisions recognized this inherently un-
stable situation and gave the HA, the executive arm of the
Community, a "reasonable time" to square the requirements
of Article 65 with the cartellized reality of the coal market.[11]

10. Ibid., pp. 350–51.

11. Article 65 is not applicable to the public cartels, and the HA acted
under Article 86 in such cases. While the problems are thus legally distinct,
they have been in practice indistinguishable. This is true, in part, because
the Court has never had to define the obligations of this aspect of Article 86.

To dismantle the cartels was a delicate task not only because the cartel structure was so much a part of European market habits but also because the coal market had to be protected from any sudden changes which might upset its equilibrium.[12]

While all of these cartels were not directly connected, they were certainly interdependent in operation. The French government, for example, considered its import monopoly, l'Association technique de l'importation charbonnière (ATIC), a defensive mechanism. ATIC was seen as the only effective way to protect French buyers from exploitation by the collective strength of the Ruhr sales cartels which faced them across the Rhine.[13] ATIC, by controlling imports with an iron hand, was able to insulate the French market from the disruptive influences of competition. Accordingly, the Ruhr objected that it could not compete effectively in this protected market.

It was clear from the outset that the HA would need the time afforded by the transitional provisions in order to arm itself with the necessary facts to answer legal questions and untangle the complex web of interdependence. The obvious assumptions of this approach were that the standards set by the treaty would not be met immediately. The approach called for a planned but limited period of illegality. Strictly speaking, the Convention itself authorized this approach, and while the Convention was applicable the HA was on firm legal ground.

Time was required to determine the facts. Then, once the facts were known, the HA had to engage in patient multi-

12. This requirement was dictated not only by common sense but also by Sections 12 and 24 of the Convention.

13. Louis Lister, *Europe's Coal and Steel Community*, pp. 269–371. See also A. de Laubadère, "Réglement amiable du contentieux opposant le Gouvernement français à la Haute Autorité de la C.E.C.A. au sujet du régime juridique de l'importation charbonnière en France," *L'Actualité juridique*, 17 (1961), 477.

lateral negotiations aimed at inducing a retreat from mutually illegal positions. Given the significance of the issues, it was reasonable to assume that these retreats would be slow, step-by-step withdrawals hinged on the appropriate reciprocal concessions from the other parties to the dispute. By its nature, this is a process in which judicial action can be of extremely limited utility.

Courts ordinarily deal with one suit at a time and are not in a position to initiate action on related questions. Judicial action can advance the final solution to the kinds of interdependent problems discussed above only when the issues are presented to the court simultaneously or when the judges can manipulate the docket to permit a coordinated approach. The sage court will be reluctant to tackle such problems. The situation becomes perplexing when the administrative process lags and the judges are faced with the claim of a party whose rights are violated by the admittedly illegal situation. The Court of Justice was continually under this type of pressure as the High Authority sought to bring the coal market in line with the treaty.

III

Between 1953, the beginning of the Coal and Steel Community, and 1958, the HA engaged in patient negotiations with the Ruhr and ATIC aimed at bringing the operations of the two organs into accord with the treaty. However, the course of the negotiations was slow and halting. The result was that those parties who considered themselves injured by the operation of the cartels were continually pressing the HA to act. Moreover, they were not beyond carrying their grievances to the Court.

In the first suit (6/54), brought by the Dutch government in May 1954, the attack on the cartel was indirect. The HA had decided to maintain ceiling prices in two of the Community's coal fields, the Ruhr and Nord et Pas de Calais, despite a buyers' market in coal. The Ruhr cartel was strong enough to neutralize the price depressing effects of the coal surplus, and the HA had learned that the cartel was unlikely to lower prices and might, in fact, raise them.[14]

The HA wished to use ceiling prices to deal with the undesirable consequences of cartel control of the market during the period when the best methods for dealing with the cartels themselves were being sought. The Dutch government, however, feared that the ceiling prices would become the general price level and that the advantages of the buyers' market would never be realized by the consumers.[15] Accordingly, it pressed for speedy action and pointed out to the Court that the HA had already taken thirteen months.

The Court responded by authorizing the HA to use its price powers, under Article 61, to deal with the results of situations contrary to Article 65. However, the basis of this decision was in Section 12 of the Convention, which gave the HA unlimited discretion "within the limits of the transitional period" in which to apply prohibitions against cartels.[16] The result, then, was to leave the HA free to continue attempts for negotiated settlement. It was, in fact, in a stronger position, because the Court had confirmed its right to take the time necessary for dealing with these problems. Within the limits of the transitional period, the cartels would become illegal only when so declared by the HA.[17]

14. Duplique, 6/54 (annex I). In the French basin the arguments for maintenance of ceiling prices were slightly different. Here, an already concentrated market was further protected by various discriminatory practices of ATIC. The Dutch were concerned, however, with the Ruhr cartel. When the HA consulted the Council of Ministers, only Belgium and Italy sided with the Netherlands. *Europe CECA,* 13 March 1954, p. 1.

15. Réplique, 6/54.

16. 6/54, Netherlands v. H.A., 1 Rec. 200, 222 (1955). 222 (1955).

17. As for the Dutch, by the time the decision was rendered on 21 March 1955, the coal situation had changed. It was now distinctly a sellers' market with considerable upward pressure on prices. One can assume that HA ceil-

IV

Freed to resolve cartel problems through its own devices, the HA took definite steps in the first half of 1956 against all of the remaining cartels, GEORG, ATIC, and Cobechar. With Cobechar, the Belgian organization, there seems to have been no serious problem and the Court was never called upon to ratify the settlement, which closely approximated the rules laid down for the Ruhr.[18] In the Ruhr, the HA's solution was to break up GEORG and replace it with three independent sales agencies, connected by common organs which were to perform solely technical and financial functions. Only in the case of very large consumers were orders to be channeled through the Joint Office, one of the common organs. The three agencies were allowed to work out their own rules of operation, subject to HA approval. A warning note for the future was sounded when the three presented the HA with jointly derived and identical rules of operation. The HA, however, accepted those regulations rejecting only one of the rules that had been formulated.[19]

In the meantime, HA negotiations with the French government over the future of ATIC were verging on deadlock. The French refused to permit French buyers to make direct contact with Community producers and dealers. Moreover, it was judged imperative that ATIC continue to make and sign, as purchaser, all contracts for Community coal.[20] The HA's decision in June 1956 gave ATIC just three months to cease signing contracts as purchaser, but gave ground on the ques-

ings were by then a welcome fixture, although the Dutch enthusiasm for freeing the coal market of cartels, concentrations, and restrictive practices had not waned.

18. See Diebold, pp. 395–96. The HA had difficulties with the Oberrheinische Kohlenunion (OKU), the organization charged with sale of coal in Southern Germany. But these problems were also settled without Court action although the OKU did figure indirectly in later suits involving the Ruhr.

19. HA 5–8/56, *J.O.C.E.C.A.*, 13 March 1956, pp. 29–80.

20. HA, *Fourth General Report* (1956), pp. 149–50.

tion of direct access to Community producers and dealers. The HA merely invited further observations on the latter question, thus separating two issues which, in its *Fourth General Report,* had been considered equally contrary to the treaty.[21] Despite the HA's concessions, the French government appealed to the Court (5/56) against the HA's decision. However, following several months of negotiations the government conceded and withdrew its suit in January 1957.

In retrospect, it seems clear that the compromise agreement left ATIC pretty much intact, retaining both its strong bargaining position and its effectiveness as an insulator of the French coal market. ATIC's commitment to abandon its veto over imports offered some ground for optimism. However, it appears that, pending a satisfactory solution of the Ruhr problem, the HA felt that ATIC was entitled to the increased bargaining power which it gained by being able, as agent, to group orders.[22]

To the extent that the ATIC and Ruhr problems were interdependent, there seems to have been good reason to avoid a court test. The Court could, of course, have invalidated the illegal portions of either system. If, however, economic circumstances dictated only a gradual freeing of the Ruhr market, it could be argued that the HA had to make adjustments in dealing with the remainder of the common market. As suggested above, a court is in no position to accept one illegal situation because of the existence of another.

V

Between 1956 and 1960, the HA worked hard to deal with one of ATIC's principal objections to the Ruhr system: high barriers to direct access to the Ruhr mines. During that

21. Ibid.

22. Because all orders were passed through ATIC, it was also in a position to assure the full utilization of the French Rhine fleet. Since it had only begun to deal with transport questions, the HA presumably did not press ATIC to give up these arrangements for Rhine traffic.

period, the HA was under continual attack from two direc-
tions: from two wholesalers who had been denied direct
access, and from the Ruhr sales organs which objected to the
continual downard pressure the HA was applying to the access
criteria. Initially, the Ruhr sales agencies asked that wholesalers wishing to buy directly, and thereby entitle themselves
to a 3 per cent rebate, meet the following standards: [23]

> Sale of 75,000 tons of Community coal.
> Sale of 40,000 tons out (of the 75,000 tons) in its own
> zone of sale.[24]
> Sale of 25,000 tons of *Ruhr* coal out of the 40,000 tons
> sold in its own zone.
> Purchase of 12,500 tons from the sales agency to which
> direct access was sought.

The HA invalidated the 25,000 ton criterion, and one of the
Ruhr sales agencies, Geitling, promptly filed suit (2/56).

The HA believed that the Ruhr coal requirement was discriminatory. To force a wholesaler to sell a specified amount
of Ruhr coal in order to gain direct access to the agencies
would certainly aid the distribution of Ruhr coal. However,
this sort of standard had little—if anything—to do with a
wholesaler's capacity to make effective use of direct access.[25]

The Court accepted the HA's argument: the required purchase of Ruhr coal meant that wholesalers wishing to gain
direct access to one of the sales agencies got credit for
purchases made at the other two. These reciprocal credits
evidenced a measure of joint operation. According to the
judges, the permissible limits of cooperation among the sales
agencies had been set forth in the rules governing the operations of the joint organs.[26] The Court concluded that the
invalidated criteria would not benefit operations of "each" of

23. All figures are annual.
24. The Community market was divided into seven geographic zones.
25. Mémoire, 2/56.
26. 2/56, Geitling v. H.A., 3 Rec. 9, 42 (1957).

the sales agencies, considered individually. Accordingly, the requirement that a wholesaler wishing direct access must sell 25,000 tons of Ruhr coal was held to be "more restrictive than is required by its purpose." [27]

But what of the remaining criteria? Was it not possible that they, too, were unnecessarily restrictive? Of course, neither the HA—which had approved the system—nor Geitling was interested in raising this central question. Geitling did argue that all the criteria were essentially the same, and held that the HA had failed to justify the distinction between the valid and invalid criteria.[28] But obviously it had no interest in a judgment holding all the criteria equally invalid. The Court accepted the limited scope of the litigation, refusing to force a fuller justification from the HA [29] and failed to raise any questions about the remaining criteria.

Just two years later, the Court began a retreat from its initial position in a suit (18/57) brought by a wholesaler, Nold, who was denied direct access to the Ruhr sales agencies.[30] The HA, as part of its continuing pressure on the sales organ, had lowered each of the access criteria—to 60,000, 30,000 and 9,000 respectively—in August 1957.[31] At the same time, the sales agencies were authorized to cut off wholesalers who, to that date, had been allowed direct access even though they did not satisfy the established criteria.[32]

27. Ibid., p. 43.

28. Réplique, 2/56.

29. "A sufficient justification can be deduced from the context of all the statements in support of the entire decision." 2/56, Geitling v. H.A., 3 Rec. 9, 36 (1957). Article 15 of the treaty requires that "the decisions, recommendations and opinions of the HA shall include the reasons therefor."

30. To be precise, let us note that Nold sought the right to purchase his coal through the OKU. This organization was allowed to group coal purchases of South German wholesalers. However, only those wholesalers who satisfied the criteria for direct access to the three Ruhr sales agencies were admitted to OKU.

31. HA 16–18/57, J.O.C.E.C.A., 10 August 1957, pp. 319–51.

32. The exemption had been granted only to those wholesalers who, prior to the establishment of three sales agencies, had been supplied directly.

The Court refused to deal with issues raised by Nold, holding that the HA's justification of its decision was so unsatisfactory that a judicial determination of how the access criteria aided distribution, or whether or not they were unnecessarily restrictive, was impossible.[33] In fact, this unsatisfactory justification was exactly the same as that accepted in the first Geitling case. This was not only the "new" Court's first cartel decision, but also seemed to be the first judicial intrusion into the HA's cartel approach.

A closer look, however, disclosed that there was, in fact, no intrusion. In the period between the Geitling case (2/56) and the Nold decision (18/57), there had been a growing disenchantment on the part of the HA with the acitivities—particularly the lack of independence—of the three sales agencies. By the time the Court delivered its opinion in March 1959, the HA had unequivocally denounced the coal sales organs for failing to develop "independent commercial policies" and for applying a "uniform marketing system . . . in defiance of the Treaty."[34]

Consequently, the Court was actually supporting the new direction taken by the HA. By the time the Nold decision was handed down, the HA had acted upon its denunciation of the Ruhr marketing arrangements. In the first place, the direct access criteria had been further lowered. Secondly, the life of the system had been extended for one year in the interest of stability—the Community by this time was in a severe coal surplus crisis. However, while the possibility of an additional year's life was held out for the three coal sales agencies, common organs and joint financial arrangements were limited to one year "and no longer."[35]

The HA's methods had obviously changed: it had despaired

33. 18/57, Firme I. Nold KG v. H.A., 5 Rec. 89, 115–16 (1959).
34. HA, *Seventh General Report* (1959), pp. 150–51.
35. HA 17/59, *J.O.C.E.*, 7 March 1959, pp. 279–86. See also HA, *Eighth General Report* (1960), pp. 185–88.

of a cooperative solution through indirect negotiation and had acted directly. The solution was thus more appropriate for the unequivocal action that characterizes the legal process. During the period that the HA had been merely chipping away at an illegal organization in the hope of cutting it down to size, the Court was faced with degrees of illegality—hardly suitable fare for a court of law. Now with the whole scheme under fire, it was possible to force the HA to defend not just individual criteria but the whole system.

One final round remained: the lowered criteria were again attacked in court from two sides (36–38 & 40/59).[36] The Ruhr sales agencies contended that the old criteria had been authorized by the HA, which had failed to show any changes in the market justifying the new reduction. Nold supported the Ruhr's attack.[37] Of course, Nold wished the criteria lowered even further and raised not only general issues, but its own more specific difficulties; it was willing to settle for special concessions, while allowing the system to continue.[38]

The HA accused the Ruhr of wishing to control distribution by maintaining restrictive ties from the mines through the sales agencies to the wholesalers. It was held that the 60,000 ton limit was not only too high, but that it also included a concealed discrimination in favor of Ruhr coal.[39]

36. After the Court decision in the first Nold case (18/57) the HA amended that part of HA 17/59 dealing with the quantitative criteria. The new decision (HA 36/59, *J.O.C.E.*, 8 July 1959, pp. 736–42) maintained the same criteria, but was justified in greater detail. The remainder of HA 17/59 was attacked by the three coal sales agencies (16–18/59).

37. Requête, 49/59.

38. 36–38 & 40/59, Comptoirs de Vente du Charbon de la Ruhr v. H.A., 6 Rec. 857, 890 (1960).

39. Mémoire, 36–38/59. It was charged that the 60,000 ton limit eliminated the middle-sized wholesalers and also the need for the other criteria. The demand pattern was such that any wholesalers who sold 60,000 tons of coal would automatically sell from 40,000 to 50,000 tons of Ruhr coal. Within this latter total, one could be certain that the two remaining standards— 30,000 tons of zonal coal and 9,000 tons from each sales agency—would be met.

Nold's difficulties were attributed to its own poor management and, in any case, were held to be quite independent of the Ruhr sales system.[40]

The Court responded to these arguments by not only accepting the suppression of the 60,000 ton criterion but, in addition, by sweeping away the remaining HA-approved criteria. It was clear from the judgment that, in the Court's view, the time had come for the HA to cease chipping away at illegal operations. The Court wanted a systematic inquiry based on the only legitimate purpose of access criteria: the distinction between wholesalers and retailers.[41] Within the limits of this standard, the Court seemingly retained an open mind about the 6,000 ton criterion, which it held inadequately justified. However, the Court ruled that the two larger criteria both resulted in reciprocal credits for Ruhr purchases, thus accepting and extending the HA argument of concealed discrimination.[42] The Court pointed out that such reciprocal credits had already been declared illegal in the first Geitling decision,[43] but neglected to mention its failure to raise any question of *concealed* reciprocity in the earlier judgment, which involved substantially larger criteria.

At first glance, it might appear that the Court was assuming the initiative, but once again closer examination reveals that the Court's approach was entirely consistent with the tack being taken by the HA. The decision advanced the cause of cartel control but without altering its direction. It did, however, bolster the HA's determination to resist pressure from the German wholesalers and the German government —through State Secretary Westrick—to retain the 20,000 ton criterion.[44] Only the 6,000 ton criterion was maintained, the HA arguing that it feared not only another lawsuit to annul

40. Duplique, 40/59.

41. 36–38 & 40/59, Comptoirs de Vente, 6 Rec. 817, 895 (1960).

42. Supra, note 39.

43. 36–38 & 40/59, Comptoirs de Vente, 6 Rec. 817, 892 (1960).

44. *Europe CECA,* 7 February 1961, p. 1.

the new criteria but a suit claiming an official fault by the HA.[45]

After eight years of the common market and five years after the first HA attempts to regulate the Ruhr cartel, all semblance of joint access criteria with reciprocal credit thus disappeared. Whether or not the 6,000 ton criterion serves as a correct gauge of wholesalers is really not important, because it can hardly be an instrument of illicit cooperation among the sales agencies. Besides establishing a general level of 6,000 tons for direct access, the HA's decision set the level for French dealers at 2,500 tons. This removed the last trace of the French government's "defensive" justification for ATIC, and paved the way for settlement of a dispute which had been dragging on for several years. The most interesting aspect of the ATIC dispute was its parallel, its virtual synchronization, with the course of events in the Ruhr.

VI

The unsatisfactory character of the initial 1956 HA–ATIC agreement was evidenced by the almost immediate reopening of negotiations.[46] The HA pressed the government to allow French purchasers to negotiate directly with Community dealers. The HA further demanded that ATIC cease its intervention as agent in all imports of Community coal. The French government was unwilling to satisfy these requirements, and in December 1957 a decision was issued ordering ATIC to cease its objectionable practices, particularly acting as agent, a role that was to be ended within one year. ATIC was given two years, or until the end of 1959, to allow direct access to Community dealers outside France and to end its obligatory role as representative in all imports.[47]

45. See Article 34.
46. Supra, p. 233. See also A. de Laubadère, *L'Actualité juridique, 17* (1961), 476.
47. HA, *Sixth General Report, 2* (1958), 93–96.

This crackdown on ATIC followed the July 1957 decisions lowering the criteria for direct access to the Ruhr. However, when in September 1957 the HA observed the identical price increases of the three coal sales agencies, it limited itself to taking steps to prevent such a coordinated pricing policy. Since it was clear that the HA was still not prepared to undertake the dismantling of the Ruhr sales system and was content to treat the symptoms rather than the disease, it is not surprising to learn that the French appealed the ATIC decision to the Court (2/58).

Although the written procedure in this suit advanced at a normal pace—being completed in early 1959—the hearing was repeatedly postponed. During 1959 and 1960 there was little activity and no apparent progress. It was at the end of 1959 that the entire HA decision was to have become executory; ATIC, however, continued its normal operations. While it might be said that France used Court action to delay application of HA decisions, this would only be part of the story. As a rule, Court action is not suspensive, and HA decisions are valid and executory until the Court decides to the contrary. It was not the suit that delayed application of the decisions; the HA had the legal power to force ATIC to comply. However, it failed to assert this power just as it continued to agree to postponement of Court action despite a lack of progress in negotiations.

The HA was willing to mark time with ATIC pending settlement of the Ruhr question.[48] At the same time, in February 1961, that the Ruhr criteria issue was settled—including its special provision for French dealers—the HA announced that an agreement had been reached with ATIC.[49] French con-

---

48. *Europe CECA* reported in March 1960 that the HA decided to delay dealing with a new question concerning the Belgian agency, Cobechar, until after the Ruhr problem had been resolved. *Europe CECA,* 7 March 1960, p. 2.

49. HA 3/61, *J.O.C.E.,* 18 February 1961, pp. 413–18, and *Europe CECA,* 15 February 1961, pp. 1 & 2.

sumers and dealers were permitted direct access to both Community producers and Community dealers. In addition, ATIC was no longer allowed to act as agent in coal imports which meant that it could no longer group orders. On the other hand, ATIC retained a role in concluding contracts and arranging payment and transport. It seems clear that the compromise left ATIC in a position to interfere with coal imports. There are those in the HA who argue that although it will be administratively more difficult for ATIC to exercise an illegal influence on French imports, its effectiveness will not be materially reduced.

Of course, the result of the agreement was the withdrawal of the suit. Again, the Court was denied an opportunity to pass on the legality of ATIC by the HA's commitment to a gradual approach. It is true that on the peripheral issue of direct access criteria, the HA had acted decisively. However, its campaign to establish the independence of the three sales organs had only just begun. Accordingly, it is not surprising that the HA was reluctant to have the Court make the general assessment of ATIC that the suit seemed to call for. The period of programmed illegality was still in process, and the HA had obtained a concession from ATIC on the one issue where the grounds for action were strong.

VII

It would seem likely that another reason for the HA's cautious policy was the coal surplus which began to develop early in 1958. Since the essential function of the sales cartel had always been to stabilize production and employment during alternations in the business cycle, it is hardly surprising that whatever independence the sales agencies had previously maintained ended with the crisis. The Joint Office began to distribute all orders,[50] and by 1959 it became gen-

50. It was authorized to deal only with large consumers whose annual purchases exceeded 50,000 tons. HA, *Fourth General Report* (1956), p. 143.

erally known that the common organs were welding the three Ruhr agencies into a single cartel.

When in February 1959 the HA announced its crackdown on the three sales agencies and their common organs,[51] it was immediately clear that a nerve had been touched: the Ruhr took the offensive and asked the HA to authorize a single cartel. Unfortunately, the HA had decided to test the strength of the Community's commitment to the stringent provisions of Article 65 at just the moment when support for cartels could be expected to be the strongest. Both the mine owners and the unions stood behind the cartel, and on February 25, 1960, State Secretary Westrick announced that the German government, under considerable political pressure, would support the request for a single cartel.[52]

While the views of the remainder of the Community were not immediately apparent, a general willingness to compromise soon asserted itself. Final agreement crystallized around the idea of rationalization as the raison d'être of a compromise scheme to amend the treaty.[53] If cartel authorization were tied to rationalization it would be self-liquidating. In addition, the HA insisted that it be given the *right* to authorize cartels. It stressed that this should be a

51. Supra, p. 236.

52. *Europe CECA,* 4 March 1960, p. 1.

53. Just prior to this time, the HA began to revise its attitude about treaty changes. Because the tide had been running against supranationalism for some years, the HA was very hesitant to recommend changes in the treaty. It feared that the opponents of supranationalism would use such a project as an excuse for making major reductions in the powers of the HA. The cartel deadlock forced the HA to reexamine its policy. Perhaps the real danger was a ten-year-old treaty, out of step with economic conditions: a coalition might form without the HA's knowledge—and certainly without consulting the HA. Such a coalition could build up irresistible pressure for just the kind of changes the HA wished to avoid, by playing on the gap between treaty and economic reality. If the HA took the lead it might be able to channel pressure for change within desirable limits and at the same time mobilize support for its own position. *Europe CECA,* 30 March 1960, p. 1.

right and not an obligation, and that, accordingly, it be allowed to withdraw authorization without having to *prove* that the cartel had abused its position.[54]

Of course, the Ruhr would have preferred a single cartel to the temporary rationalization program. It had agreed to compromise on the latter, although the restrictions included in the amendment proposal at the behest of the HA had made the whole idea rather unpalatable.[55] The compromise had been hammered out in long, hard negotiations, beginning with a trip by President Malvestiti of the HA to Bonn in March 1960. Once the Council of Ministers had committed itself to seeking an acceptable amendment,[56] and with little chance of the Court's accepting the request for a single cartel, the Ruhr really had no choice.[57] The time was ripe for a political compromise, and the HA had maintained the pressure on the Council by refusing to suspend the Ruhr suit. The unpleasant possibility of a Court order to free the market was a real threat—as unwelcome to the HA and the Council of Ministers as to the Ruhr. Only when the proposal for the amendment, formulated along lines suggested by the

54. The retention of HA discretion seemed to be required by the Court's opinion in the amendment of Article 56. Supra, Chapter 11.

55. The Ruhr objected to the discretionary power given to the HA, as well as the temporary character of the change. Moreover, the commitment to rationalization was almost certain to bring unwelcome interference, since the HA and the Ruhr disagreed over rationalization procedures—particularly concerning the closure of less efficient mines. *Europe CECA,* 4 March 1961, p. 1, and 4 July 1961, p. 1.

56. HA, *Ninth General Report* (1961), p. 168.

57. The HA, determined to resist the single cartel, had argued initially that it was exposed to immediate attack before the Court—the Dutch seemed most likely to undertake such a suit—if it were to authorize a system that its own legal advisors deemed contrary to the treaty. *Europe CECA,* 12 April 1960, p. 2. Moreover, Community officials were inclined to believe that the Court's final criteria decision foreshadowed a rejection of the Ruhr suit. The sales agencies were also pessimistic about their chances before the Court. *Europe CECA,* 4 March 1961, p. 1.

HA, had been agreed upon was action on the suit inter-rupted.[58]

What was being requested was a temporary relaxation of Article 65. Because the major amendment involved the awk-ward and time consuming process of ratification by national parliaments, the petite revision was decided upon. Accord-ingly, for virtually the first time in the cartel litigation the Court was put in a vital position. The judges decided, on both procedural and substantive grounds, to reject the changes proposed by the Ruhr. The proposed change is too long to reproduce here, but the disputed portion read as follows:

> In the event of a fundamental and persisting change in marketing conditions for the coal mining and/or the iron and steel industry, the High Authority may grant the following further authorizations.
>
> (a) It may authorize agreements *concerning adjustments to the new marketing conditions.*[59]

The Court held that the open-ended character of the amendment would result in a power without limits. Thus, instead of an adaptation of HA powers, which was permitted by Article 95, an entirely new power would be conferred.[60]

While it might have been possible to redraft the proposal to meet these procedural criticisms, the substantive objec-tions presented a seemingly impregnable legal wall against the plans of the Council and the HA.[61] The essential obstacle

58. The Dutch government, which objected, was unable to block action in the Council but did file a dissent.

59. Avis 1/61, 7 Rec. 481, 510 (1961). Italics are supplied and indicate the wording objected to by the Court.

60. Ibid., pp. 514–15.

61. In response to a series of written questions advanced by the Court, the Council and the HA indicated that it was "impossible to make a complete enumeration of the conceivable agreements" for adjusting to the new condi-tions. See *Annexe II de l'Avis, Réponses aux questions posées par la Court de Justice des communautés européennes au sujet de la demande d'avis 1/61,*

raised by the Court was its interpretation of Article 65 #2(c), which prohibited the HA from authorizing "joint buying or selling" agreements "capable of giving the interested enterprises the power to determine prices, or to control or limit the production or selling of a substantial part of the products in question within the common market, or of protecting them from effective competition by other enterprises within the common market."

The principal objective of the amendment proposal was to loosen this restriction, but under the control of the HA and only temporarily. The Court, however, argued that Article 65 was the concrete application of one of the fundamental principles of the treaty, Article 4(d), which prohibits "restrictive practices tending towards the division or the exploitation of the markets." Article 65 #2 permitted certain exceptions to this rule, but only if the limitation of Article 65 #2(c) were met. The Court concluded that to eliminate this restriction would be an unacceptable derogation of Article 4(d),[62] and Article 95 did not permit amendments which modified "the provisions of Articles 2, 3, and 4." By the same token, the proposal was more than an adaptation of HA powers. In allowing the HA to ignore the restrictions of Article 65 #2(c), the amendment would have invested the HA with an altogether new power.[63]

Of course, the distinction between new powers and adaptations of old powers is hardly precise.[64] Moreover, at the be-

---

7 Rec. 526 (1961). Nonetheless, some examples were given, and it would seem that a more explicit statement of the nature and objectives of the agreements would have been possible.

62. Avis 1/61, 7 Rec. 481, 519 (1959).

63. Ibid., p. 518.

64. There was a dispute over this question at the time Article 56 was revised. The Court had then taken a rather permissive view of the possibilities for change. *Procédure de révision au titre de l'article 95, alinéas 3 et 4 du traité C.E.C.A.*, 5 Rec. 533 (1959). See also Hans Jürgen Lambers, "Les Clauses de révision des traités instituant les communautés européennes," *Annuaire français de droit international*, 7 (1961), 618–22.

ginning of its opinion the Court pointed out that Article 95
permitted changes in Article 65 which would make possible
authorization "of agreements of another nature than those
provided for by the present text, but pursuing the same end,
or of agreements of the same nature as those provided for by
the text in force, but pursuing another end, or, finally of
agreements of another nature and pursuing other ends." [65]
It is difficult to see how this statement is consistent with the
judges' refusal to authorize a temporary and conditional relaxation of the restrictions of section 2(c).

The Court itself was aware of this apparent inconsistency,
but denied that there was any real contradiction. Yet the
wording of the Court's denial emphasized the problem: "The
Court recognizes . . . that changes . . . permitting authorization of *other categories of cartels* not foreseen by the text in
force . . . can constitute an adaptation of the rules relative
to the exercise of the powers of authorization attributed to
the High Authority." The judges, however, drew the line at
that category of cartel which would enable enterprises "to
acquire through restrictive practices a position permitting
them to exploit or divide the market . . . *this prohibition is
rigid and distinguishes the system set up by the Treaty.*" [66]

Certainly, the Court's unwillingness to allow the concentration of economic power that was sought was in keeping
with both the text and the spirit of Article 65. But would this
concentration have been contrary to one of the fundamental
principles of the treaty—the permissible limits of a petite
revision? As the Council and the HA pointed out in response
to a question posed by the Court, the purpose of the amendment was to permit agreements which resulted in the prohibited accumulation of economic power—but to prevent the
enterprises from taking advantage of this position.[67] Given

65. Avis 1/61, 7 Rec. 481, 514 (1961).
66. Ibid., pp. 518, 519, italics supplied.
67. Avis 1/61, *Réponses,* ibid., pp. 528–29.

the background of Article 65,[68] it hardly seems that this temporary moderation of anti-cartel operations would have changed the direction of integration.

Since a major amendment to the treaty was never considered feasible, the practical consequence of the Court's rejection was to reopen the question of the Ruhr's petition for a single cartel. The HA had rejected this request, and the Ruhr had appealed to the Court of Justice. However, action on the suit (13/60) had been suspended pending a decision on the change in Article 65.

VIII

While a negative response to the Ruhr's appeal for a single cartel was in prospect, the questions raised seemed likely to lead to a judgment of signal importance. The Court was called upon to construe the crucial passage of Article 65—the rock on which the petite revision had foundered—section 2(c).

In its opinion on the petite revision, the Court had rejected a change in the treaty that would have allowed a cartel to attain the dominant position prohibited by section 2(c). The Ruhr was now arguing that, given the conditions of the market, a single cartel would not be in a dominant position. Specifically, it was claimed that the pressure on its markets from Community and third-country coal, but particularly from petroleum, would check Ruhr power to determine prices.[69] If the cartel was unable to determine prices, the Ruhr contended, the size of the cartel itself was immaterial.[70] As we shall see, however, size was not immaterial to the Court, which decided to reject the suit.

While its approach is entirely consistent with the temper

68. Supra, pp. 224–28.

69. In support of its contention the Ruhr provided figures detailing the competitive pressures and demonstrating that other coal basins did not follow Ruhr price leads.

70. See requête, 13/60.

of Article 65,[71] the Court was required by the wording of
that article to address itself to the arguments raised by the
Ruhr. Would the cartel have "the power to determine
prices" for a "substantial part of the products in question
within the common market"? [72] Two familiar, but critical,
antitrust problems were thus presented to the Court: describ-
ing the relevant market and defining the limits of permissible
restraint of competition.[73] In dealing with the problems, the
Court—despite the expected rejection of the cartel—adopted
a new approach to the cartel issue, which paved the way for a
resolution of the Ruhr problem in the summer of 1964.
Guided by its one economist—the judgment is now referred
to familiarly as the *l'arrêt Rueff*—the Court undertook to
reinterpret Article 65, paragraph 2(c). The judges sought to
apply a standard of competition which took into account the
oligopolistic character of the coal market. In other words, the
members of the Court started out by admitting that even
under the best circumstances only a restricted amount of
competiton was possible among the giants of the coal industry.[74] However, despite this more flexible attitude, the HA's
rejection of the single cartel was upheld. Let us see why.

Determination of Prices

As a starting point, the Court accepted the distinction
agreed upon by the parties between the power to *determine*
prices and the power to *fix* prices. To fix prices was simply to
set prices at levels dictated by the market, while determina-

71. Supra, pp. 224–26.

72. Article 65, paragraph 2(c). The prohibition also extended to the power
to "control or limit production or selling." The Court's analysis of this
problem, which was rather perfunctory and in accord with the remainder
of the decision, will not be treated here. See 13/60, Comptoirs de Vente du
Charbon de la Ruhr, 8 Rec. 165, 214–15 (1962).

73. Rostow, *Planning for Freedom*, pp. 286–90.

74. This problem has already been touched upon briefly in connection with
the steel industry. Supra, p. 56.

tion of prices entailed a price policy operated independently of the market, being "more or less equivalent to . . . a system from which competition had been eliminated." [75] The Court had no difficulty deciding that the cartel would, in fact, have the power to determine prices for its members; price competition was, of course, to be excluded within the cartel. Insofar as Community coal was concerned, it was concluded that the Ruhr "enjoyed a margin of geographic protection within which it has the power to determine its prices." [76]

The case for a lack of competitive pressure was strongest for Community coal; there was considerably more caution in the Court's analysis of third-country coal. However, the Court concluded that "the High Authority was founded in recognizing that the joint sales agreement gives to the interested parties such broad possibilities of directing the competition, that the competition of producers from third-countries does not exclude, for the sales organ, the possibility of determining the prices in its principal sales zones." [77]

The Court was on still weaker ground when dealing with the marketing difficulties caused by petroleum. After briefly exploring the uneven character of petroleum competition for different varieties of coal, the judges held that "relative to the competition of petroleum, there exists a price zone, in which the common sales organ can choose, not freely, but with a certain margin of freedom, its sales policy and, *in certain limits,* its prices." [78] Of course, the judgment was vulnerable at this spot since the Court had accepted as a starting point the Ruhr's contention that "determination of prices" was roughly equivalent to "elimination of competition."

75. 13/60, Comptoirs de Vente, 8 Rec. 165, 201 (1962).
76. Ibid., pp. 204–05. The Court's conclusion was based on the low Ruhr costs and correspondingly low prices, reinforced by considerable geographic protection in its principal sales zone. In fact, 73.1% of the coal consumed in Germany was in 1959 provided by the Ruhr.
77. Ibid., p. 207.
78. Ibid., italics supplied.

The Court's decision was based upon its reevaluation of Article 65 in light of the oligopolistic character of the coal market. Oligopoly, by definition, precludes the elimination of competition; the oligopolistic producer can never—in an unqualified manner—determine prices. On the other hand, all producers, because of their size, exert "a non-negligible influence on the prices and are, from this fact, conducting a true selling policy." Accordingly, the goals of Article 65 had to be limited to ensuring the continuance of a "certain measure of competition." [79] The Court concluded that it was just this "minimum measure" which the HA had attempted to protect in refusing to authorize the cartel.

The Relevant Market

It remained for the Court to determine whether or not the "certain measure" of control over prices extended to a "substantial part of the products in question within the common market." [80] But what are the products in question? Should the investigation be limited to the coal market or are the dimensions of the entire energy market relevant, as the Ruhr contended? The judges never faced up to this pivotal question.

Implicit in the Court's discussion of price determination was a broad view of the dimensions of the market: competition from petroleum, as well as from Community producers and from third countries, was considered.[81] There is, however, reason to believe that the discussion of petroleum was *obiter dictum,* because in deciding whether the pricing powers of the cartel extended to a substantial portion of the market, only coal production was considered. What mattered to the Court was relative strength: the production of the

---

79. Ibid., pp. 209 ("politique de vente"), 213.
80. Article 65, paragraph 2(c).
81. It should also be recalled that, in passing on the amendment of Article 56, the Court had agreed that competition from petroleum—and low-priced imports from America—sufficiently transformed the structure of the coal market to justify the application of Article 95. Supra, p. 206.

mines to be gathered in the single sales cartel would be four times as great as that of any other basin, and double that of the entire production of the *Charbonnages de France*. Accordingly, "statistical subtleties" aside, there could be no doubt that one was dealing with "a substantial part of the products in question within the common market." [82] The Ruhr was just too big.

The significance of the Court's restricted view of the market is most clearly brought out by the conclusions of Advocate General Roemer. Like the Court, Mr. Roemer decided that perfect competition was not possible in the coal market, but concluded that the cartel would not be in a position to exercise an unacceptable degree of influence. The advocate argued that the market envisaged by Article 65, the coal market, must be enlarged to include all forms of energy.[83] Without claiming that the advocate's argument is conclusive, it is clear that the judges would have had a more difficult time sustaining their position, given a broadened conception of the relevant market.

The Court claimed that its oligopolistic theory took into account, in accordance with the wishes of the plaintiffs, "the new tasks which are posed by the dynamics of economic life." [84] However, taken together with its rejection of the petite revision, it was clear that the judges had, in fact, set themselves squarely against the economic consensus of the remainder of the Community. At best, the Court seemed to exhibit an unsatisfactory ambivalence to the changing conditions of the market—and even to its own theory of competition in an oligopolistic market.[85] At worst, the judgment

82. 13/60, Comptoirs de Vente, 8 Rec. 165, 219 (1962).

83. See ibid., 260–64. Mr. Roemer also pointed out that a nationalized coal industry within the Community made the ideal of free competition unattainable.

84. Ibid., p. 214.

85. For an interesting and extended presentation, see Maurice Bye, "L'arrêt 13–60 du 18 mai 1962 sur les comptoirs de la Ruhr," *Droit Social, 26* (1963), 257–67.

seemed merely to adapt the Court's uncompromising, treaty-anchored opposition to cartels to an oligopolistic market. Either way, it was certain that the Court had no sympathy for the abuse theory; the power concentration of the Ruhr cartel was unacceptable regardless of the checks imposed on the utilization of that power.

IX

The Court's rejection of the Ruhr suit sent the parties back to the drawing board in search of a legally acceptable solution. However, there was general agreement that the single cartel was economically justified, and President Malvestiti was to assure the Ruhr that a majority of the members of the HA shared this position.[86] Nevertheless, given the Court's decision and pending a major amendment of the treaty, the HA argued that it was compelled to push on toward a legally acceptable solution. Accordingly, the Ruhr was invited to make proposals before the end of December 1962, with a view to final settlement by March 31, 1963. Permission was granted to continue the temporary regulations—in fact, a single cartel system—until this latter date.[87]

The solution finally agreed upon by the Ruhr and the HA after more than six months of negotiation was a division of the Ruhr cartel into two independent sales organs.[88] Throughout the negotiations the controversy centered on the degree of independence of the sales organs. At issue were four potential ties:

86. *Europe CECA,* 29 November 1962, pp. 2, 3. See also Louis Sizaret, "Chronique générale de jurisprudence européenne," *L'Actualité juridique, 18* (1962), 428.

87. Ibid., 7 June 1962, pp. 1, 2. Ironically enough, as *Europe CECA* pointed out, it was just this date which had been sought by the Ruhr when it submitted its initial request. See also HA, *Ninth General Report* (1961), p. 167.

88. *Europe CECA,* 31 January 1963, pp. 1–2. See HA 5 & 6/63, *J.O.C.E.,* 10 April 1963, pp. 1173–1208.

1. a common export organ
2. a common office to handle accounting and other technical operations
3. the joint agency which has handled market analysis and public relations
4. the government-owned mines

The HA had been particularly insistent on including all the government-owned mines in one of the sales organs, but the Ruhr, backed by the German government, flatly refused.[89] As to the various joint agencies, it was decided that they would be revised, so their operations would not interfere with the pursuance of independent policies. Moreover, the HA was to maintain a close watch over the operation of the entire system and was to intervene if the state mines followed a collective policy, or if either the letter or the spirit of the agreement was violated.[90]

The settlement did not go long unchallenged, for in May 1963 the Dutch government filed suit against the two-cartel arrangement.[91] Taking its cue from the objections raised by the HA during the preliminary negotiations, the Dutch government charged that the cartels were so similar in structure —with, for example, the government-owned mines and those mines exporting to third countries divided evenly between the two sales agencies—that "parallelism" was bound to result.[92] The Dutch also argued that the control system set up

89. See details of negotiations between State Secretary Westrick and the HA. *Europe CECA,* 17 December 1962, p. 3. In opposition to the HA position, it was argued that the government mines had different industrial interests, pursued independent policies, and were always guided by sound principles of business management.

90. Again the parallel with ATIC is instructive. As part of the "final" settlement with ATIC, a permanent representative of the HA was attached to the French cartel to make certain that it did not abuse the strategic position it retained.

91. See *Europe CECA,* 30 May 1963, p. 1.

92. 66/63, Netherlands v. H.A., 10 Rec. 1047, 1062–65 (1964).

by the HA violated the opinion expressed by the Court when it rejected the proposal to amend Article 65. They claimed that the elaborate controls revealed that the cartels were in a position to violate Article 65. Instead of striking directly at this potential, the HA had confined itself to a system of subsequent control.[93] The executive had, in other words, introduced the abuse theory, or so it was contended.

The heart of the HA's defense was that, in accordance with the judgment of the Court on the matter of the single cartel, the Ruhr sales operations had been divided between two independent organs of equal size, each in turn about equal to the Charbonnages de France. A situation had thus been created in which the necessary minimum of competition became possible.[94] However, since there was no way of knowing how the cartels would act, the system of control had been set up to make certain that the sales agencies operated in an independent fashion. Mere suspicion that the two cartels would drift back into unified operations was not enough to justify a refusal.[95]

The Court accepted the position of the executive without reserve, pausing only to note that, barring flagrant errors, Article 33 prevented the judges from challenging the executive's assessment of the economic situation. The judges did not deny that the sales agencies might adopt parallel policies but held that this was to some extent inevitable in an oligopolistic market. Only conscious parallelism was to be avoided. So long as there was no agreement, "even tacit," the HA was not in a position to interfere.[96] On the other

93. Ibid., pp. 1060–61.

94. Ibid., p. 1067. The Dutch objected that the HA was attempting to transform the Court's negative thesis into a positive rule of law. According to the plaintiffs, the judges had merely said that the single cartel, which would have been twice as large as the Charbonnages de France, could not be permitted. Ibid.

95. Ibid., pp. 1061–63.

96. Ibid., pp. 1075–77. The judgment was rendered after this chapter had been completed and too late to allow an extended analysis of its contents.

hand, should the cartels violate the rules accepted by the executive, the HA must act. Since the history of the Ruhr could, to say the least, give rise to suspicion that it might violate these agreements, the HA was entitled, perhaps obligated, to set up some control.[97]

While there is no way of knowing whether the new system will be effective, one wonders how the HA will be able to force independent policies on two sales agencies when it was unable to maintain the independence of the three original agencies.[98] Here as in no other case one is struck by the frailty of judicial review when it is confronted by powerful economic and political forces. In a formal sense, the judgment of the Court seems sound and defensible. In fact, it is hard to see what the alternative would have been. On the other hand, in a practical sense, the position of the Dutch government is sensible and convincing. One has the feeling that the parties were, in fact, talking past one another.

To put it another way, it can be argued that the Court did, in fact, adopt the abuse theory as charged by the Dutch government. The potential for joint operation is enormous. In the first place, the similarity of the two agencies and the transparency of the market make the step between accidental parallelism and conscious parallelism a small one.[99] Secondly, there are not only some common organs remaining, but these common organs together with the two sales agencies themselves are housed in the same building.[100]

Perhaps even more disquieting to the Dutch was the general atmosphere in which the new agencies were authorized

---

But I was fortunate enough to discuss the matter with persons close to the case, and I am confident that the basic issues are treated fairly.

97. Ibid., pp. 1072–74.

98. On the very day the HA's decision was announced, reservations were expressed in the Ruhr about the HA's control operation. *Europe CECA*, 31 January 1963, p. 3.

99. Cf. 66/63 Netherlands v. HA., 10 Rec. 1047, 1076 (1964).

100. Ibid., p. 1065.

and established. The spirit of the negotiations seemed to imply that the agreement was a temporary accommodation pending a major revision of the treaty,[101] which, in turn, will deal in a systematic manner with the entire energy question. Moreover, given the sympathy of the HA with the goals of the Ruhr,[102] it is reasonable to assume that control will be limited. Even the Court noted that, with the coal market under considerable pressure, the needs of rationalization take precedence over protection of competition—so long as all competition is not eliminated from the coal market.[103] In other words, it would seem that the solution finally agreed upon will not differ markedly from the rationalization cartel which had been rejected by the Court.

One is naturally forced to wonder whether respect for the rule of law can be advanced by operations of this sort. The Court seems to have fought and lost a battle to protect the treaty from political incursions. Throughout the initial years of the Community, the judges had gone along with the HA's halting efforts to implement the cartel provisions of the treaty. During this time, the rule of law simply was not extended to cartel activity, and the Court was content to march in step with executive action. However, the judges seemed to grow increasingly restive under what was for them an untenable situation. By the time of the petite revision, judicial patience was exhausted. Once the judges decided to act, they were not in the mood for compromise.

However, the economic argument for a single cartel was compelling and no other country was prepared to accept the rules which were being forced upon the Ruhr.[104] At the

101. State Secretary Westrick held in December that, with the question of British entry still to be settled, a general revision of the treaty was out of the question. *Europe CECA,* 17 December 1962, p. 3.

102. Supra, p. 252. At the time of the Dutch suit, there were even rumors that the HA and the Council were ready to agree on a single cartel. *Europe CECA,* 30 May 1963, p. 1.

103. 66/63, Netherlands v. H.A., 10 Rec. 1047, 1077 (1964).

104. In France, and by and large in Holland, the coal industry is na-

political level, too, there was support for a change of Article 65, evidenced, of course, by the acceptance of the petite revision by the HA and the Council of Ministers. All told, it would seem that the Court was trying to lay the foundation for a normative pattern of cartel control on political and economic quicksand. By giving legal recognition to the new Community consensus, the Court could have established a framework within which realistic norms could take shape. Accordingly, it is not surprising that the Court ended by adopting a more flexible attitude to the cartel problem.

Still, one should not minimize the dilemma faced by the Court. The changes sought by the Ruhr and accepted by the HA and the Council were designed to bring the rules of the treaty and the "living law" into agreement. However, the treaty as it stood did not really permit the adjustment, and the legality of the method chosen to amend Article 65 was at least open to question. Recall that it was not on the basis of legality, but expediency, that the petite revision was chosen instead of the grande revision. In other words, the Court's approach was in keeping with its obligation to the treaty, and it maintained its "tough line" long enough to make it clear that the judges can stand firm in the face of considerable political pressure.

That the Court finally came around must be attributed not to weakness but to an acceptance of reality—to a recognition that Article 65 was unsatisfactory as it stood. We have a perfect example of a situation in which the fluid character of integration and the rigid nature of the Community's political process—particularly, its mechanism of formal change—put the Court in an extremely awkward position.[105] At the same time,

---

tionalized; in Belgium, a single cartel is authorized and operating. Just two weeks before the HA decision on the double cartel in the Ruhr, the authorization of the Belgian cartel, Cobechar, had been extended to 31 December 1965.

105. See Bye, p. 257, "The role of the Court on this occasion has been so decisive that one could speak of the 'government of the judges.'"

the rule of law was placed under considerable pressure. What was ultimately at issue was the proper relationship between law and politics in the Community. It is to this broad and vital problem that Part Six, the concluding section of this study, is devoted.

6 PERSPECTIVE

INTRODUCTION

This study has presented in considerable detail the case law of the Court of Justice of the European Coal and Steel Community. We have seen that, even at this early date, the work of the Court is extensive and varied. Still the litigation has proven amenable to grouping, and these groups reflect the distinctive kinds of difficulties faced by the Court in its attempt to fit judicial review into an experiment in regional integration. A sense of development and progressive adaptation is conveyed by the manner in which the materials have been organized and presented; and a proper posture for the Court is suggested.

But should we not go one step further and assess the total performance of the Court of Justice? Because of their signal importance and because they can serve as focal points for the general inquiry, two questions stand out:

1. Is the rule of law compatible with the integrative process?
2. What contribution can judicial review make to integration?

These two problems will be explored in detail in the final chapters.

The real significance of this inquiry is not so much in what it tells us about the Coal and Steel Community as in the lesson it conveys for the future of European integration. With the Common Market in its early stages, it is important to know what can be expected from judicial review. No analysis of the judicial process in the Common Market will be attempted here. However, problems of the Coal and Steel Community will be described in terms of the broader questions of regional integration, thus raising issues relevant to the Common Market. Of course, if the lesson of the Schuman Plan is to serve as a reliable starting point for understanding the relationship of law and politics within the European Community in general, it is essential to know what features of the development of judicial review are unique to the Coal and Steel Community setting. Fortunately, the rather narrow compass of the Schuman Plan offers a manageable amount of material for a necessarily precise analysis.

To date, the Court of Justice has written only the first chapter in the story of judicial review in the European Communities. During the roughly ten years covered by this study, the Court of Justice has been concerned almost exclusively with the operations of the Coal and Steel Community. Now the balance of the Court's docket seems to be shifting toward the Common Market. Moreover, as this is being written, a merger of the executives of the three Communities seems imminent. With the first chapter virtually complete, it seems an appropriate time to seek patterns and attempt generalizations.

14

REGIONAL INTEGRATION: THE RULE OF LAW

In order to properly assess the strength of the rule of law in the Coal and Steel Community, we must break down the problem into two component parts: the *opportunities* for asserting legal rules and the *response* of the Court of Justice to these opportunities. In the second section of this chapter [1] we shall focus on the performance of the Court. First, it is important to consider the opportunities with which the judges have been presented.

As a starting point, the quantity and significance of litigation offer a rough but meaningful gauge of the importance of law in the Coal and Steel Community. To what extent has the judicial process been used to resolve disputes within the Community? While it is true that a number of major problems have not reached the Court, most of the significant Community controversies have been litigated,[2] and, as we

1. Infra, p. 273.
2. Among the important matters which the Court has not been called upon to treat are industrial mergers and labor problems. The former category is rather surprising, because there have been significant disputes, particularly over reconcentration of the German steel industry. (See Diebold, *The Schuman Plan*, pp. 356–78.) On the other hand, because trade unions have no standing to bring suit, it is altogether understandable that Community difficulties in establishing policies for labor mobility and harmonization of wages and working conditions have not been subjected to litigation.

have seen, the judges have been presented with vital issues, not just peripheral aspects.

PATTERNS OF CONFLICT

There is another way in which the Court of Justice is at the center of Community conflict. Interviews with participants in the system, together with my own observations, lead me to conclude that suits are likely to be brought to the Court only after attempts to negotiate settlements have proved fruitless.[3] In other words, the participants are not concerned with the *nature* of the dispute, be it political or legal. For the protagonists, the failure of the political process to provide a settlement is sufficient to transform a political dispute into a legal question. However, to what extent can the Court of Justice be expected to compensate for such political weaknesses? If we are to gauge the performance of the judges, we must understand how these systemic flaws impinge on the judicial process and, specifically, how they influence the Community's patterns of litigation.

The Evolution of Supranationalism

The most striking fault in the Coal and Steel Community system has been the failure of the HA to use the supranational powers with which it was endowed by the treaty. The decline of the HA can in general be traced to the 1955 departure of its first president, the remarkable Jean Monnet.[4] Both by the force of his own personality and by capitalizing on the initial enthusiasm which had given rise to the Community, M. Monnet molded the HA into an active and enterprising executive organ. If, under M. Monnet, the HA often tested the outer limits of supranationalism, it has become increas-

3. For a more systematic and detailed presentation of this position, see supra, pp. 3–6.
4. See Haas, *Uniting of Europe,* Chapter 12.

ingly a mediator since his departure.[5] However, there has been more to the decline of the HA than the personality of its first president.

It is particularly important to note that in March 1957 the Rome Treaty establishing the European Economic Community was signed. The impact of the Common Market upon the Coal and Steel Community has been twofold. In the first place, the principle of supranationalism was sharply muted, the Common Market Commission being primarily a proposing organ which can act only with the approval of the Council of Ministers.[6] Secondly, the new community represented a change in approach to the problem of European integration. Originally, there were to have been a series of coordinate communities, each with its own responsibility, topped off eventually by a European Political Community. The European Defense Community was, for example, to have dealt with military integration and the "Green Pool" was to have handled agricultural problems. This grand design crumbled after the French National Assembly rejected the Defense Community.

When Europe turned to the Common Market it became immediately clear that the Coal and Steel Community would have to give up its identity. There is little likelihood that the Coal and Steel Community, including only two industries—albeit large and vital—can, in the long run, exist on a basis of coordinate equality with the Common Market, which incorporates the remainder of the economy. While the Common

5. Only recently, under the guidance of President Dino Del Bo, have there been signs of a revival.

6. Ironically, the Commission has used its relatively meager formal powers most effectively and has consequently become a much stronger body than the HA. For a convincing analysis of the institutional evolution of the Commission, see Leon N. Lindberg, *The Political Dynamics of European Integration* (Stanford, Stanford University Press, 1963); "Decision Making and Integration in the European Community," *International Organization, 19* (1965), 56–80.

Market was in its embryo stage an argument could be made for maintaining the separation, but it has become increasingly clear that problems like transport and energy require an integrated solution. However, a joint executive seemed altogether likely to take the less supranational approach of the newer and larger Community—thus further supporting the HA's disinclination for an aggressive role.[7]

There is a still more fundamental explanation for the decline of the HA. Despite a sufficient, even impressive, array of legal powers, the HA has failed to mobilize the political support necessary for more vigorous action, a failure that stems directly from the problems already considered. However, all these difficulties notwithstanding, a strong European parliament would have immeasurably strengthened the hand of the executive. Indeed, an enthusiastic parliament could have prodded the HA to a more vigorous assertion of its formal powers. Unfortunately, the treaty is not particularly generous in granting powers to the parliament. Even more important has been the failure of the parliament to generate effective political support on the national level to back its own enthusiasm for Community solutions.[8]

Traditionally, parliaments have been raised as a check against a demagogic executive or an unruly monarch. What powers the Coal and Steel Community treaty invests in the parliament follow orthodox lines. Thus, the HA is made responsible to the parliament and may be forced to resign by a parliamentary vote of censure. If the HA had developed along vigorously supranational lines, a method to assure political responsibility would have been particularly impor-

7. The HA, as noted earlier, was extremely hesitant to undertake any amendments to the treaty for fear that the "opposition" would use the occasion as an excuse to reduce the supranational powers of the HA. Supra, Chapter 13, note 53.

8. See, for example, Kenneth Lindsay, *European Assemblies* (New York, Praeger, 1960), p. 25.

tant.[9] Yet at the present juncture this parliamentary control of the HA is largely academic. The treaty divides "legislative" power between the HA and the Council; the HA has, of course, given up the initiative and the Community's center of gravity has shifted accordingly. The Council, which has assumed the major legislative role, is not answerable to the parliament.

While it has been persuasively demonstrated that the Council of Ministers has operated as an effective organ for advancing Community interests,[10] there is no use closing one's eyes to the consequent distortions in the Community system. The resultant pitfalls for the Court of Justice—the Community's most federal organ—are obvious. Generally speaking, the Court is responsible for the integrity of the treaty and any distortions are likely to put the judges under pressure. If the Council of Ministers bends the treaty slightly in order to deal with a difficult problem, or if the HA fails to fulfill the role charted for it in the treaty, Court action offers the obvious avenue for redress. Moreover, as we have seen, both enterprises and member governments have been willing to use the judicial process to press their claims. It is, in other words, clear that the weaknesses of the Community's political structure have impinged directly and unmistakably on the Court of Justice. However, for a precise picture, a systematic analysis of litigation over the life of the Community is required.

Litigation

Categorization of litigation by parties makes it relatively easy to pick out the power relationships lying beneath the

9. Moreover, despite its political weakness, the HA has become a formidable bureaucratic organization. It is altogether understandable that there would be strong desires to maintain control over the "technocratic" possibilities of a European bureaucracy.

10. Haas, Chapter 13.

surface.[11] The categories which follow are set up to disclose the impact of HA weakness on the Court of Justice, to demonstrate the legal consequences of the general inflexibility of the Community system, and finally to gauge the extent to which the judges are called upon to resolve disputes involving member governments—a priori, the most highly charged politically. Table 2 presents in summary form, by year, five categories of disputes brought to the Court.

For the most part suits have been tabulated singly, but there has been a certain amount of grouping, as indicated in the supporting data. To present each of the suits on scrap and rail transport as a single unit of litigation would have been to badly distort the qualitative aspects of the Court's work. Categorization also represented something of a problem. Take, for example, the Monnet Margin cases. While HA action was directed against the steel companies, the result was to engage the executive in litigation with both steel companies and the French government. In this instance, the suits were divided between categories I and II. On the other hand, in the rail rate cases a similar ambiguity was treated by placing all the litigation in category II. Although enterprises did file suit, the entire Community operation against discriminatory rates was directed against nationalized railways in Germany and France.

---

11. Unfortunately, the formal designation of the parties is not a reliable guide to the real disputants. Because of the procedures that govern the operations of the Court (see supra, pp. 41–43), the HA has been the plaintiff in virtually all of the suits brought under the Coal and Steel Community Treaty. In fact, the executive may be only peripherally concerned, while the real dispute is among or between enterprises and member governments. Such is the case, for example, when an enterprise attempts to prod a reluctant HA to impose a provision of the treaty on one of the member governments. Consequently, the categories shown in Table 2 are based on the real parties rather than the officially designated plaintiff and defendant.

TABLE 2. SUITS FILED[a] WITH THE COURT OF JUSTICE BY YEAR AND BY CATEGORY[b]

	1953	1954	1955	1956	1957	1958	1959	1960	1961	1962[c]	1963	1964	TOTAL
I		1	2	3	2	1[d]	4	1	1	1	2	3	21
II		1	1	2		3							7
III				1	1		2				1		5
IV		2			1	2		2					7
V	2						2	1	1		1		7
TOTALS	2	4	3	6	4	6	8	4	2	1	4	3	47

a. These figures are based on grouping of similar suits in certain cases. For a detailed tabulation see accompanying list of categories. Suits which were filed with the Court but withdrawn before a judgment could be rendered are included. Very few of these abortive legal actions have been treated in the preceding chapters; the problem of out-of-court settlement will be dealt with in Chapter 15.

b. For an explanation of the categories, see supra, pp. 271–72.

c. Only a portion of the suits filed after 1961 have been treated in this study. Nevertheless, the tabulations for 1962 to 1964 are complete. While no basic changes in the patterns of litigation are to be noted, there has been some revival in litigation between the HA and the enterprises.

d. The scrap problem has not really been discussed in detail for the period after 1958. For this reason and because the multitude of appeals can be considered as one continuous operation, the individual suits have not been tabulated. To indicate the dimensions of the problem, suffice it to say that between January 1, 1959, and December 31, 1964, 99 scrap suits were filed.

CATEGORIES OF LITIGATION

I. ENTERPRISE VS. HIGH AUTHORITY

 1. Monnet Margin (3 & 4/54: decision 1954)
 2. Belgian coal – transition program (8 & 9/55: decision 1956)
 3. Scrap – pig iron bonus (11 & 12/55: withdrawn 1956)
 4. Ruhr cartel (2/56: decision 1957)
 5. Price list deviations (8/56: decision 1957)
 6. Scrap – general (9 & 10/56 and 2 & 15/57: decision 1958)
 7. Investment (1 & 14/57: decision 1957)
 8. Scrap – penalty (8–13/57: decision 1958)
 9. Scrap – mopping up (1958 to date)
10. Price list deviations (1/59: decision 1959)
11. General levy – Italian (22/59: withdrawn 1960)
12. Ruhr cartel (36–38/59: decision 1960)
13. General levy – German (41 & 50/59: decision 1960)
14. Ruhr cartel (13/60: decision 1962)
15. Price list deviations (16/61: decision 1962)
16. Imposition of sanctions by the HA (12/62: withdrawn 1964)
17. Participation in the Oberrheinische Kohlenunion (67/63: decision 1964)
18. Merger of August Thyssen and Phoenix–Rheinrohr (86/63: withdrawn 1964)
19. Price list deviations (3 & 4/64: action pending as of December 31, 1964)
20. General levy (21/64: action pending as of December 31, 1964)
21. Participation in the Oberrheinische Kohlenunion (36/64: action pending as of December 31, 1964)

II. MEMBER GOVERNMENT VS. HIGH AUTHORITY

1. France & Italy vs. Monnet Margin (1 & 2/54: decision 1954)
2. Luxembourg vs. HA cartel dissolution order (2/55: withdrawn 1955)
3. Italy vs. double scrap price (3/56: withdrawn 1957)
4. France vs. HA order against ATIC (5/56: withdrawn 1957)
5. France vs. HA order against ATIC (2/58: withdrawn 1961)
6. Special German rail rates (3–18, 25 & 26/58; 19/58; and 24 & 34/58: decisions 1960)
7. Special French rail rates (27–29/58: decision 1960)

III. ENTERPRISE VS. ENTERPRISE

1. Comicoke vs. Ruhr (4/56: withdrawn 1956)
2. Ruhr cartel (18/57: decision 1959)

3. Comicoke vs. gas coke exporters (35/59: withdrawn 1962)
4. Ruhr cartel (40/59: decision 1960)
5. Applicability of the cartel article (12/63: decision 1963)

IV. ENTERPRISE VS. MEMBER GOVERNMENT

1. Holland vs. Ruhr cartel – price ceilings (6/54: decision 1955)
2. Luxembourg vs. Luxembourg steel (7 & 9/54: decision 1956)
3. Holland vs. German miners' bonus (17/57 & 30/59: decision 1961)
4. Holland vs. German steel – trucking rates (39/58: withdrawn 1960)
5. Germany vs. French steel – Venlo rail rates (43/58 & 26/59: withdrawn 1960)
6. France vs. Vloeberghs (9 & 12/60: decision 1961)
7. Holland vs. Ruhr cartel (67/63: decision 1964)

V. INTERGOVERNMENTAL DISPUTES

A. *Disagreement*

1. France vs. Belgium – coal ceilings (3/53: withdrawn 1953)
2. Belgium vs. France – ATIC (4/53: withdrawn 1953)
3. Italy and Holland vs. Community (20 & 25/59: decision 1960)
4. Italy and Holland vs. Community (9 & 11/61: decision 1962)

B. *Adapting the Treaty*

1. Article 56–petite revision (proposed 1959: rejected 1959)
2. Article 65–petite revision (proposed 1960: rejected 1961)
3. Article 37–Belgian coal emergency measures (2 & 3/60: decision 1961)

With these caveats out of the way, what does Table 2 indicate? The bulk of the cases are to be found in category I. These are disputes between the HA and the enterprises, stemming from executive action taken against the firms. By adding suits in category II, the result of executive operations against the national governments, we account for more than half of the total number. Since both categories are symptomatic of a vigorous executive the chart would seem to belie the conclusion of executive weakness drawn in the preceding section. However, most of this litigation occurred during the early and middle periods of the Community. This is particularly true of executive collisions with the member governments—the real test of a bold executive. There have been none since 1958.[12]

While the Court has in recent years been spared direct confrontations between the Community executive and the national governments, equally explosive problems have been presented to the judges. Depite the general reduction in litigation,[13] an increasing number of disputes brought to the Court of Justice fall into the last three categories. All of this litigation can be traced either to executive weakness or to the difficulties the Community has experienced in adapting to changing conditions. Suits in categories III and IV—among enterprises or between enterprises and member governments —resulted from the failure of the HA to act against alleged violations of the treaty. In each instance, the failure advantaged certain parties and disadvantaged others, and the disadvantaged party took its complaint to the Court of Justice. The final grouping is a little more complex and is therefore divided into two subgroups. However, both subgroups evidence a breakdown of the Community's political institutions, that is, the failure to arrive at a generally acceptable solution to a Community problem. The disputes in subgroup A are the result of simple disagreement over the application of the treaty, while those in subgroup B stem specifically from attempts to adapt the treaty to change.

What are we to conclude from this analysis? It is clear, in the first place, that the weaknesses of the Community's political structure have impinged directly and unmistakably on the Court of Justice. There has been an obvious tendency to thrust upon the Court difficult jobs that the other institu-

12. Of the three recorded in 1958, two dealt with the single problem of rail rates and the third, concerning ATIC, ended in political compromise and withdrawal before a judgment could be rendered.

13. To the members of the Court, inundated with scrap problems, this assertion might seem laughable. However, it remains true that all of these suits raise similar questions and date back to executive action in the early years of the Community.

tions have failed to deal with in a satisfactory manner. At the outset it was not unusual for a member government to bring a dispute with the HA directly to the Court of Justice. Now the tendency seems to be to work informally or in the Council to arrive at some sort of agreement. Only after all else has failed, or after an unsatisfactory compromise has been challenged by an enterprise, does the dispute reach the Court of Justice. The judges' first opportunity to deal with the matter comes after the battle lines have been formed and rigid positions have been taken. In other words, the Court is increasingly being asked to do the work of the other institutions of the Community.[14] How have the judges reacted to this pressure? How well have they acquitted their obligation to the rule of law?

RESOLUTION OF CONFLICT

For purposes of this discussion, we need not develop a sophisticated "rule of law" model. The basic issue is the distinction between polar methods of resolving conflict: law and negotiation. Successful negotiation is anchored in mutual adjustment, with the concessions made by each party likely to be in direct proportion to influence. Law, on the other hand, is based on established rules, and it is these norms which determine how a conflict will be resolved.[15]

14. For a summary of this problem with respect to the weakness of the HA, see Werner Feld, "The Court of Justice of the European Communities: Emerging Political Power? An Examination of Selected Decisions of the Court's 1961–1962 Term," *Tulane Law Review, 38* (1963), 53–54.

15. Recall our earlier discussion, supra, pp. 9–13. The same idea has been expressed in terms of law and politics as follows: "Perhaps the purest analytical concept of law is that in which an impartial judge objectively applies a pre-established rule to decide a controversy. And perhaps the purest analytical concept of 'politics' is that in which the stronger influence or interest regulates the social distribution of values. Morton A. Kaplan and Nicholas de B. Katzenbach, *The Political Foundations of International Law* (New York, Wiley, 1961), p. 3.

In practice, the distinction between the legal and the negotiated settlement is not likely to be nearly so marked. The
application of *established* rules is a notoriously inexact
process, and negotiation always precedes and often continues
in parallel with litigation. Nevertheless, the dual goals of the
judicial process are the development of predictable patterns
of rules and equal application of these norms to all parties
subject to the legal system. It is this double standard—stable
rules and equal protection—that we must now apply to the
Coal and Steel Community in general, and the Court of Justice in particular.

By and large, the rule of law has been established within
the Coal and Steel Community. The Court has certainly not
buckled before political pressure, and its adoption of functional methods has provided a solid foundation for a workable system of rules. The judges have regularly asserted the
primacy of the law, and they have generally sought to explain
and defend their decisions, thus providing guides for the
future. These favorable conclusions must, however, be quali-
fied if we are to gain a balanced picture of the Court's accom-
plishments.

Judicial Caution

Both the milieu in which the Court operates and the traditional attitudes of the continental judges tend to moderate
judicial activism. A hesitancy to assume a public and educa-
tive role is bolstered by the anonymity which cloaks judicial
decisions. The connection between anonymity and judicial
caution is indirect, stemming from the fact that as a general
rule continental courts are without dissenting and concur-
ring opinions. In the absence of these two devices, whatever
may be their shortcomings, judicial decisions resemble a
patchwork quilt rather than even-textured, well-reasoned
arguments. Before signing a decision, each judge is eager to
insert a particular point or perhaps soften the phrasing of a

holding to make it more acceptable. At any rate, judgments can seldom become consistent and persuasive documents.

It is this difficulty, perhaps, which accounts for some of the criticism I encountered when speaking with attorneys for the enterprises as well as with officials of the member governments and the HA. They charged the Court with excessive and confusing obiter dicta. Ironically, the judges who favor the Court's obiter dicta practices defend the extra words as the appropriate way of clarifying the Court's position and thus avoiding additional litigation.

It is difficult to generalize on the practical results. The Court has often used its obiter dicta to good advantage. Even in marginal situations—like scrap and cartel litigation—a general idea of the attitude of the Court emerges. However, in such cases, the precise position of the judges is left in doubt, and this doubt tends to foster additional litigation. The multinational character of the Court of Justice compounds the problem. National judicial traditions call for different sorts of decisions, ranging, for example, from the extreme brevity of the Franco–Belgian style to the longer discursive judgments characteristic of Italy and Germany.[16]

Finally, the judges are painfully aware of the dynamic character of the Community project and, to a lesser extent, of the essentially economic nature of the rules they must propound. For these reasons, they are again reluctant to assume an active position. Among the members of the Court with

16. The multinational composition of the Court has created no problems which are of basic relevance to this study. Consequently, there has been no attempt to touch on the multitude of bothersome and time-consuming difficulties of this sort which have plagued the Court since it first began to sit. Suffice it to say that the comparative technique has become part and parcel of the Community process and has resulted—with varying degrees of success—in a synthesis of the legal concepts of the six member states; it is generally felt that the French tradition is dominant. For the most explicit example of comparative jurisprudence, see Advocate General Lagrange's study of *détournement de pouvoir,* 3/54 Assider v. H.A., 1 Rec. 123, 143–75 (1955).

whom I spoke there was real concern that too audacious a resolution to current conflicts might restrict the future growth of the Community. Yet these pressures do not weigh upon the Court in a uniform manner; they may vary with the nature of the issue presented for litigation.

The Brink of Politics

Where the jurisdiction of the Community is clear the Court has generally been willing to indulge in extensive and illuminating explorations of the treaty. On the other hand, the judges have had major difficulties with suits raising issues bearing on the partial character of the Community. The other problem area for the Court has been, of course, suits growing out of the Community's rather awkward efforts to adapt the treaty to changing conditions. Yet even in these matters the Court has often taken firm and unequivocal stands.

The judges did not let *partial integration* stand in the way of an impressive resolution of the rail rate cases. The decisions of the Court brought unity and clarity to a vague and diffuse article of the treaty and, at the same time, cleared away substantial obstacles to transport harmonization. As in the miners' bonus and the trucking cases, the judgments tended to force the treaty to its integrative limits. Treaty rules were pressed, even though the result was to expose weaknesses in the system, weaknesses stemming directly from the partial commitments of the member governments.

In thus probing the limits of the treaty, Court action compels member governments to face the logic of integration. The miners' bonus decision, for example, obliged the German government to make some unpalatable adjustments. By the same token, the Dutch government has been put under pressure by the judgment in the trucking cases.

On the other hand, the Court failed to operate in the same forthright manner in the Vloeberghs case. The national coal import monopoly, ATIC, remained free to continue its restrictive operations. Why? The explanation seems to lie in the nature of the problem of partial integration. The treaty's failure to deal with such matters as fiscal and commercial policy was not an oversight; a positive political decision is required to fill this gap. Individual enterprises are in no position to make these decisions, or to influence them substantially. Accordingly, the Court's unwillingness to permit enterprises to precipitate constitutional crises is both understandable and appropriate. Moreover, let us recall that the treaty itself, in restricting enterprise access to the Court, makes a similar kind of distinction.[17]

Analogous, in this sense, to the obstacles of partial integration are the difficulties of coming to grips with problems of *change*. Here again the Court has generally asserted the rules of the treaty in a strong and unequivocal manner. On the two occasions when attempts were made to amend the treaty, the Court took a firm stand in the face of substantial political opposition. Before taking a closer look at these two matters, let us examine the one instance in which the Court's answer to the problem of change was to avoid the issue completely.

The judges rejected on procedural grounds the suits brought by the German coal companies against the Community's emergency measures to deal with the Belgian coal crisis. They held that enterprises were not entitled to challenge executive action undertaken on the basis of Article 37, action based upon "the political responsibilities of the Governments of the member states and of the High Authority, particularly in that which concerns the reconciliation of the general interest of a member state and the general interest of the Community." [18] The rationalization program for the Belgian coal industry was the result of high level political negotiations. The program was the response of the Community to genuine political and economic crisis. Since the enter-

17. Supra, pp. 43–44.
18. 2 & 3/60, Niederrheinische Bergwerks AG v. H.A., 7 Rec. 261, 289 (1961).

prises are hardly in a position to offer constructive alternatives to the emergency action, it is not surprising—and again, let us recall their second class status—that they should be denied an opportunity to block action agreed upon by the member governments.

On the other hand, the judges have not hesitated to stand against agreements arrived at by the member governments, even when they have been stamped with the Council of Ministers' seal of approval. The Court, as we know, rejected proposals to amend both Articles 56 and 65. While in both instances the Court successfully blocked the proposed change, there is little doubt that it was more successful in asserting the claims of the treaty in regard to readaptation procedures than with respect to cartels.

The reasons for the contrast are patently clear; they are partially political and partially legal. Legally, the Court was on strong ground when it refused to accept the reservations added by the German government—an obvious attempt at a de facto continuation of the transitional period. In contrast, the interpretation of the treaty on which the Court based its rejection of the cartel amendment is open to attack. Politically, the differences between the two situations are instructive. In both cases the problem was to adjust an inadequate treaty to the demands imposed by changing economic conditions. Moreover, in both instances, a major revision of the treaty which would not have been subjected to judicial review was considered time consuming and hazardous. But at this point the similarity between the two situations ends.

It was clear that the German government stood alone in its opposition to a legally acceptable scheme to extend the possibilities of readaptation assistance. In the cartel dispute, in contrast, the Court took on not just one or two member governments, but a unanimous decision of the Council of Ministers. Given the fluid character of integration and the strong national bias of the Community's institutions—a bias reinforced by the tentative operations of the HA—it is not un-realistic to look at the Council as the de facto constituent organ of the Community. This impression is reinforced by the makeup of the European Economic Community in which "almost all the rules spelled out in the Treaty may be changed by the Council, aided by the Commission and com-pelled to submit its desires to the consultative deliberation of the parliamentary Assembly. *Formal amendment seems un-necessary.*" [19]

All this is simply to suggest that there are times when a bold assertion of the rules of the treaty is not in order; when, on the contrary, arbitral-type solutions are more appropriate. Arbitration resolves the immediate dispute but entails no obligation for the future, nor is it necessarily consistent with decisions previously rendered. The arbitral decision either defers to the political authorities directly, or, by avoiding—or treating in a restricted fashion—the substantive issues, leaves open the future course of action. In any case, the result of arbitration is, on the one hand, to allow the political authori-ties freedom of action to deal with the problems and, on the other hand, to shut the enterprises off from effective legal relief.

There is no intent, in this analysis, to suggest that the Court is altogether at liberty in politically awkward situa-tions to shirk its obligations to the rule of law. The Court's reluctance to articulate effective rules for steel pricing prac-tices has already been criticized, and undeniably the refusal of the judges to deal with the substance of the suit brought by the German enterprises against the general levy is vulner-able to attack.[20] Certainly the issues raised were of general

19. Haas, p. 309, italics supplied.
20. It is not my intention to question the procedural grounds upon which the judgment stands. This analysis seeks simply to determine when the judges are entitled to sidestep sensitive problems. Even if the Court felt

and far-reaching importance. The significance of executive access to an independent purse hardly requires elaboration. Yet, we are not faced with an unresolved political question or with the adaptation of the treaty to the changing demands of integration. If the treaty provisions are ambiguous, the ambiguity is that of the unprovided case, the classic opportunity for judicial activism. Moreover, it should be recalled that the enterprises and not the member governments pay the Community's bills. Accordingly, in this instance, the protection of the law should have been extended.

PROSPECTS

The legal system of the Coal and Steel Community may be said to have burst full grown upon the scene. The Community has been spared the Hobbesian anarchy which has so long characterized the international legal order. Not only has there been no resort to physical violence, but effective limits have been placed on other sorts of self-help. However, it is clear that the Court has come under increasing pressure in recent years as a result of weaknesses in the Community political system. Since these weaknesses have their counterparts in the structure of the Court, and since the Court, too, is part of the Community system, it is not surprising that application of the rule of law has been tentative and incomplete.

Legal rules have not been applied to all conflicts nor has the protection of the law been fully extended to the enterprises. While the enterprises are thus partially excluded from the protection of the law, the Court has certainly opened up an effective, if limited, grievance channel to the enterprises; neither the HA nor the member governments have escaped judicial censure. That confidence in the Court of Justice continues is demonstrated by the tribunal's crowded docket,

---

that these procedural shortcomings were compelling, some obiter dicta guidance would have been possible.

which includes the ample beginnings of a body of Common Market litigation. In part, this willingness to overlook the Court's weaknesses is attributable not only to concrete gains achieved by litigation, but to an assumption that the tribunal —still in its judicial infancy—will remedy whatever defects have appeared.

Law and Politics

Undoubtedly, as the Court matures solutions will be found to some of the problems that now plague the judges. However, it seems unlikely that any legal system—particularly at the constitutional level—can support a pervasive and unyielding application of the rule of law. The United States Supreme Court, for example, finds shelter from time to time in a vaguely defined category of political questions. Despite sporadic efforts to stabilize this category and invest it with a fixed meaning, the concept remains amorphous. The failure of the Supreme Court to develop a stable and well defined category attests to the determination of the judges to maintain a free hand and suggests that the category cannot by its nature be formalized. The temper of the times, the prestige of the Court, and the availability of alternative solutions are often more important determinants of the "political" than the nature of the dispute itself.

Continental doctrine accepts the proposition that certain questions are political and thus ought not be dealt with by courts.[21] However, a significant number of officials with whom I spoke held that explosive political problems could be defused simply by bringing them before a court. It is, no doubt, true that legal procedure in general and the judicial

21. In French administrative law the notion is embodied in the category, *acte de gouvernement*. See M. Waline, *Droit administratif* (8ᵉ ed. Paris, Editions Sirey, 1959), pp. 190–99, and Charles E. Freedeman, *The Conseil d'Etat in Modern France* (New York, Columbia University Press, 1961), pp. 116–17 and 126–27. See also Hans G. Rupp, "Some remarks on Judicial Self-Restraint," *Ohio State Law Journal, 21* (1960), 503–15.

process in particular do perform this service. *Within limits*
tensions can be reduced by a measured dose of legal tran-
quilizers,[22] but it is not surprising that the judges of the
Court of Justice who are caught in the cross fire between law
and politics are cognizant of these limits. President Donner
has indicated his—and presumably the Court's—awareness of
the problem. He has also suggested that there are those whom
the Court serves who are not sufficiently sensitive to these
difficulties:

> By virtue of the principles admitted in the law of the
> Community, according to which the judge interprets,
> himself, with authority, the rules relative to his own
> competence, it is incumbent upon us to put in concrete
> form the principles and dispositions requiring the sep-
> aration of powers. Experience shows that the application
> of these abstract and rather vague norms to concrete
> cases can vary according to the period, to the place, and
> to the subject. Only those who know the two provinces
> can fix the limits between that which is proper to the
> political and administrative powers and consequently
> must be respected by the *jurisdictions.*
>   . . . There is these days a fatal tendency which envi-
> sions too rigid a distinction between the governmental
> and administrative functions, on the one hand, and the
> judicial function on the other.[23]

While it would be premature to say that the Court of Justice
has explicitly formulated and applied a political questions

22. As Talcott Parsons has written, "One of the very important aspects of
legal procedure is to provide a mechanism for the 'cooling off' of the pas-
sions aroused. . . . The important thing . . . is that a person under strain
should have some opportunity for 'tension release' that is treated as institu-
tionally legitimate." "The Law and Social Control" in William M. Evan,
ed., *Law and Sociology* (Glencoe, Ill., Free Press, 1962), p. 68.

23. From the address of President Donner at the swearing in of Judge
Lecourt, 18 May 1962 (Document #11, 444—mimeo., p. 2).

doctrine, the seeds of such a doctrine are certainly to be found in the refusal of the Court to permit the German coal firms to challenge the isolation of the Belgian market.

Law and Politics: Regional Integration

Whatever may be the normal dimensions of the conflict between law and politics, it is clear that they are enlarged by the nature of regional integration. It can be argued with some truth that the crux of the problem in the Coal and Steel Community is institutional. If the political institutions could respond to the changing demands of integration in the prescribed manner, the integrity of the treaty could be preserved. Substantive change would be softened by procedural stability, and the Court of Justice would be in the clear. This argument, while sound as far as it goes, passes over real problems.

The procedural difficulties of the Community stem directly from deep-seated substantive failings. Judicial review must make its peace with the partial and fluid character of the Community system. Ordinarily, judicial review rests on a constitutional document which is both complete and stable; it designates and regulates all relevant relationships among the parties. Even in a federal system the constitution seeks a definitive distribution of power, and so can be used as a standard for resolving all disputes. A category of political questions, which offers an avenue for sidestepping certain sensitive issues, does not detract from the essential integrity of the constitutional document.

In the Coal and Steel Community the picture is altogether different. It is not just that the system is partial; federalism, too, is a partial system. Nor is it that the system is bound to change; the evolutionary character of federalism is too well known to require repetition. What really matters is that the Coal and Steel Community is purposefully tentative. The limits placed on Community authority are experimental; the boundary traced by partial integration is, in reality, the Community's growing edge. It is not only that integration is likely to follow an evolutionary course—this dynamic is actually the instrument of integration.

The "expansive logic of partial integration" is, in other words, an organic kind of development, not readily amenable to a system of prior rules. Moreover, because the member governments are determined to keep a firm hand on the progress of integration, the Community has been hobbled with incomplete institutions which are often unable to respond in a constitutional manner to the changing demands of integration. It is the assumption of the leaders of the European movement that an autonomous Community will slowly develop as the integrative process advances—in other words, that the organic nature of the process will ultimately wrest control from the member states. Nonetheless, in the Community system as it now stands, organic growth must coexist with national control.[24]

The rule of law is thus caught between two opposing but equally hostile forces: on one side, the claims of the member governments and, on the other, the fluid mechanics of integration. Each in its own way offers formidable obstacles to settled norms. However, the effectiveness of the Court of Justice will not depend on the extent to which it can purge itself of these influences. Pristine adherence to traditional standards is likely to thwart the Community's legal experiment. Only by understanding the forces which buffet the Court, and by continuing to bend before them at appropriate times, can the judges live a reasonably legal life in relatively uncongenial surroundings. The judges of the European Communities must, in other words, tread a particularly narrow path between law and politics.

24. For a recent critique, see Stanley Hoffmann, "Discord in Community," in Francis O. Wilcox and H. Field Haviland, Jr., eds., *The Atlantic Community: Progress and Prospects* (New York, Praeger, 1963), pp. 10–13.

15

REGIONAL INTEGRATION:

THE CONTRIBUTION OF JUDICIAL REVIEW

The preceding chapter focused on the underlying conflict between the commitment of the legal system to stable and determinate rules and the singularly fluid process of regional integration. It was demonstrated that legal rules have not been applied to certain categories of Community disputes and it was suggested that insofar as the lacunae reflected weaknesses in the political system, judicial prudence was appropriate. But how will these limitations in application of judicial review affect the contribution the Court can make to the development of the Community? Indeed, what specifically is that contribution? It will be the task of this final chapter to explore these questions.

Generally speaking, the Court of Justice plays both an active and a passive role in the political process which is guiding the growth of the Community. The active contribution of the Court flows directly from its case law, which will be shown to have leavened the fluid process of integration with a vital measure of stability. Secondly, it will be argued that by its very existence the Court of Justice effectively and positively influences the bargaining process which is the driving force of integration. Let us first study the active participation of the judges in the community building process.

A FRAMEWORK OF ORDER

There can be no doubt about the rather disruptive character of the integrative process. The Coal and Steel Community is dedicated to changing the commercial, economic, and ultimately the political methods of the enterprises and member governments. Almost without exception, the litigation analyzed in earlier chapters resulted from an unwillingness to change established practices: sales cartels, national subsidies, trade protection, secret rebating. Given the stake of a judicial body in a substantial degree of stability, the awkward position of the Court of Justice—particularly at the outset—is patently clear.

However, even in its early stages, the Community cannot operate in a setting of unrestricted change. Both the businessman and the politician must be offered the vital minimum of security to permit effective planning and policy making. Certainly, assurance of the continued pursuit of common goals is essential. Otherwise, the numerous immediate sacrifices make no sense at all. In more general terms, there must be a reciprocal certainty that other members of the Community will not

> pursue their ends by means selected only on the basis of instrumental efficiency. Though the choice of means on this basis may result at times in co-operative combinations, these combinations are by definition subject to immediate dissolution, if, for example, exploitation or annihilation becomes more advantageous for any one member. *Hence a state of indeterminate flux rather than a system of action exists.*[1]

The following discussion will seek to demonstrate the distinctive manner in which judicial review has contributed to this necessary stabilization of the integrative process.

1. D. F. Aberle et al., "The Functional Prerequisites of a Society," *Ethics*, 60 (1950), 103. Italics supplied.

Legitimation and Interpretation

The Treaty of the Coal and Steel Community does not simply evidence a positive commitment to a common goal. It reveals the dimensions of that joint effort by defining the structure of a *specific* system of action. If the rules that the Court formulates are to contribute to the development and stabilization of patterns of behavior, they must be integrally linked to the goals and methods of that system of action. To put it more simply, the judgments of the Court must be both clear and convincing.

The successful decision involves legitimation and interpretation.[2] Interpretation makes habitual performance *possible* by rendering the rules of the Community determinate. In applying the general and potentially discordant norms of the treaty to specific conflicts, the Court supplies a vital lubricant to the operations of the Community: the immediate dispute is resolved and the rule is made clear, not just for the parties to the dispute but for the entire Community.

Legitimation, on the other hand, is an important element in *motivating* habitual performance. Settled norms may provide a significant social lubricant, but litigants are not likely to be so easily satisfied; they must be convinced that the judgment is correct. The Court must argue persuasively that the rules it articulates are, on the one hand, functionally effective and, on the other, that they correspond to the methods of the Community as they were sealed in the original compact. By thus demonstrating that legal norms serve the common goal in an already agreed upon manner, the judges make a strong case for compliance and thereby serve the cause of stabilization.

However, the norms articulated by the Court fall into distinctive categories, and both the degree of stabilization attainable and the techniques for its attainment differ according to the category being considered. Essentially we are faced

2. Talcott Parsons, in Evan, ed., *Law and Sociology*, pp. 58–59.

with three kinds of norms: the *primary rules* of the treaty, which impose duties and grant rights to the enterprises and member governments; the *values* of the Community, which define in a more general way the integrative consensus; and the *secondary rules*—the rules of the game—which grant the power to make and change rules and even to redefine the initial consensus.[3] In the discussion which follows the contribution of the Court of Justice in each of these areas will be considered. Specifically, we shall examine the potential for stability and the progress made by the Court in that direction.

The Methods of Integration: Primary Rules

The Treaty of the Coal and Steel Community is quite specific; it is made up principally of primary rules which are immediately applicable, requiring only direct executive action.[4] Given this specificity, it stands to reason that the rules are going to be put under enormous pressure by the process of integration. There is no chance at all that the framers of the treaty could have foreseen the twisting course of integration with sufficient clarity to have set forth anything but a most tentative set of primary rules. What chance is there, then, to put tolerable limits on the inevitable changes? The most fundamental element of stability is the relationship of these rules to the more general goals of the treaty. In other words, while the rules themselves may change, the ends they serve are likely to be more permanent. It is for this reason that, throughout this study, emphasis has been placed on the relationship of means to ends—on the functional solution to legal conflicts within the Community.

In analyzing the litigation, the Court was constantly tested by functional standards: had it adopted an empirically

3. For a fuller treatment, see supra, Chapter 1.

4. The E.C.S.C. Treaty thus stands in contrast to the Common Market Treaty which is classified as a *traité cadre,* a framework treaty. See Paul Reuter, "Juridical and Institutional Aspects of the European Regional Communities," *Law and Contemporary Problems, 26* (1961), 382.

grounded, teleological approach? In each of the problems considered an attempt was made to sketch the substantive relationship between the litigation and the goals of the treaty. The decision was then judged primarily in terms of whether or not it took account of, and accommodated itself to, this relationship. Since the preceding chapters of analysis of litigation have explored this particular judicial task, there seems no reason to attempt a recapitulation here. Suffice it to say that the Court has generally abandoned the strict textualism of 1954 decisions on the Monnet Margin and accepted, in its stead, functional techniques.

The minimum contribution of functional methods is to ensure that norms will not be self-defeating. It is this kind of service that the Court performed when it held that the HA was entitled to withhold the benefits of the Belgian coal program from some enterprises, provided only that the denial served the objectives of the program. However, the judges have gone beyond this significant minimum, indicating how programs (for example, the scrap scheme) and specific rules (for example, the transport regulations) serve the goals of the Community. In doing this, the Court certainly stamps the rule in question with a significant measure of legitimacy. Moreover, by developing the functional relationship between specific rules and Community goals, the judges provide a solid foundation for stable norms. While the dynamic nature of integration may dictate frequent changes in given rules, the Court's functional analysis furnishes a blueprint of legally permissible dimensions of those changes. The primary rules of the Community are likely to be ephemeral, but the commitment to goals will, it is to be hoped, be more enduring.

Community Values

The means–ends relationship sketched in the preceding section is not self-contained. The link between primary rules and goals is not simply empirical, or objective. The adoption of means obviously involves a value choice, and in Articles 2 to 5 of the treaty the fundamental principles of the Community, the values which were to guide the process of integration, are set forth. This value commitment is more enduring than the attachment to detailed primary rules and more specific than the generalized pursuit of integration.

The Court's job is to transform these values into operative standards for judging primary rules. The task is complicated by the rather ambivalent character of these values,[5] but the judges, as we shall see, have grappled with the problem quite successfully. While the values of the Community are spelled out at some length in Articles 2 to 5, the key provision is Article 2. The second paragraph indicates both the orientation and the ambivalence of the treaty:

> The Community must progressively establish conditions which will *in themselves* assure the most rational distribution of production at the highest level of productivity, while safeguarding the continuity of employment and avoiding the creation of fundamental and persistent disturbances in the economies of the member states.[6]

The Court of Justice has taken its cue from the italicized words. Again and again, the judges have attacked both major and minor obstructions to the market process. While sympathetic to temporary measures to avoid "fundamental and persistent disturbances" or to protect "the continuity of employment," the Court has consistently shaped the rules of the treaty to serve the rationalizing force of a free common market.

The judges have strenuously resisted subsidies, which of course distort the normal conditions of competition and in-

5. Supra, pp. 16–19.
6. Italics supplied.

hibit a rational adjustment to the common market. In the rail rate cases it was held that transport subsidies for weak or poorly placed industries were contrary to the treaty and must be eliminated—even at the cost of some unemployment.[7] As a matter of fact, let us recall that the unity which the Court imparted to Article 70 in the rail rate cases was predicated on purifying the market process.[8] It was by a similar line of reasoning that the German miners' bonus was rejected in 1961. The rejection was based largely upon what the tribunal termed "the essential ends" of the common market as defined in Article 2: "the most rational distribution of production at the highest level of productivity." [9]

The Court accepted the isolation of the Belgian coal market and the consequent distortion of the common market. However, the measure was endorsed only because its goal was to further the ends of Article 2.[10] Much the same point was made somewhat obliquely in the first Belgian coal cases (8 & 9/55). The Court held that to grant the benefits of the coal levy to all Belgian coal producers, without reference to rationalization, would be to make the scheme an illegal subsidy.[11] Again, somewhat indirectly, the judges invalidated the exemptions from the scrap levy which were accorded for "group scrap" because it was held that these exemptions, based on financial ties, encouraged cartels.[12]

In the cartel area the Court has pressed the claims of the free market with particular vigor. In its initial rejections of

7. 3–18, 25 & 26/58, Barbara Erzbergbau AG v. H.A., 6 Rec. 367, 407–08 (1960).

8. Supra, pp. 145 and 148.

9. 30/59, De Gezamenlijke Steenkolenmijnen in Limburg v. H.A., 7 Rec. 1, 39–40 (1961).

10. 2 & 3/60, Niederrheinische Bergwerks AG v. H.A., 7 Rec. 261, 288 (1961).

11. 8/55, Fédération Charbonnière de Belgique v. H.A., 2 Rec. 199, 314 (1956).

12. 32 & 33/58, Société nouvelle des usines de Pontlieue-Aciéries du Temple v. H.A., 5 Rec. 275, 306–07 (1959).

the direct access criteria, the Court's distaste for cartels was inferential. Even in 1960 when the judges snatched the initiative from the HA by eliminating one of the direct access criteria and forcing the executive to better justify the remaining criterion, the Court was rather circumspect. However, in rejecting the proposal to amend Article 65, the judges took a particularly bold and uncompromising stand against cartels and in favor of a competitive market. It is true that in its two most recent decisions the Court's position has become more flexible. No doubt this change of direction signals a curtailment of the judicial assault on cartels. Yet the Court's new posture seems to be dictated by the economic reality of the coal market, not by diminished enthusiasm for a competitive market. Suffice it to recall the Court's expressed determination to protect "the measure of competition necessary to safeguard the fundamental requirement of Article 2." [13]

Taken together, the decisions of the Court disclose a tribunal committed to a free market economy and to the general efficacy of the rationalizing pressure of natural market forces. In paying tribute to Judge Rueff on his retirement from the Court, President Donner noted: "Your economic views were clearly allied to the conception of the authors of the treaties and upon which the E.C.S.C, especially, was founded." [14] Given Judge Rueff's fervent commitment to liberal economic principles, the remarks of the President of the Court hardly require amplification.

The Court's attachment to competition and a market economy is bounded by a vigorous and uncompromising assertion of the principle of equal treatment. The rules of fair trade are not necessarily in contradiction to a free market. Certainly, destructive competition must be suppressed, and the elimination of subsidies is a prerequisite to a market

13. 13/60, Comptoirs de Vente v. H.A., 8 Rec. 165, 212 (1962).
14. Document #11440, p. 3 (mimeo), italics supplied.

economy. However, the Court's stress on published rates and alignment has evidenced a clear choice of equal treatment over maximum competition.[15]

The judges' inflexible insistence on fair trade is open to criticism on a number of grounds. For present purposes, it is sufficient to say that a limited assertion of fair trade would be altogether consistent with the Court's commitment to a competitive market. However, by pushing their stand beyond reasonable limits, the judges have to some extent detracted from an impressively consistent implementation of the fundamental principles of the treaty. Symptomatic of the difficulties that the Court has created for itself has been its failure, to date, to make a very convincing application of functional techniques to problems of discriminatory pricing.[16] However, this departure from the general pattern has been confined to a restricted series of problems. The judges' reading of the major portion of the treaty will certainly be shaped by the requirements of a competitive market. This judicial orientation imposes limits on the changes which may be made in primary rules, thus imparting reassuring continuity to the treaty.

The Structure of Integration: Secondary Rules

The ultimate goal of the treaty, integration, is certainly permanent. Were this goal to be abandoned, the treaty would obviously have to be scrapped. It is, after all, this very general commitment to integration which transforms the relations among member governments and enterprises from one of indeterminate flux into a system of action.[17] However, without exception, all the intermediate goals as well as the Community values are tentative. While circumscribing changes in the primary rules and thus contributing a measure of stability,

15. Supra, Chapters 3 and 4.
16. Ibid.
17. Supra, note 1, this chapter.

these goals and values can also be modified. Yet even at this juncture order is possible.

Probably the most characteristic contribution of law to any social system is its support of procedural regularity, the respect it confers on the rules of the game: who shall have the power to change rules and what procedures must be followed? The judges have shown considerable concern for structural questions. The Court's most explicit defense of the Community system per se came in the first Meroni decision (9/56) and served as the cutting edge of its sweeping attack on the HA's administration of the scrap program: "The power balance which characterizes the institutional structure of the Community is a fundamental guarantee accorded by the Treaty, particularly to the enterprises and associations of enterprises." [18]

Perhaps more important than such a generalized defense of the system has been the Court's continuing preoccupation with the powers of the HA. Certainly the problem of defining the proper constitutional role for the Community's supranational executive is the most vital procedural issue with which the judges have been faced. In this matter, the Court of Justice has given legal support to a vigorous—although not unrestricted—application of HA initiative and discretion. While it might seem that support of executive intervention is not in accordance with a commitment to liberal economic principles, there is in fact no inconsistency. Specifically, the executive action supported by the Court has almost without exception been taken to bolster the strength of the free market.

It is perhaps an irony of economic integration that central intervention is necessary if a free market is to be established. Direct barriers to trade, like tariffs and quantitative restrictions, must be removed, and other distortions of trade—often

18. 9/56, Meroni & Co., Industrie Metallurgische, S.P.A. v. H.A., 4 Rec. 9, 44 (1958).

the product of member government intervention—must be eliminated. As we have seen, the six countries of the Coal and Steel Community had more than their share of such distortions and alert policing operations were a necessary prerequisite to establishing a free common market. Even the more positive programs of the HA have been accepted by the Court primarily on the basis of their contribution to a healthy free market. Both the transitional program for Belgian coal and the emergency operation undertaken on the basis of Article 37 were required to prepare Belgian coal to compete in the common market. The scrap program, too, was in the service of the regular supply conditions necessary for a sound market.

Admittedly, the Court substantially freed HA's investment opinions from legal restraint, but the executive's authority over investment is meager indeed. Of more significance, at least potentially, was the refusal of the judges to interfere with the HA's power to tax. However, in this instance the Court's endorsement was only lukewarm, if that. The judgment avoided an appraisal of the arguments raised by the German firms, taking refuge in a procedural rejection of the German suit; the Court remains uncommitted as to the dimensions of executive authority. Finally, let us recall how very cautious the HA has been in asserting its powers. In a practical sense, there has just not been any threat of *dirigisme*.

The real conflict between initiative and procedural regularity revolves around the problem of executive discretion. Here, it would seem that the Court has been most aware of the fluid nature of integration and has accordingly allowed considerable discretionary authority. The judges have, for example, refused to confine the utilization of HA powers to the purposes of the articles in which they were authorized. The measure in question must bear some positive relationship to the goals of the article under which it is ostensibly taken.[19] The Court may even require that the ruling be directly motivated by the purposes of that article. However, the simultaneous pursuit of other goals is perfectly proper. As early as the Monnet Margin cases, the Court held that pricing powers could be used for other goals. Similarly, the judges have recognized that the financial mechanisms of the scrap program might purposely influence the investment plans of the enterprises. As noted earlier,[20] this sort of interpretation tends to give each HA power a life of its own—a life based on objectives beyond those incorporated in the article granting the power.

Certainly the most significant avenue to broad executive discretion was the judicial determination that the HA could temporarily subordinate certain of the fundamental principles of the treaty.[21] The executive has been charged with the duty of reconciling the individual interests of the enterprises and the member governments with the general or Community interest.[22] On the other hand, the Court's willingness to back HA efforts to establish a free market and promote Community goals is not unrestricted. It is the Court which stands as the final arbiter of the general interest, testing the executive's reconciliation of Community interests. Moreover, the judges have demonstrated a genuine concern for fair administration of HA programs and have at times been sharply critical of procedural shortcomings. The Court has stated that reasonable standards of administration call for prompt HA response to investment proposals,[23] and has indicated a continuing concern for clear and detailed justification of all executive decisions.

Recall also that the avalanche of scrap litigation stems di-

19. 6/54, Netherlands v. H.A., 1 Rec. 201, 227 (1955).

20. Supra, p. 129.

21. Supra, p. 128.

22. Supra, p. 123.

23. 1 & 14/57, Société des usines à tubes de la Sarre v. H.A., 3 Rec. 201, 220–21 (1957).

rectly from the Court's condemnation of the HA's failure to keep adequate control of the powers delegated to the scrap office. Moreover, the judges insisted strenuously on the importance of procedural purity in the first trucking rate cases. In both of these latter situations the decisions expressed an explicit judicial determination to maintain the integrity of the system established by the treaty. Given the Court's permissive attitude toward executive action, a narrow construction of procedural requirements should offer welcome security to both the enterprises and member governments— eliminating the temptation of administrative short cuts. In other words, the judges seem to have combined a necessary measure of flexibility with a real determination to maintain the balance of the Community's institutional structure.

The Integrated Social System

It should be abundantly clear from the foregoing analysis that the Court of Justice has gone a long way toward establishing a firm foundation for a system of rules. The judges have manifested a flexible attitude toward specific textual rules but have worked to confine change within limits dictated by the purposes, methods, and values set forth in the treaty. By explicitly formulating and articulating the links among these factors, the Court has provided guides for the participants and thus offered to the process of integration that necessary minimum of stability which was discussed at the opening of this chapter.[24]

However, this process is only the means to an end: the goal is an integrated social order at the supranational or regional level.[25] What is the nature of the Court's contribution to this ultimate goal? Of course, a stable pattern of norms,

24. Supra, p. 286.

25. For a discussion of this distinction—integration as a process vs. integration as a condition—and its general significance in the study of European unity, see Lindberg, *Political Dynamics of European Economic Integration,* pp. 4–8.

which makes behavior mutually predictable, is a kind of indispensable minimum for a viable social system.[26] But in addition, by identifying and implementing the values of the integrative commitment, the Court has helped to create a mutually intelligible framework for *communication*. In other words, even if the values articulated by the Court are not universally shared, misunderstandings as to the terms of the discourse about integration are avoided. Similarly, the Court's functional techniques have breathed life into the specific goals of the Community. By constant exploration of the relationship between individual problems and these goals, common aims have become more concrete and determinate, and the reasons for abiding by Community norms more compelling. Finally, it must be noted that the Court's functional inquiry has extended to secondary as well as primary rules; the position of the HA in the Community's institutional apparatus has been critically analyzed and its potential as well as its limits spelled out.

What finally emerges, then, is not merely an undifferentiated set of rules but a series of supports necessary to the development of a viable social system. The Court has helped to specify the *who*, the *what*, the *how*, and to some extent the *why* of the emerging Community system.[27] Understandably,

26. Aberle et al., *Ethics*, p. 103.

27. The obvious resemblance to the functional theories of society developed by the sociologists is, of course, not accidental. Many of the categories used in these functional theories, the so-called "functional prerequisites of a society," are readily adaptable to the analysis of legal rules and thus provide an obvious link between the two disciplines. The well-known article cited above (note 1), "The Functional Prerequisites of a Society," specifies, inter alia, the following categories: "a shared articulated set of goals," "the normative regulation of means," and "role differentiation and role assignment" (pp. 104–11). The utility of these functional prerequisites is described as follows: "Role differentiation specifies *who* is to act, while the common articulated set of goals defines *what* is to be done. The normative regulation of means tells *how* these goals may be won" (p. 108). Of course, this functional assessment rests on assumptions about the nature of society which

the normative base is not complete at this early date in the life of the Community. Still, the direction is clear, and the purposeful and structured stability that the Court is imparting to the rules of the Community seems likely to make a vital contribution to the building of an integrated common market.

BARGAINING: THE CORPORATIVE ELEMENT

Let us now turn to the passive contribution of the judges. Simply stated, we shall view the Court as a "fleet in being." Even without asserting rules, the Court has been able to influence the Community's political process. While the active and passive contributions of the Court are separable, both in theory and in fact, they are certainly interdependent. The passive role depends on the threat of judicial veto; only because the Court has established a reputation for firm adherence to rule of law standards has it been able to influence the bargaining process.

The Political Process

We have seen that the Community's political process is dominated by the Council of Ministers. In other words, the "federal" organ in the institutional structure, the High Authority, has been subordinated. Supranationalism, insofar as it envisaged the imposition of fixed Community norms on enterprises and member governments, has been replaced by a process of negotiated settlement conducted by the member governments. While at this early stage any conclusions are necessarily tentative, the success of the techniques adopted by the Coal and Steel Community is hard to deny. Both in its

---

are not yet verifiable. However, the hypothesis is suggestive and provides clear and meaningful, if not definitive, standards for gauging the work of the Court of Justice.

own right and as a catalytic agent in the creation of the Common Market and Euratom, the integrative achievement of the Schuman Plan is impressive. The methods developed by the Community seem to be leading in the proper direction at a reasonable rate of speed.[28]

In this connection, the distinctive nature of the Community system must be noted. It is true that supranationalism has been considerably watered down and that the rules established are rather plastic. Still, the Community should not be mistaken for the ordinary international organization, whose member states are characterized by a fierce determination to guard national interests—a determination backed by an effective veto power: "The symbiosis of interministerial and federal procedures has given rise to a highly specific, *and certainly corporate,* series of techniques whose tendency to advance integration is patent even though it is neither clearly federal nor traditionally intergovernmental." [29]

The point is that decisions are made at least in part with an eye to the Community and its welfare and advancement. A procedural consensus guards against permanent obstruction by the member governments, and a substantive consensus has emerged which commits the governments to the realization of Community goals.[30] The HA contributes to this process by capitalizing on its technical competence:

> It has been extremely difficult for recalcitrant governments to resist the facts and recommendations put before the Council by the High Authority, partly because

28. Needless to say, the usefulness of testing judicial review according to how well it fits into the political pattern is entirely dependent upon whether or not the Community has been pursuing the proper course. If the path chosen is a blind alley, it could be argued that the Court would make its most valuable contribution by swimming against the tide. On the other hand, in these circumstances it is unlikely that the Court would be capable of forcing a more rigidly supranational pattern on the member governments.

29. Haas, *The Uniting of Europe,* p. 526, italics supplied.

30. Ibid., p. 523.

government experts had been bound to the accuracy and relevance of the necessary statistics while they were being compiled.[31]

The Court of Justice is in a position to influence the Community bargaining process in a similar way. That is to say, the constant threat of judicial veto, when combined with a continuing commitment to the goals of the Community, can keep negotiated settlements within acceptable limits.

Out-of-Court Settlement

What evidence is there that the Court of Justice has influenced the bargaining process? While difficult to document, the most striking evidence is provided by the settlement of suits withdrawn before the Court could render a judgment. Given the secrecy which cloaks out-of-court negotiations, it is difficult to determine the precise basis of the final agreement. However, enough information is usually available to make possible a satisfactory, it not absolutely reliable, analysis.

For the most part, only suits resulting in judgments have been treated in this study. Aborted litigation was included in the tabulation in Chapter 14, but only in two instances have these suits been discussed. The HA's efforts to control the operations of ATIC were analyzed in some detail in Chapter 13, and the German steel association's prodding of the executive in the Dutch trucking rate cases was noted in Chapter 8. However, as the listing below indicates, a considerable number of suits have been settled out of court.

The cases listed are rather a mixed bag. The suits range over a large proportion of the problems which have faced the Coal and Steel Community, and they have reached the Court along a variety of paths. However, the twelve cases fall readily

31. Ibid., p. 524. This process has been much more pronounced in the Common Market. Working in the same general manner, the Commission has exercised considerably more initiative and demonstrated more skill in prodding the Council of Ministers. See Lindberg, pp. 65–73.

into two groups: (1) suits stemming from a HA decision to which an enterprise or a member government objected; (2) suits which sought to prod a reluctant HA to act. In either situation the imprint of the Court is unmistakable. The HA always responded to the prodding with vigorous executive activity. Moreover, in all instances, the party which had reason to expect an adverse decision from the Court of Justice ended by making some concessions. Finally, in most cases the bargained settlements evidence the influence of treaty rules. Let us examine the suits in more detail, focusing on the above categories.

TABLE 3. OUT-OF-COURT SETTLEMENT

Number of the Litigation	Subject Matter	Plaintiff	Withdrawn
3/53	Coal price ceilings, Belgium	France	1953
4/53	Coal price equalization, France	Belgium	1953
2/55	Coal import monopoly, Luxembourg	Luxembourg	1955
11 & 12/55	Scrap – pig iron bonus	Assider & I.S.A.	1956
3/56	Scrap – double pricing	Italy	1957
4/56	Ruhr cartel	Coke industry, Italy	1956
5/56	ATIC	France	1957
2/58	ATIC	France	1961
39/58	Trucking rates – publication	Steel industry, Germany	1959
22/59	General levy	Macchiorlatti	1960
43/58 & 26/59	Rail rates – discrimination	Steel industry, Lorraine	1960
35/59	Price discrimination – gas coke	Coke industry, Italy	1962

Executive Initiative

Four of the twelve suits fall into this group, and the lesson of legality is clearest in the Luxembourg (2/55) and the Macchiorlatti (22/59) cases. The details are not altogether clear with regard to the Italian enterprise suit, but only reservations about Macchiorlatti's rather dim chances before the Court seems to account for the withdrawal.[32] Luxembourg dropped her suit against a HA order to dissolve its coal import monopoly when the government's legal advisers made it clear that the case would be lost.[33] Without the threat of a judgment, there can be little doubt that Luxembourg would have put up stiffer resistance to the HA's dissolution order. The government had already resisted similar pressure applied by its steel industry—far and away the overwhelming national economic factor.

The legal quality of the above settlements seems beyond question. The same is not true of the two remaining suits in this category (5/56 and 2/58). Both involve ATIC and both were of questionable legality.[34] The background "presence" of the Court does indeed reinforce the position of the party standing on the firmest legal ground. But that party must be willing to take advantage of the leverage thereby provided. In its negotiations with ATIC, the HA was never interested in squeezing all the benefits out of its advantageous position. Still, it cannot be denied that each settlement pushed ATIC a little closer to the rules of the treaty, thus again evidencing the beneficial impact of the Court of Justice on the bargaining process.

Prodding the HA

The HA was permissive in its dealings with ATIC largely because of its go-slow policy for dealing with the Community's cartel problems. There are instances—some in the

32. The firm questioned the HA's right to tax on the basis of estimates made by the executive of Macchiorlatti's production. The HA had been forced to take these steps because the steel company had failed to forward the necessary information.

33. A Luxembourg official who was involved in the litigation explained to me that the suit had been undertaken against the advice of legal counsel and then, on more careful consideration, withdrawn.

34. Supra, pp. 233 and 240–41.

cartel field—that illustrate how a cautious HA can find itself trapped between opposing parties with the threat of judicial veto hanging over its head. While the results of such situations vary, the record indicates that the HA is vulnerable to this sort of prodding. The outcome depends almost entirely on how insistent the "troublemaker" is. If he is willing to rock the boat with dedication, the cause of the treaty is virtually certain to be advanced.

It was the suit filed in 1958 by the German steel association (39/58) that led the HA to withdraw a questionable concession it had made on the publication of trucking rates.[35] Moreover, after the Court had invalidated the HA decision withdrawing the concession, it was the threat of the steel association to file a suit that stimulated the HA to take advantage of the opportunities for action which were opened up by the judgment.[36] Similarly, a group of French steel enterprises galvanized the HA into action when they pressed their claim against the Bundesbahn in the Court of Justice (43/58 and 26/59). The enterprises wanted the HA to force the Bundesbahn to compute the rates for Ruhr coal going to the Lorraine over the shortest route, through Venlo on the German–Dutch border. Although the suit was finally rendered superfluous when the German government introduced trainload rates,[37] the HA's response to the legal attack was a vigorous campaign to negotiate a settlement.

But what happens when the injured party is not interested in advancing the rules of the treaty? In two cases, involving the Italian coke industry, the interests of the injured party were clearly separable from the legal principles involved. In one case (4/56), again involving the early stages of the HA's cartel program, the executive was clearly vulnerable to charges that the three "separate" coal sales agencies were, in

35. Supra, p. 152.
36. Supra, p. 162.
37. Supra, p. 146.

fact, operating as a single cartel, contrary to provisions of Article 65. Consequently, the HA took the initiative and managed to bring off a negotiated settlement. The Ruhr made concessions on the one point which interested the Italians— access to the short supply of Ruhr coal. The suit was then withdrawn, and questionable operations of the cartel continued unhampered and untested.[38]

The other case was similar but more complicated. The Italian coke makers again appealed to the Court (35/59) in an effort to win concessions from the producers of gas coke in Germany. It was claimed that gas coke was being "dumped" on the Italian market, causing appreciable disturbances. When the HA refused to act the suit was filed, but once again both sides preferred to avoid a judgment. A compromise was reached giving the HA continuing authority to collect information on shipping and pricing practices and to *arbitrate* disputes which arise.[39] Obviously, the settlement bypasses Community rules and gives the HA ad hoc responsibility for dealing with subsequent disputes.[40]

There remain four out-of-court settlements which have not been discussed. While they could have been divided between the two basic categories, they differ from the other cases in that the legal merits of the questions are very much in doubt. Since these settlements are of little importance for our purposes, they can be disposed of in rather summary fashion. Suffice it to say that in three of the four instances the parties obtained some relief. In the fourth case, the failure to gain concessions can be attributed to the vulnerable position of the plaintiff. With a legal skeleton in the closet, it apparently seemed wiser to retreat. In short, these cases again demon-

38. See the Italian communication withdrawing its suit, dossier 4/56.

39. *Europe CECA,* 8 June 1962, p. 3.

40. It should be noted that gas coke is only peripherally a treaty product (see Annex #1 of the treaty). Moreover, there is good reason to believe that the pricing rules of the treaty will at least set a framework for the negotiations.

strate the impact of legal pressure on the political process.[41]

In closing, we may note the likelihood of innumerable out-of-court settlements which cannot be documented because they never even reach the initial stages of formal litigation. When an attorney advises a client that a suit would be useless, a species of out-of-court settlement is taking place. Whether such advice follows preliminary conversations with officials of the HA, or whether the attorney decides simply on the basis of his own reading of the treaty and prior decisions of the Court, the result is the same: the law becomes the accepted standard of action. A responsible, well informed bar and a stable jurisprudence are the necessary prerequisites of this kind of development.[42]

What are we to conclude from these twelve out-of-court settlements? Clearly, the success of the suit as a bargaining technique indicates a general respect for the authority of the Court. The result is that bargaining strength in Community negotiations is roughly proportional to legal strength. Although there is no way of being assured that out-of-court

41. Of the four settlements, two concern scrap: 3/56, brought by the Italian Government, and 11 & 12/55, filed by two Italian steel associations. (On the final compromise, see *Europe CECA*, 9 February 1956, p. 1.) The other two cases concern coal problems. The French objected to the prices set by the HA for Belgian coal, and when the government filed suit (3/53) Belgium retaliated with a court attack (4/53) on some of the practices of ATIC. For an explanation of the French withdrawal, see HA, *Second General Report* (1954), p. 82. The Belgians, who backed off without concessions, explained their position rather cryptically in a note to the Court withdrawing their suit (see the dossier, 4/53). In this latter case the Court was spared the difficult task of dealing with the HA's admission, in the written procedure, that the program under fire was in itself illegal but that its elimination depended upon a prior solution to other problems.

42. It would be misleading to speak about a special bar of Community attorneys, because the Court is open to any attorney who is permitted to plead cases in his own country. However, it is becoming clear that a relatively small group of lawyers is devoting a rather large portion of its energies to the legal problems of the European Communities.

settlements will be in accordance with the treaty, the choice is in the hands of the injured party. With the threat of a vigorous assertion of legal rights hanging over negotiations, real concessions may be obtained. Certainly the position of the HA in its bargaining with enterprises and member governments is strengthened.

Even if it prefers accommodation to a strict application of Community rules, the executive can still use its legal leverage to record substantial gains. Recall the case of ATIC: a hesitant HA, unenthusiastic about going as far as a Court decision, still managed to extract real if not conclusive concessions. Recall also the bargaining over the amendment to Article 65. Although the amendment was finally rejected by the Court, it was clear that *both* the provisions of the treaty and predictions of the attitude of the Court had a significant impact on the final proposal.

These conclusions are substantiated by interviews with responsible officials at the HA and the Commission, the executive organ of the Common Market: both find that the threat to begin legal proceedings is a potent weapon against both the enterprises and the member governments. One highly placed Common Market official, who also had considerable experience in the Coal and Steel Community, indicated that the passive role of the Court is among its most important attributes. He contended that the existence of the Court tends to force negotiations and settlements to cluster around the treaty.

The advantage of the bargaining process over the judicial process is its flexibility. Out-of-court settlements can be forced into constitutional paths, but undesirable rigidity can be avoided. If political decisions do not follow the precise course which a rule of law commitment would call for, emerging practices are channeled and stabilized. This productive interaction between the judicial and the political processes thus fits well into the regional pattern. In this sense, the Court becomes the perfect partner in the Community's corporative political process.

THE ESSENTIAL DILEMMA

There can be no doubt that the Court of Justice is an integral part of the Coal and Steel Community's institutional structure and that it is making a positive contribution. The rules promulgated by the Court provide direction and stability; its commitment to the rule of law offers security; and its presence exercises a salutary effect on the political process which is the driving force of integration. Yet, linking these three roles is a basic contradiction—an interesting sort of irony—which is a continuing threat to the Court.

In order to maintain the momentum of the Community's political process, departures from the federal pattern are often necessary. Since the Court is in no position to take the integrative initiative, it has been suggested that the judges must adopt a rather permissive attitude toward these departures. Generally speaking, the argument has been that so long as the political process is keeping the Community on course, the Court must give rather a wide berth to the political authorities.

The problem is that the Court's possibilities for influencing the political process rest on its continued ability to project a vigorously federal image. This is best illustrated by the cartel dispute. The judges chose to make an uncompromising defense of Community rules and procedures, assuming at times a position open to criticism for its inflexibility. Still, in retrospect, it seems clear that in the cartel field the Court has exercised a deep and continuing influence on the bargaining process. This influence has been because of, not in spite of, its strong stand.

What are we to conclude? Logically, there is no resolution. Perhaps, as integration progresses and the weaknesses which give rise to the Court's difficulties are remedied, the judges will be able upon occasion to take the initiative in awkward situations. Until that time the Court is well advised to remain in the wings, giving the political dynamic of integration its head.

To date, the Court has managed to escape being torn apart on the horns of the resultant dilemma. Perhaps judges have an intuitive ability to avoid a collision course with the political authorities. More likely, it is the fortunate vagaries which surround the application of rules that make judicial life bearable: stabilization does not imply a social deep freeze in which rules calcify and perfect security is attained. On the other hand, even in the early stages of integration we have learned that the political process cannot be perfectly plastic. At any rate, despite occasional—and generally appropriate—retreats from the rule of law, the judges have been able to foster the necessary respect for the judicial process.

BIBLIOGRAPHY

BIBLIOGRAPHICAL NOTE

The Court of Justice itself publishes the most complete bibliography of legal writings on the European Communities. This bibliography is regularly brought up to date with supplements and is certainly invaluable to any student of Community law. Since it runs to hundreds of pages, it could not be reproduced here. The following listing of books and articles has been carefully pruned; only materials with considerable relevance to this study have been included. Similarly, the documents included are either standard sources upon which I have drawn heavily, or miscellaneous publications closely related to questions I have treated.

A full collection of documents on Community litigation can be found in mimeographed form at the Library of the Court of Justice in Luxembourg. The dossiers of the suits filed contain all of the written proceedings plus transcripts of the hearings. In addition, the dossiers include mimeographed copies of the Court's decisions as well as the conclusions of the Advocate General. These latter two documents are available at the Court of Justice on the day of delivery. Finally, it is also possible on occasion to obtain mimeographed copies of the pleadings of the attorneys.

DOCUMENTS

British Iron and Steel Federation, *Treaty Establishing the European Coal and Steel Community,* London, undated.

Charter of the United Nations—Statute of the International Court of Justice, New York, 1946.

European Coal and Steel Community, High Authority, *General Reports on the Activities of the Community,* with annexes, Luxembourg, 1953–1963.

————, *Investment in the Community Coalmining and Iron and Steel Industries,* Luxembourg, September 1960 and July 1961.

————, *Rapport financier pour l'année 1959.*

————, *Rapport sur l'harmonisation des tarifs de Transport concernant le charbon et l'acier,* Luxembourg, August 1958.

European Community, *Journal Officiel des Communautés Européennes,* édition de langue française, serial.

European Community, Cour de Justice, *Conférence à la Faculté Internationale de Droit Comparé le 27 avril 1961,* by A. M. Donner (Document #10159).

————, *Discours prononcé par le Président de la Cour de Justice à l'occasion de la prestation de serment de Monsieur Lecourt le 18 mai 1962* (Document #11440).

————, *Discours prononcé par le Président de la Cour de Justice à l'occasion du départ de Monsieur le Juge Jacques Rueff le 18 mai 1962* (Document #11440).

————, *Recueil de la Jurisprudence de la Cour,* serial.

————, *Indices, Recueil de la Jurisprudence de la Cour,* vols. 1–5, Luxembourg, 1961.

————, *Réponse de M. Jacques Rueff au discours de Monsieur le Président de la Cour de Justice des Communautés, prononcé à l'occasion du départ de M. Jacques Rueff, le 18 mai 1962* (Document #11447) .

European Community, Information Service, *Bulletin from the European Community,* serial.

France, Ministère des affaires étrangères, *La Communauté européenne du Charbon et de l'Acer. Rapport de la Délégation Française sur le Traité et la Convention Signés à Paris le 18 avril 1951,* Paris, Imprimerie nationale, 1951.

Netherlands, Ministry of Transport and Waterstaat, *Memorandum Concerning the Common Transport Policy in the European Economic Community,* The Hague, 1961.

BOOKS

Bebr, Gerhard, *Judicial Control of the European Communities,* New York, Praeger, 1962.

Bok, Derek C., *The First Three Years of the Schuman Plan,* Studies in International Finance, No. 5, Princeton, Princeton University Press, 1955.

Bowie, Robert and Carl Friedrich, *Studies in Federalism,* New York, Little, Brown, 1954.

Carlston, Kenneth S., *Law and Structures of Social Action,* London, Stevens, 1956.

Corwin, Edward S., ed., *The Constitution of the United States,* Washington, U.S. Government Printing Office, 1953.

David, René and Henry P. de Vries, *The French Legal System,* New York, Oceana, 1958.

De Visscher, Charles, *Theory and Reality in Public International Law,* Princeton, Princeton University Press, 1957.

Diebold, William, Jr., *The Schuman Plan,* New York, Praeger, 1959.

Easton, David, *The Political System,* New York, Knopf, 1953.

Federal Bar Association, *Institute on Legal Aspects of the European Community,* Washington, Federal Bar Association, 1960.

Feld, Werner, *The Court of the European Communities: New Dimension in International Adjudication,* The Hague, Nijhoff, 1964.

Freedeman, Charles E., *The Conseil d'Etat in Modern France,* New York, Columbia University Press, 1961.

Friedmann, W., *Law in a Changing Society,* Berkeley, University of California Press, 1959.

Friedrich, Carl I., *Constitutional Government and Democracy,* New York, Ginn, 1946.

———, ed., *Community,* Nomos, New York, The Liberal Arts Press, 1959.

Fuller, Lon, *Forms and Limits of Adjudication,* unpublished lecture delivered at The Center for the Study of Democratic Institutions, Santa Barbara, California (undated).

Galeatti, Serio, *The Judicial Control of Public Authorities in England and Italy,* London, Stevens, 1954.

Haas, Ernst B., *The Uniting of Europe,* Stanford, Stanford University Press, 1958.

Haines, C. Grove, ed., *European Integration,* Baltimore, Johns Hopkins Press, 1957.

Hamson, C. J., *Executive Discretion and Judicial Control: An Aspect of the French Conseil d'Etat,* London, Stevens, 1954.

Hart, H. L. A., *The Concept of Law,* Oxford, Oxford University Press, 1961.

Hartz, Louis, *The Liberal Tradition in America,* New York, Harcourt, Brace, 1955.

Kaplan, Morton A., *System and Process in International Politics,* New York, John Wiley & Sons, 1957.

——— and Nicholas de B. Katzenbach, *The Political Foundations of International Law,* New York, John Wiley & Sons, 1961.

Lawson, F. H., *A Common Lawyer Looks at the Civil Law,* Ann Arbor, Michigan, University of Michigan Law School, 1953.

Lindberg, Leon N., *The Political Dynamics of European Integration,* Stanford, Stanford University Press, 1963.

Lindsay, Kenneth, *European Assemblies,* New York, Praeger, 1960.

Lister, Louis, *Europe's Coal and Steel Community,* New York, Twentieth Century Fund, 1960.

Mathijsen, Pierre, *Le Droit de la Communauté Européenne du Charbon et de l'Acier,* The Hague, Nijhoff, 1958.

Niemeyer, Gerhart, *Law Without Force,* Princeton, Princeton University Press, 1944.

Pound, Roscoe, *An Introduction to the Philosophy of Law,* New Haven, Yale University Press, 1954.

——, *Social Control Through Law,* New Haven, Yale University Press, 1942.

Reuter, Paul, *La Communauté Européenne du Charbon et de l'Acier,* Paris, Librairie Générale de Droit et de Jurisprudence, 1953.

Rostow, Eugene V., *Planning for Freedom,* New Haven, Yale University Press, 1962.

Schwartz, Bernard, *French Administrative Law and the Common Law World,* New York, New York University Press, 1954.

Scitovsky, Tibor, *Economic Theory and Western European Integration,* Stanford, Stanford University Press, 1958.

Stein, Eric and Thomas L. Nicholson, eds., *American Enterprise in the European Common Market: A Legal Profile,* 2 vols. Ann Arbor, Michigan, The University of Michigan Law School, 1960.

Stone, Julius, *Legal Controls of International Conflict,* New York, Rinehart, 1954.

Timasheff, N. S., *An Introduction to the Sociology of Law,* Cambridge, Harvard University Committee on Research in the Social Sciences, 1939.

Valentine, D. G., *The Court of Justice of the European Coal and Steel Community,* The Hague, Nijhoff, 1954.

Waline, M., *Droit Administratif,* 8e éd. Paris, Editions Sirey, 1959.

ARTICLES

Aberle, D. F., A. K. Cohen, A. K. Davis, M. J. Levy, Jr., and F. X. Sutton, "The Functional Prerequisites of a Society," *Ethics, 60* (1950), 100–11.

Amram, Philip W., "Dissent in Germany," *American Journal of Comparative Law, 6* (1957), 108–11.

Anonymous, *Le Droit européen* (1960), 427–31.

Bachof, Otto, "German Administrative Law with Special Reference to the Latest Developments in the System of Legal Protection," *International and Comparative Law Quarterly, 2* (1953), 368–82.

Bebr, Gerhard, "The Balance of Power in the European Communities," *European Yearbook, 5* (1959), 73–79.

———, "The Concept of Enterprise Under the European Communities: Legal Effects of Partial Integration," *Law and Contemporary Problems, 26* (1961), 454–63.

———, "The Development of a Community Law by the Court of the European Coal and Steel Community," *Minnesota Law Review, 42* (1958), 845–78.

———, "The European Coal and Steel Community: A Political and Legal Innovation," *Yale Law Journal, 63* (1953), 1–43.

———, "Protection of Private Interests Under the European Coal and Steel Community," *Virginia Law Review, 42* (1956), 879–925.

———, "The Relation of the European Coal and Steel Community Law to the Law of the Member States: A Peculiar Legal Symbiosis," *Columbia Law Review, 58* (1958), 767–97.

Buergenthal, Thomas, "The Private Appeal Against Illegal State Activities in the European Coal and Steel Community," *American Journal of Comparative Law, 11* (1962), 325–47.

Buxbaum, Richard M., "Antitrust Regulation within the European Economic Community," *Columbia Law Review, 61* (1961), 402–29.

Bye, Maurice, "L'arrêt 13–60 du 18 mai 1962 sur les comptoirs de la Ruhr," *Droit Social, 26* (1963), 257–67.

Chevallier, Roger, "L'arrêt 30/59 de la Cour de Justice des Communautés Européennes," *Revue générale de droit international public, 66* (1962), 546–80.

Coppé, Albert, "The Economic and Political Problems of Integration," *Law and Contemporary Problems, 26* (1961), 349–63.

Corwin, Edward S., "The Passing of Dual Federalism," *Virginia Law Review, 36* (1950), 1–24.

Delvaux, Louis, "Le Contrôle de la Cour de Justice de la Communauté Européenne du Charbon et de l'Acier sur les faits et circonstances économiques," *Annales de droit et de sciences politiques, 18* (1958), 41–58.

Deutsch, Karl W., "The German Federal Republic," in Roy C. Macridis and Robert E. Ward, eds., *Modern Political Systems: Europe* (Englewood Cliffs, New Jersey, Prentice Hall, 1963), pp. 267–398.

Donner, Andreas M., "The Court of Justice of the European Communities," *Legal Problems of the European Economic Community and the European Free Trade Association* (International and Comparative Law Quarterly Supplementary Publication, 1961), pp. 66–75.

Dumon, F., "La formation de la règle de droit dans les Communautés européennes," *Revue internationale de Droit comparé, 12* (1960), 75–107.

Easton, David, "An Approach to the Analysis of Political Systems," *World Politics, 9* (1957), 383–400.

Europe CECA, Agence internationale d'information pour la presse, daily bulletins, Luxembourg, 1953–1964.

Feld, Werner, "The Court of Justice of the European Communities: Emerging Political Power? An Examination of Selected Decisions of the Court's 1961–1962 Term," *Tulane Law Review, 38* (1963), 53–80.

———, "The Significance of the Court of Justice of the European Communities," *North Dakota Law Review, 39* (1963).

———, "The Judges of the Court of Justice of the European Communities," *Villanova Law Review, 9* (1963).

Freund, Paul, "The Federal Judiciary," in Robert Bowie and Carl Friedrich, *Studies in Federalism* (New York, Little, Brown, 1954), pp. 106–72.

Gaudet, Michel, "The Legal Framework of the European Economic Community," *Legal Problems of the European Economic Community and the European Free Trade Association* (International and Comparative Law Quarterly Supplementary Publication, 1961), pp. 8–22.

———, "The Legal Systems of the European Community," *Proceedings of the 1960 Institute on Legal Aspects of the European Community* (Washington, Federal Bar Association, 1960), pp. 202–17.

Heidelberg, Franz C., "Parliamentary Control and Political Groups in the Three European Regional Communities," *Law and Contemporary Problems, 6* (1961), 430–37.

Hoffmann, Stanley, "Discord in Community," in Francis O. Wilcox and H. Field Haviland, Jr., eds., *The Atlantic Community: Progress and Prospects* (New York, Praeger, 1963), pp. 3–21.

———, "International Systems and International Law," in Klaus Knorr and Sidney Verba, eds., *The International System,* Princeton, Princeton University Press, 1961.

Jeantet, Fernand-Charles, "Note doctrinale," *Revue du droit public et de la science politique en France et à l'étranger, 71* (1955), 618–31.

Kopelmanas, Lazare, "Note doctrinale," *Revue du droit public et de la science politique en France et à l'étranger, 71* (1955), 88–97.

Lagrange, Maurice, "Les pouvoirs de la Haute Autorité et l'application du Traité de Paris," *Revue du droit public et de la science politique,* 77 (1961), 40–58.

———, "The Role of the Court of Justice of the European Communities as Seen Through its Case Law," *Law and Contemporary Problems, 26* (1961), 400–17.

Lambers, Hans J., "Les Clauses de révision des traités instituant les Communautés européennes,"*Annuaire français de droit international, 7* (1961), 593–631.

Lang, Norbert, "Trade Regulation in the Treaty Establishing the European Coal and Steel Community," *Northwestern University Law Review, 52* (1957–58), 761–72.

Laubadère, A. de, "Règlement amiable du contentieux opposant le Gouvernement Français à la Haute Autorité de la C.E.C.A. au sujet du régime juridique de l'importation charbonnière en France," *L'Actualité juridique, 17* (1961), 476–79.

Lievens, Robert, "Conseil d'Etat in Belgium," *American Journal of Comparative Law, 7* (1958), 572–89.

McMahon, J. F., "The Court of the European Communities," *Journal of Common Market Studies, 1* (1962), 1–21.

Marsh, Norman S., "Supranational Planning Authorities and Private Law," *American Journal of Comparative Law, 4* (1955), 189–207.

Mehren, Arthur von, "The Judicial Process in the United States and in France—A Comparative Study," *Revista Jurídica de la Universidad de Puerto Rico, 22* (September 1952–April 1953), 235–65.

Nadelmann, Kurt H., "The Judicial Dissent," *American Journal of Comparative Law, 8* (1959), 415–32.

Parker, William N., "The Schuman Plan—A Preliminary Prediction," *International Organization, 6* (1952), 381–95.

Parsons, Talcott, "The Law and Social Control," in William M. Evan, ed., *The Law and Sociology,* Glencoe, Illinois, Free Press, 1962.

Polach, Jaroslav G., "La conception du pouvoir politique dans le Plan Schuman," *Revue française de science politique, 1* (1951), 256–75.

———, "Le droit de la C.E.C.A.," *Journal du droit international, 80* (1953), 4–23.

———, "Harmonization of Laws in Western Europe," *American Journal of Comparative Law, 8* (1959), 148–67.

Reuter, Paul, "Les interventions de la Haute Autorité," *Actes officiels du Congrès international d'Etudes sur la Communauté européenne du charbon et de l'acier,* Milan-Stressa, *5* (1957), 7–75.

———, "Juridical and Institutional Aspects of the European Regional Communities," *Law and Contemporary Problems, 26* (1961), 381–99.

————, "La publicité des barèmes et des écarts de prix dans le Marché Commun du Charbon et de l'Acier," Plaidoirie devant la Cour de Justice de la C.E.C.A. (Affaire 1/54), *Droit Social, 18* (1955), 7–13.

Reynaud, R., "Les Syndicats et la construction européenne," *Revue de l'action populaire* (1961), 787–805.

Rheinstein, M., "An Approach to German Law," *Indiana Law Journal, 34* (1959), 546–58.

Riesenfeld, Stefan, "The French System of Administrative Law," *Boston University Law Review, 18* (1938), 48–82 and 400–32.

————, "Protection of Competition," in Eric Stein and Thomas L. Nicholson, eds., *American Enterprise in the European Common Market: A Legal Profile* (Ann Arbor, The University of Michigan Law School, 1960), pp. 197–342.

Robertson, Arthur H., "Legal Problems of European Integration," *Recueil des cours de l'Académie de droit* (The Hague, Académie de droit international, 1957), pp. 105–211.

Rupp, Hans G., "Some Remarks on Judicial Self-Restraint," *Ohio State Law Journal, 21* (1960), 503–15.

Schindler, M., "Judicial Review of Administrative Acts in Germany," *British Journal of Administrative Law, 2* (1956), 113–21.

Sizaret, Louis, "Chronique générale de jurisprudence administrative européenne," *L'Actualité juridique, 18* (1962), 157–63.

Stein, Eric, "The Court of Justice of the European Coal and Steel Community," *American Journal of International Law, 51* (1957), 821–29.

————, "The European Parliamentary Assembly: Techniques of Emerging 'Political Control,' " *International Organization, 13* (1959), 233–54.

————, "The New Institutions," in Eric Stein and Thomas L. Nicholson, eds., *American Enterprise in the European Common Market: A Legal Profile,* 2 vols. Ann Arbor, Michigan, The University of Michigan Law School, 1960.

———— and Peter Hay, "New Legal Remedies of Enterprises: A Survey," in Eric Stein and Thomas L. Nicholson, eds., *American Enterprise in the European Common Market: A Legal Profile,* 2 vols. Ann Arbor, Michigan, The University of Michigan Law School, 1960.

Stewart, Stephen, "The Court of the Coal and Steel Community," *British Journal of Administrative Law, 1* (1955), 123–28.

Teitgen, Pierre-Henri, "Jurisprudence récente en matière de droit économique et professionnel: Organization du commerce du charbon dans la C.E.C.A.," *Droit Social, 24* (1961), 525–31.

Valentine, D. G., "The First Judgments of the European Coal and Steel Community Court," *Modern Law Review*, 20 (1957), 596–619.

——, "The Jurisdiction of the Court of Justice of the European Communities to Annul Executive Action," *British Yearbook of International Law*, 36 (1960), 174–222.

van Houtte, Albert, "La Cour de Justice de la C.E.C.A.," *Annuaire européen*, 2 (1956), 183–222.

van Kleffens, A., "De werking van het Hof van Justitie der Europese Gemeenschap voor Kolen en Staal in de praktijk," *Bestuurs Wetenschappen*, 13 (1959), 429–38.

Vernon, Raymond, "The Schuman Plan," *American Journal of International Law*, 47 (1953), 183–202.

INDEX

Italicized page numbers refer to tabular material.

Abuse theory (cartels), 252, 254, 255

Acciarieri Laminatoi Magliano Alpi (ALMA): HA action against for price publication failure, 71, supported by Court, 72

Acte de gouvernement, compared to HA executive action, 217, 281 n.

Adenauer, Chancellor Konrad, intervention in coal bonus case, 176

Adjudication: in federal system, 3–8; and political questions, 6, 7; compared with arbitration, 8, 9–12; international, 9–13; rooted in consent, 11; goal, 11

Advocates General, of Court, 27, 28, 30; role, 32; patterned after Conseil d'Etat officer, 37; opinions, 38; independence important, 38

Affectation stricte doctrine: applied to HA taxing power, 79; accepted by Advocate Roemer, 81

Alignment, price, 56–57, 163; fraudulent, 66–67, 70; requires prior publication of rates, 157, 158. *See also* Publication, price; Transport rates

Antitrust legislation (U.S.), influence on Community practice, 226

Antoine Vloeberghs Company. *See* Vloeberghs

Arbitral awards, bases of, 10

Arbitration: international, 9–13; role of consent, 9, 11; goal, 11; character-

ized Court decision on HA tax power, 83, and other politically awkward cases, 279

Association D'Enterprises Aachener Steinkohlen-Bergbau, suit against coal quotas, 214–17

l'Association technique de l'importation charbonnière (ATIC): prevented entry of third-country coal, 186, HA opposed, 187, litigation, 189–92, Court permitted continuation, 192; defensive cartel against Ruhr sales cartels, 229; negotiations with HA, 232–33, 301, 307; effect of Ruhr cartel decision, 239, appealed to Court, 240, compromise, 240–41; out-of-court settlements, 303. *See also* Coal crisis; Ruhr cartels

Bebr, Gerhard, quoted, 40

Belgian Coal Federation: suit against HA subsidy action, 92, charged discrimination, 93, HA defense, 94–95, Court decision, 95–97

Belgian coal industry: subsidies to for transitional period, 89–90; price ceilings set, 91; suits against HA subsidy action (*1955*), 92–94; compensation program failure, 97–98; import quotas established, 98; measures to ease integration into common market, 201, 219, 291, 295,